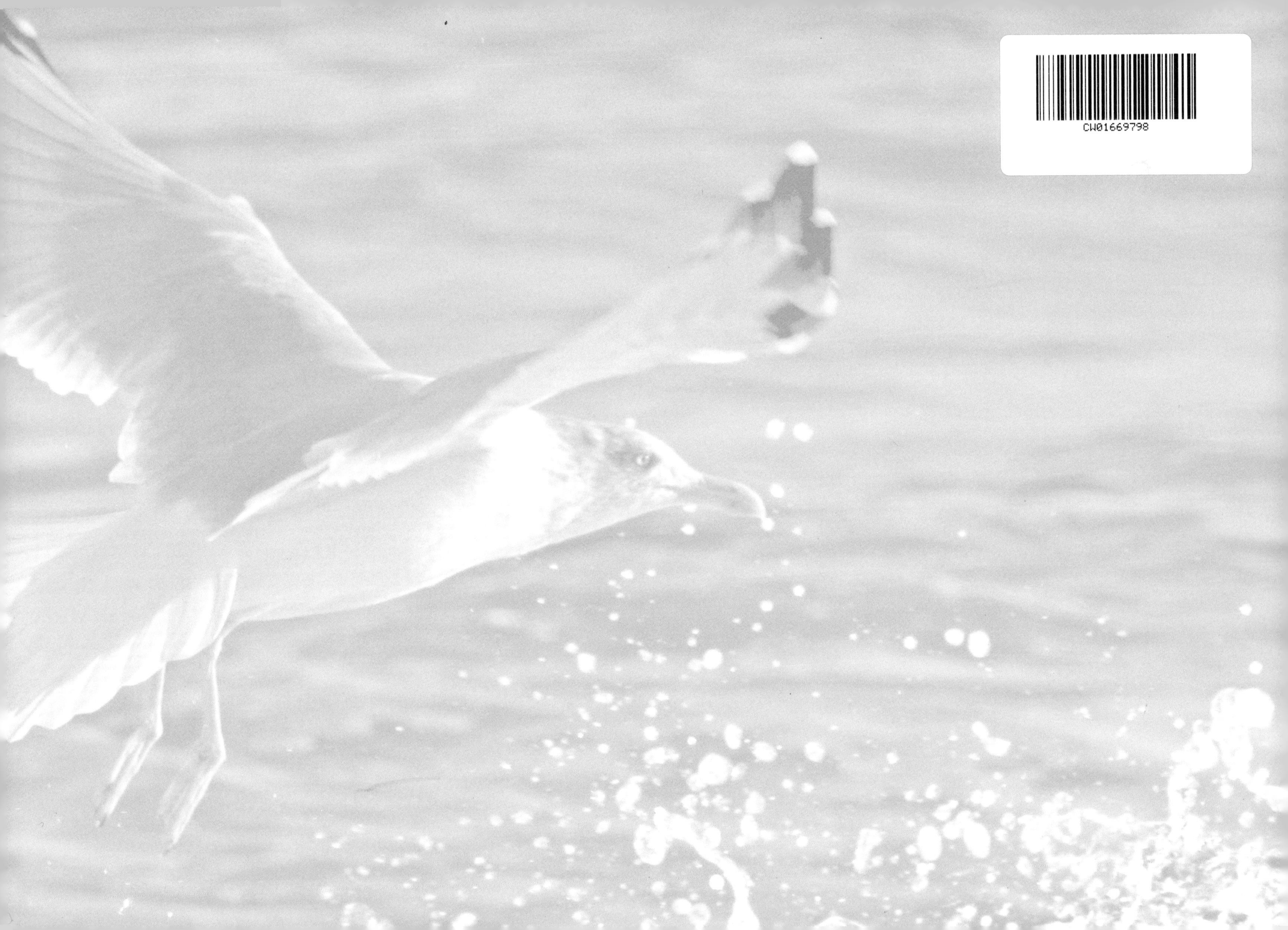

Britten's

Suffolk Heritage Coast

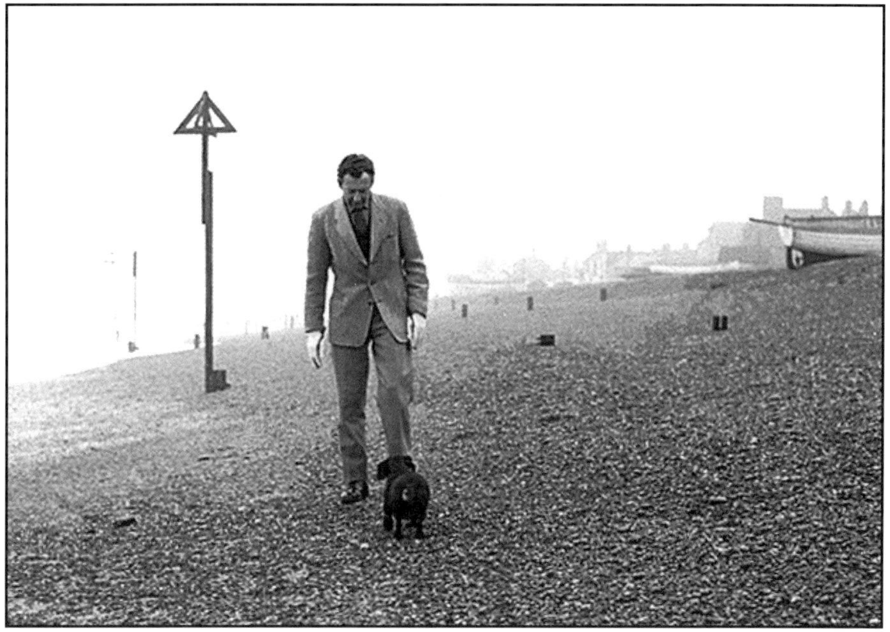

A pictorial tribute by Clive Strutt

First edition published in 2013

www.clivestrutt.com

ISBN 978-1-907938-52-8
A catalogue record for this book is available from the British Library

Printed and Published by Leiston Press
Unit 1b Masterlord Industrial Estate,
Leiston, Suffolk, England. IP16 4JD
www.leistonpress.com

Acknowledgements

Special thanks to my wife Maggie, who is herself an accomplished photographer and writer, who has been a pillar of strength and given her unflagging morale-boosting encouragement throughout this production. To good friend Pauline Whyte for her support and expertise in copy-editing and typographical matters and design suggestions. To James Bell, my brother-in-law, who is an ace on split infinitives. To Madeleine Weston for her design suggestions. To Maggi Hambling, celebrated artist and Suffolk 'gal', for her generous remarks in her foreword. To Glenn Barnes, Managing Director of Leiston Press Ltd, for publishing this book, and to his talented and enthusiastic staff, especially Penny Smith who beavered away at my InDesign mistakes to knock the book into publishing shape – all of whom have contributed to make this, not only a British produced book from start to finish, but proudly a Suffolk production. To all those, and to many more people who I have encountered during the last three years spent on researching and taking photographs for this book, I give my heartfelt thanks.

Finally, my special gratitude goes out – in this his centenary year – to Benjamin Britten who, fifty years ago, entrusted to me as a young cameraman the role of being his, and the Aldeburgh Festival's, photographer. Not only was he very generous both in kind and in words, he was also a gentle man in every respect. I feel immensely privileged to have known him as a good friend.

Contents

SUFFOLK HERITAGE COAST

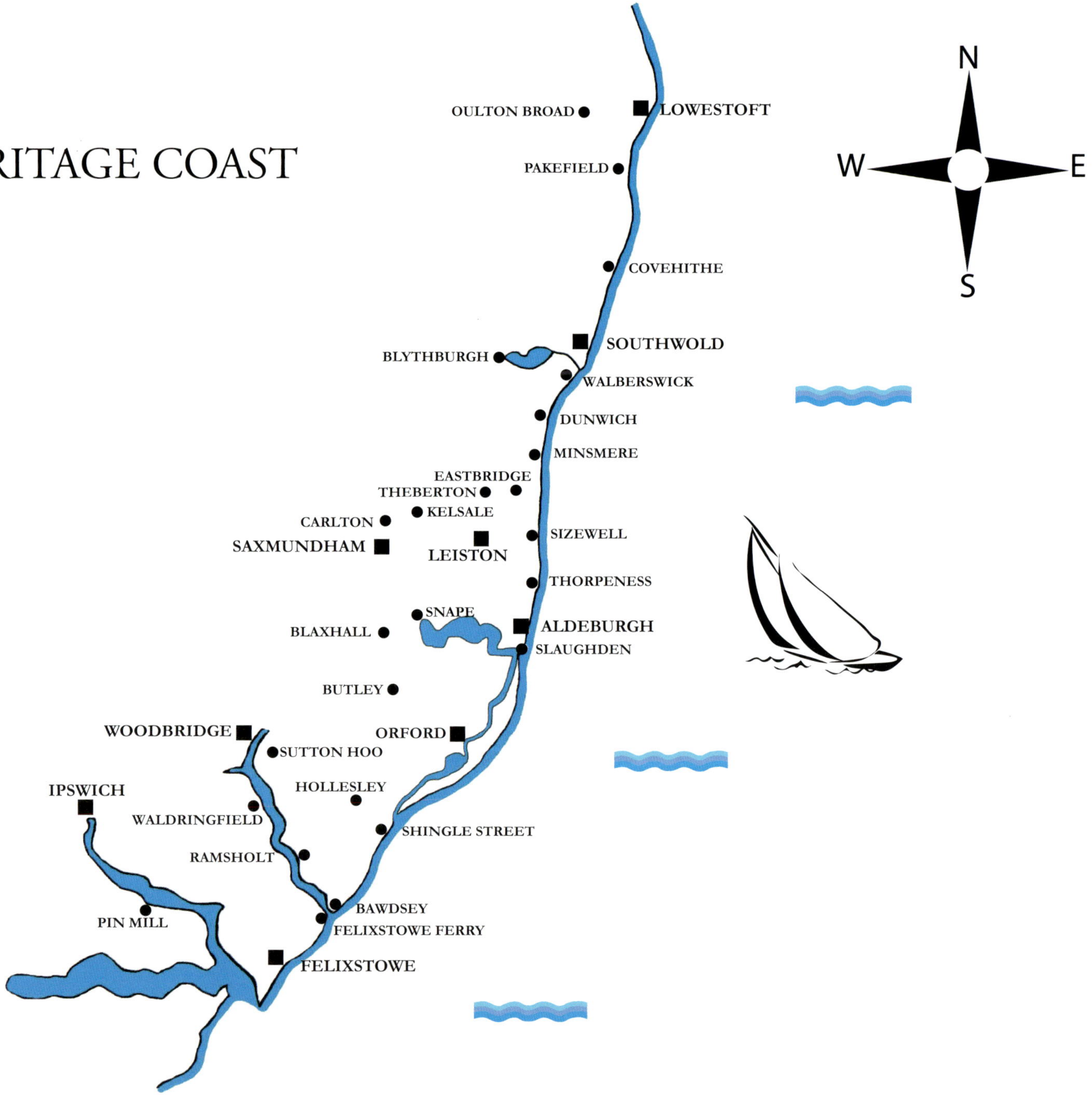

Preface

Benjamin Britten was born on this coast, lived most of his life along it, and was inspired by it when writing his music. This book is a 'local boy's take' on the coast that both he and I loved, and on those special moments I shared with him as his photographer and friend.

Ever since I was given a Kodak Brownie camera and a roll of film as an eight year old, I've been drawn irresistibly to photographing the Suffolk coastal countryside and its people. Ask any landscape artist or photographer what makes Suffolk so special, and they will inevitably say it's the clear light and the large skies that lift the ordinary into the extraordinary.

The area is rich in history, with indications of human habitation along its shores dating back some 700,000 years. There is ample evidence that the Romans and Vikings flourished when they settled on these shores. Many words have been written about the riches garnered from the wool trade here in medieval days, and we benefit today from that time of great prosperity with magnificent Suffolk churches built in celebration of that wealth, leaving us with a spectacular inheritance still to be enjoyed in our villages and towns.

After the decline of the wool trade, Suffolk's affluence waned. Small farmers eked out a miserable living from a few cows, pigs and chickens, with barely enough land to keep them going throughout the seasons. Farmers have always been tough, resigned, independent people, with an eye to making a bob or two. That pedigree has been passed down the line enabling them to sustain a livelihood during the hardest of times. These days, most of those farmers remaining are now wealthy landowners managing high tech, multimillion-pound assets.

The Suffolk coastline has been steadily disappearing into the North Sea for several hundred years. It's a harsh environment typified by the tough longshore fishermen who put to sea in their boats from the beach. The people along its shores frequently have to contend with floods that threaten to take over their homes and land. This is all part of what makes the Suffolk coastal people special, they have an inbuilt stoicism. This book truly celebrates everything best about the county, and I'm pleased to say it has been printed and published by a Suffolk firm of printers.

Clive Strutt, 2013

Foreword

'Britten's Suffolk Heritage Coast' – a book of discovery.

Here is a true Suffolk eye and a true Suffolk voice. Together they bring us the life of this place: land, sky, people, animals, birds and buildings, traced through the past into the present, with understanding and love.

Clive Strutt's fascinating black and white images combine perfectly with his stunning colouramas of today. This book both awakens the visitor to – and reminds we inhabitants of – the rich history, timeless variety and genuine pleasure of our mysterious and constantly changing Suffolk coastline.

Maggi Hambling
March 2013

The magic that is Suffolk's Heritage Coast

Turn east off Suffolk's main A12 road and you are in the county's Heritage Coast, most of which is designated as an Area of Outstanding Natural Beauty. This book covers the area from Lowestoft in the north to Felixstowe and Ipswich in the south within which lie forty miles of beautiful coastline, countryside and rivers. Like most things of beauty, it can be mysterious, moody, and full of surprises.

Abutted by an area of sandlings, verdant agricultural fields, woodlands, rivers and marshlands, interspersed with picturesque towns and villages, the sea is the omnipresent master of this low shoreline. The lost city of Dunwich, the one-time capital of East Anglia and a major seaport, is now mostly under the waves, leaving a few houses standing behind a perilously fragile shingle sea wall. Felixstowe Dock – the largest container port in the UK – is the new banner-carrier for Suffolk's proud seafaring history. Nuclear power stations at Sizewell reside harmoniously beside their next door neighbour – Minsmere Nature Reserve.

Offshore wind farms reap a plentiful harvest of dependable wind power, sharing the same North Sea with longshore fishermen who have been launching their boats here for generations.

The Suffolk coast has played its part in the defence of the realm. The quaint village of Orford has long been associated with buildings of a military nature. Henry II built a castle here in 1173. From 1913 until the 1990s the spit of land separating Orford village from the sea – Orfordness – was a top secret no-go area in the forefront of military and scientific ingenuity. It is now a wildlife area.

The summer of 1672 saw the bloody naval battle of Sole Bay played out within sight of Southwold.

Much later, and to deter territorial ambitions of the French, Martello towers were erected along the coastline.

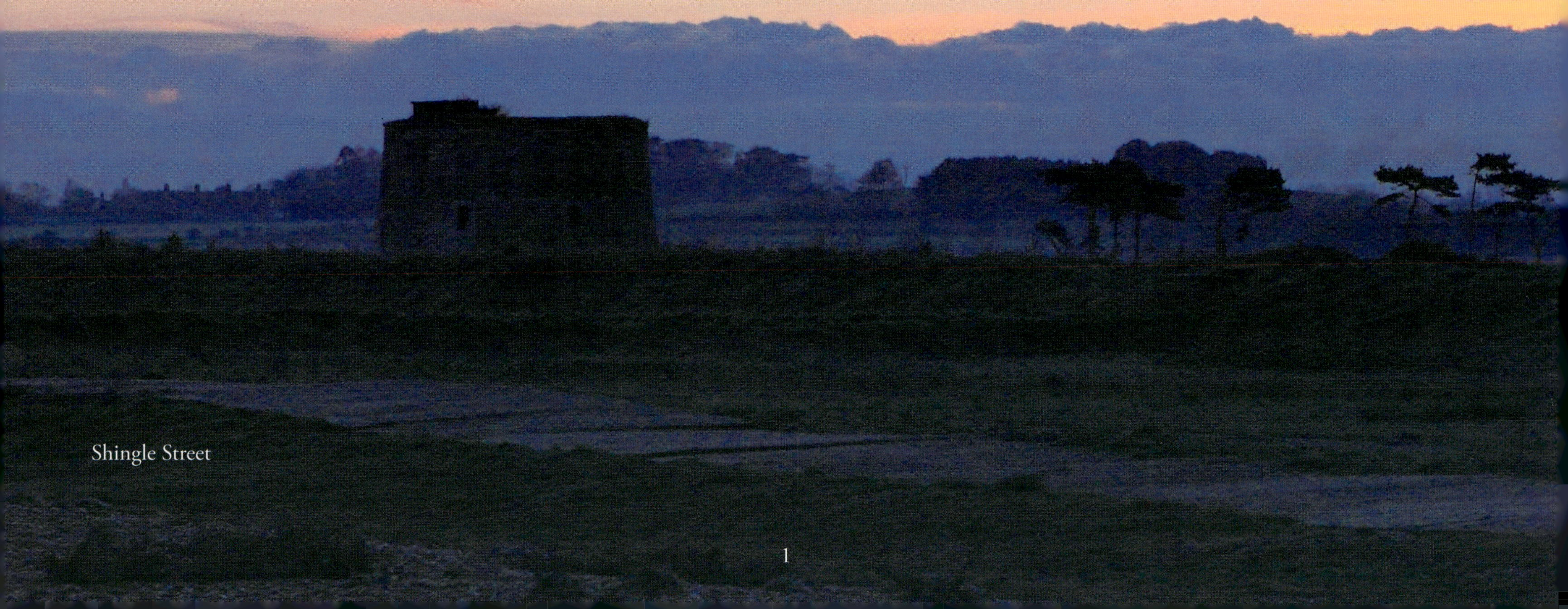

Shingle Street

A few miles south, Bawdsey Manor was another top secret research establishment for the Ministry of Defence, where Sir Robert Watson-Watt – originally based at Orfordness – carried on the development of RADAR, an invention that played a significant part in winning the Battle of Britain and the Second World War.

At the outbreak of that war, this coastline was deemed a prime invasion landing area. Grazing marshlands at Minsmere were flooded, resulting in an ideal habitat for wildlife.

Notwithstanding man's best endeavours in the past to destroy himself, nature now reigns supreme along our coastline.

The resilient and independent-minded people of this area have learned to live with change, but are fiercely proud of their unique heritage, resisting attempts to turn their high streets into yet another 'clone' for the ubiquitous plastic-fronted multinational superstores, coffee shops and eateries. They happily welcome and share their heritage with a year-round influx of visitors, who quickly fall under the tranquil charm and magic that is – Suffolk's Heritage Coast.

Composer Benjamin Britten felt most at home in this landscape, which was the inspiration for much of his acclaimed music. Born in Lowestoft on St Cecilia's Day – the patroness of musicians and church music – on 22nd November 1913, in a house fronting onto the capricious North Sea, his passion for this coastline never diminished, and apart from a short spell living in America, he lived, worked and composed here, and was hugely instrumental in turning coastal Suffolk into a regional centre for music and the arts.

To celebrate the centenary of his birth, writer and photographer Clive Strutt – who worked and was friends with Britten for a number of years – has compiled this book of his own photographs and text about the coastal area of Suffolk, as his personal tribute, not only to the man, but more importantly to this beautiful part of England that Britten loved, and that was so much a part of his music.

This pictorial journey starts at Britten's birthplace – Lowestoft – and works south to Felixstowe and Ipswich, visiting many historical and picturesque Heritage Coast towns and villages on the way.

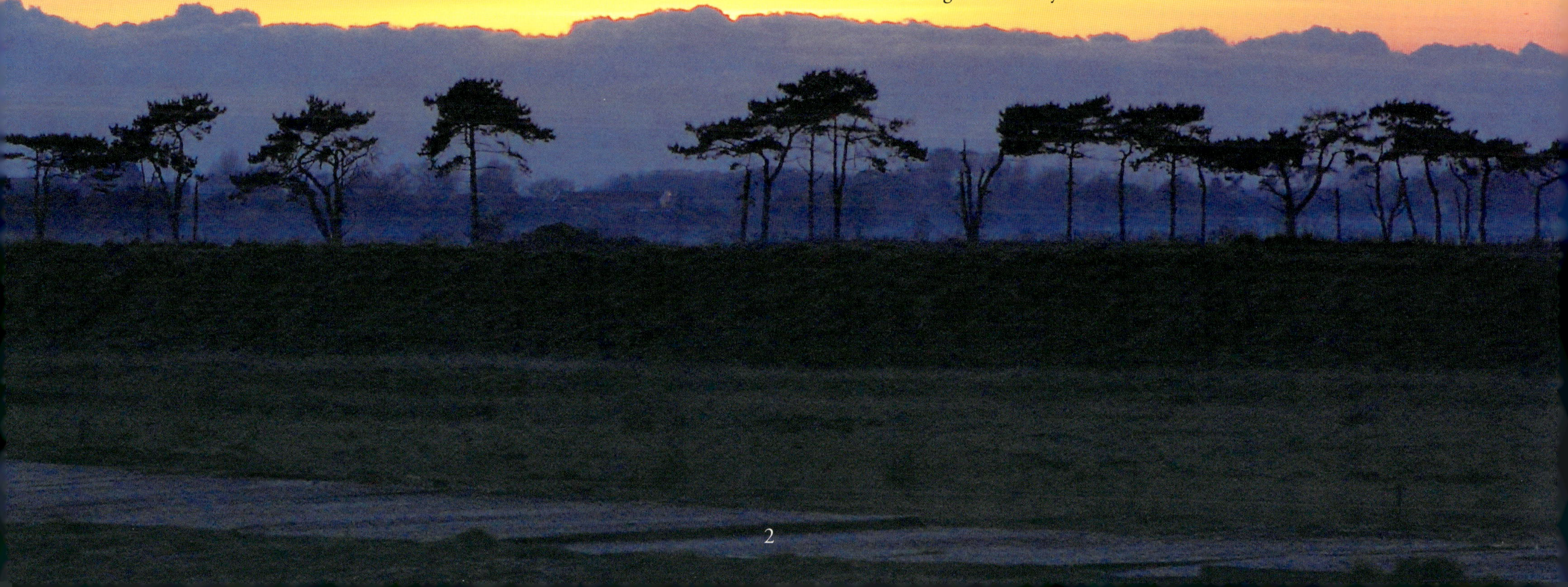

Lowestoft and the Waveney Valley

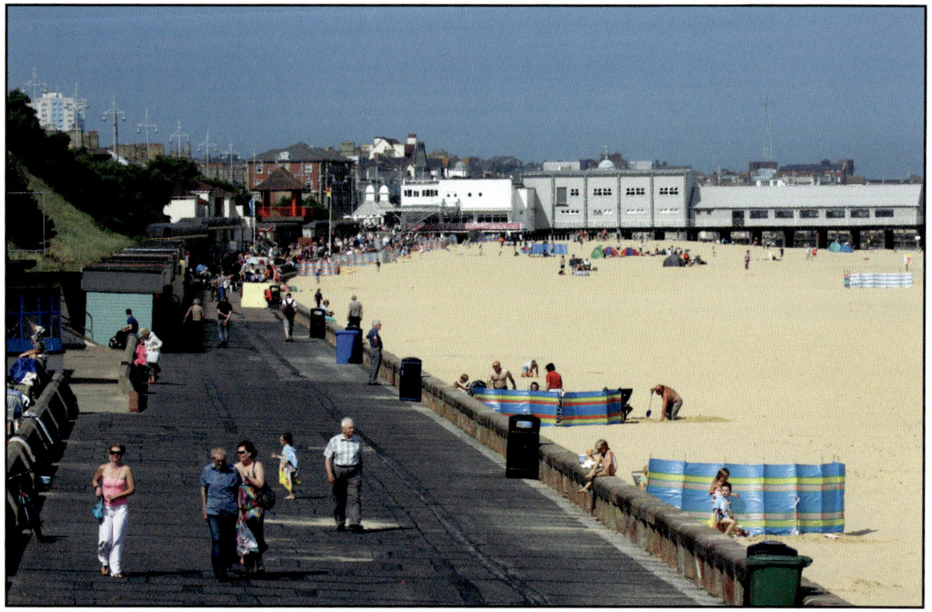

Lowestoft is the most easterly point in the UK. The town and the nearby Waveney Valley area are dubbed the Sunrise Coast, because the sun rises here before anywhere else in the country. Together with the rest of Coastal Suffolk, this area boasts the longest sunshine hours and driest climate in Great Britain, making it a popular choice as a beach holiday resort. More rain falls in Jerusalem than hereabouts. The 'big skies' and clear light of Suffolk have inspired artists, photographers, poets, writers and musicians for generations.

Edward Benjamin Britten was born at 21, Kirkley Cliff Road, Lowestoft on 22nd November, 1913. He was the youngest of four children. His first composition was attempted at the age of five, and he went on to compose prolifically when living here as a child.

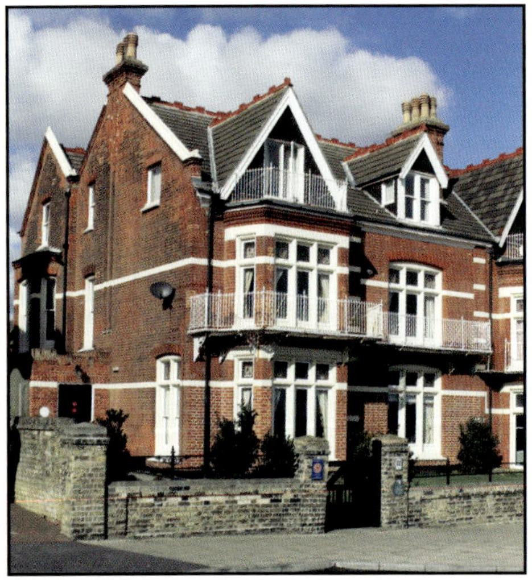

From his family house on the sea front (left) he would have watched fishing boats entering and leaving the busy harbour – once the home port to a large fleet of herring drifters and trawlers. Those boats have now disappeared from this part of the coast, with a mere handful of small fishing vessels remaining in the harbour. The decline in the Lowestoft fishing industry, and the town that was built around it, is due to reduced fish stocks, and European fishing quotas.

Ever resilient, the harbour is now a supply base for offshore activities in the North Sea for both oil and gas, and for operations on the 500-megawatt Outer Gabbard Offshore Windfarm, the world's largest offshore windfarm. There is also a popular yachting marina within the harbour complex. To the west of the town is Oulton Broad, the southern entrance to the famed boating holiday playground of the Suffolk and Norfolk Broads.

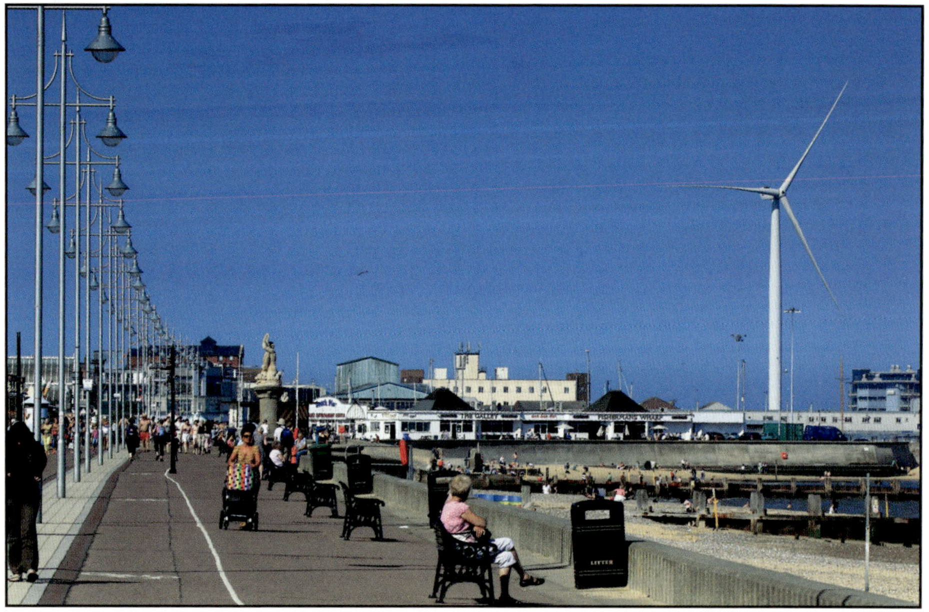

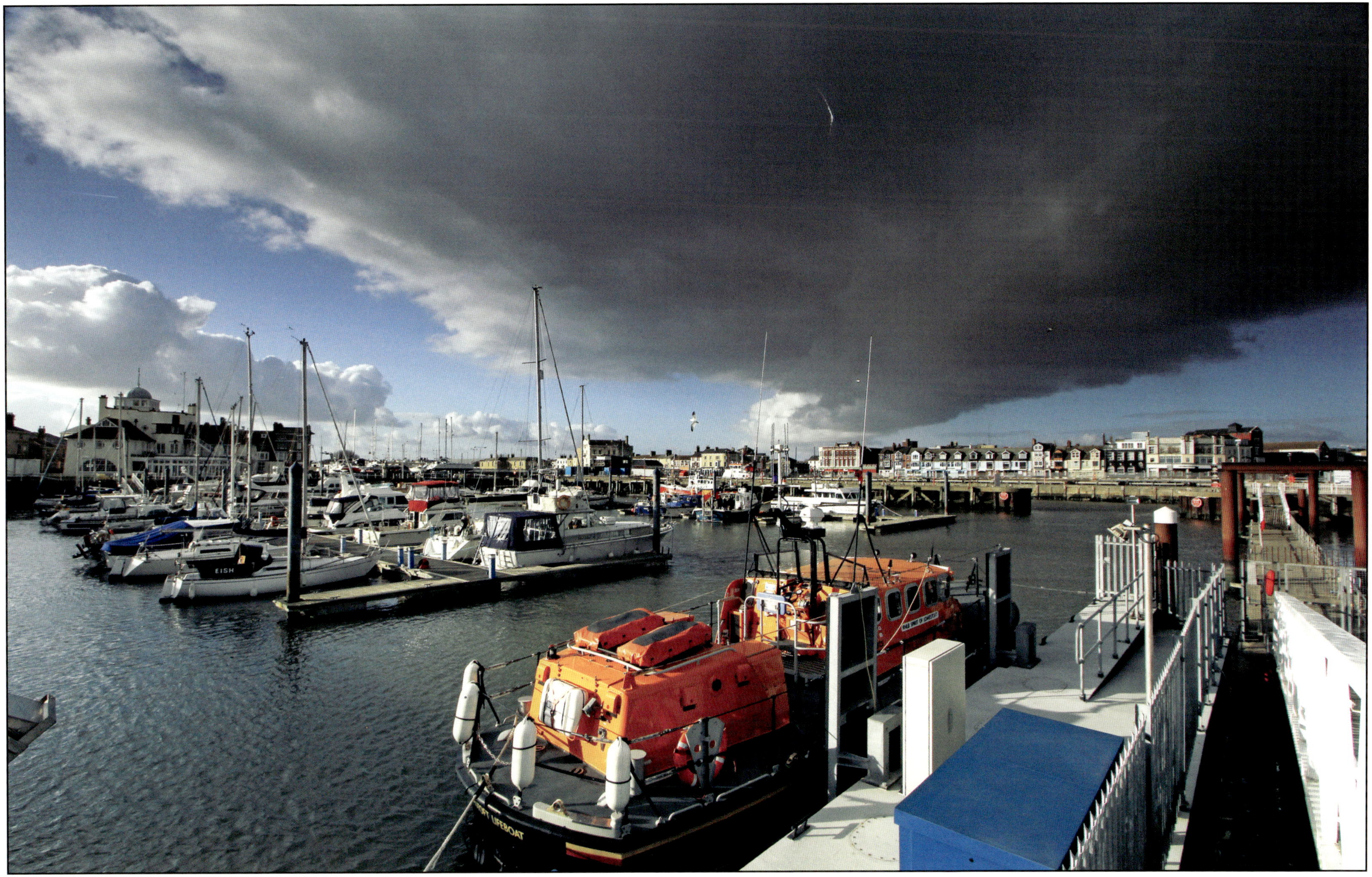

With the entrance guarded by the ever-vigilant RNLI lifeboat, pleasure craft in and around Lowestoft harbour now outnumber commercial vessels ten to one.

Early beginnings

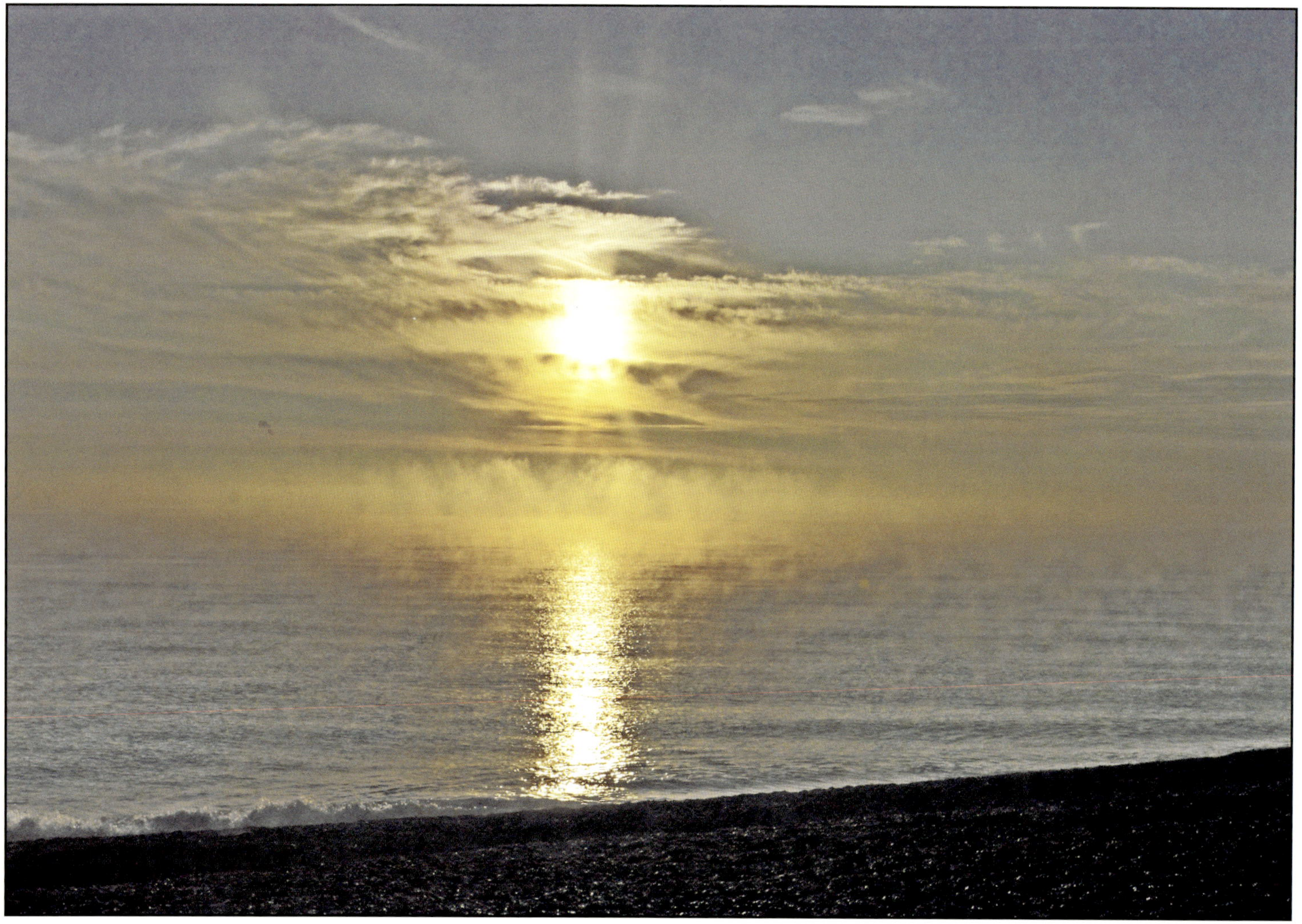

Raising its sleepy head from the morning quilt of sea mist, the golden dawn appears over the horizon at Lowestoft long before the sun rises in other parts of the United Kingdom.

Lowestoft is believed to be one of the earliest known sites of human habitation in Britain – flint tools dating back 700,000 years have been found at nearby Pakefield. With the coming of the railways in the nineteenth century, Lowestoft not only became a centre for the fishing industry, with daily railway shipments of fish to London, but also opened up the tourist trade to day-trippers attracted by the large sandy beaches that are bathed annually in above-average summer sunshine and below-average rainfall, making it a very popular seaside resort.

Ness Point, the most easterly tip of the British Isles, is marked by a large compass rose – the *Euroscope* – set at ground level (right). Around its perimeter various cities in Europe are marked, giving directions and distances from Lowestoft.

A 126 metre high wind turbine, known locally as *Gulliver,* dominates the skyline. Unlike the town beaches, this easterly section of foreshore is somewhat inhospitable, with large rocks put there to protect the point from the ever-threatening sea encroachment.

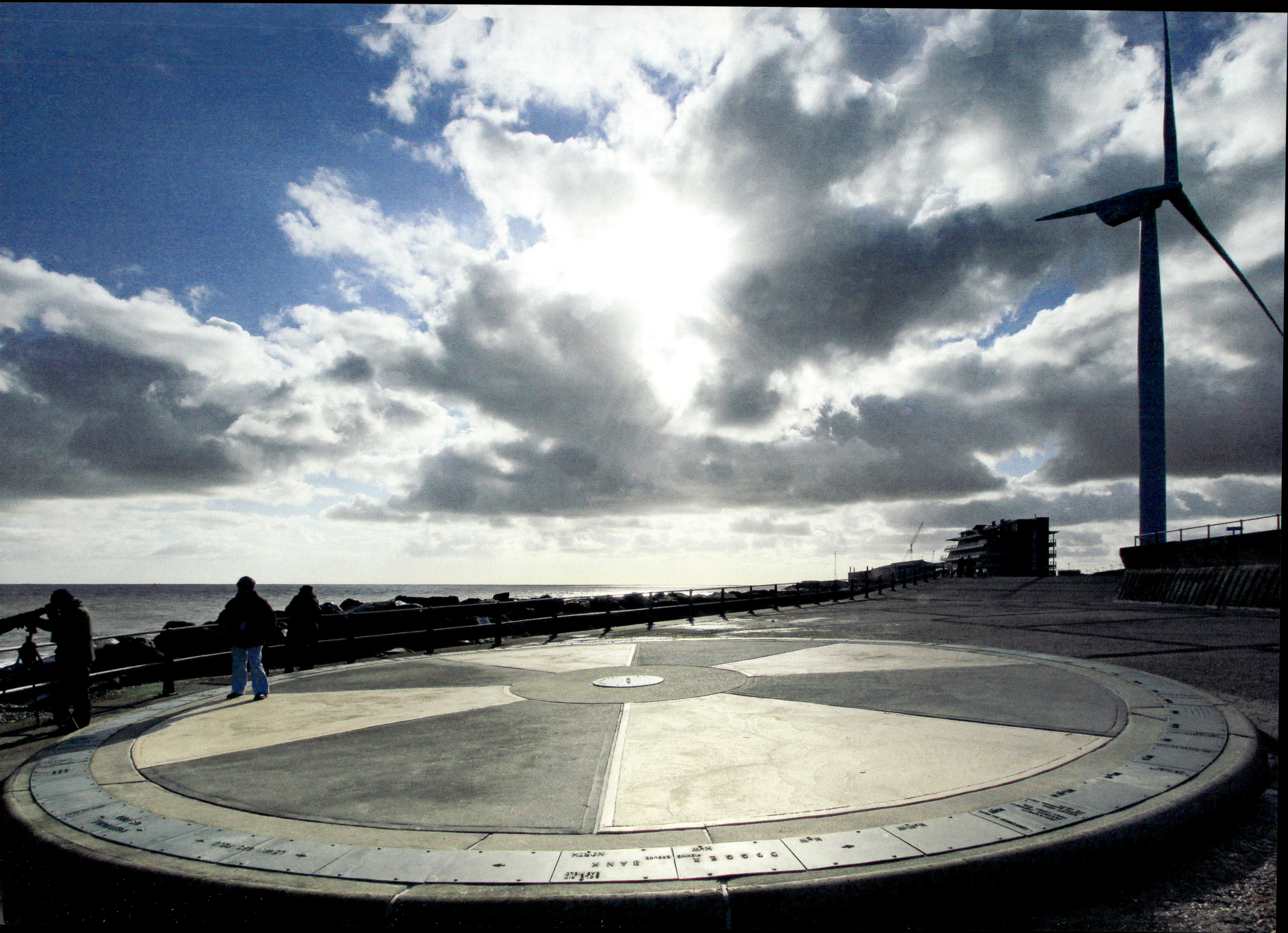
DOGGER BANK
NORTH

The Lowestoft 'Scores'

There are thirteen 'scores', or cuts (shortcuts), running from the high northern part of Lowestoft old town, down to the sea. The scores were named after local families or after a public house adjoining the score. Some of the original names have long since been changed, but they all provided a quick way to the sea for those engaged in fishing and ancillary occupations. Some originally had shops on either side making them a busy and profitable commercial area. These narrow scores, especially the ones with twists and turns, were no-go areas after dark for all but the bravest of souls – they had a reputation for harbouring ruthless robbers.

Every year the Lowestoft Scores Race is held – one of the most unique road races in the country. Covering an arduous and hilly distance of 4.75 miles, well over 100 runners run for charity.

For the less energetic, the scores trail can be walked following the sign of the fish embedded on the pavements.

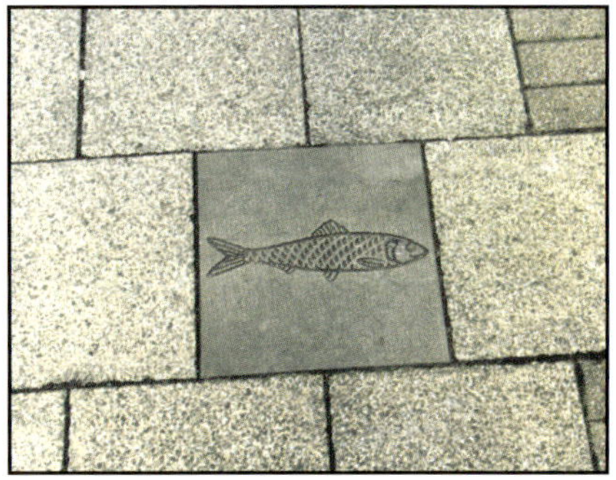

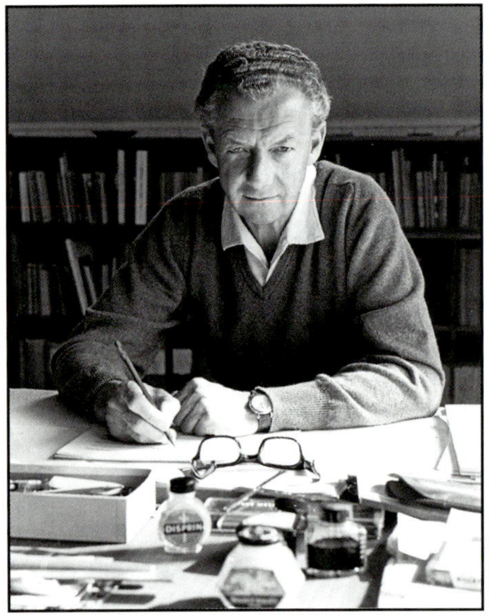

As a child Benjamin Britten would have been very familiar with the Lowestoft scores. Scores of a different kind – music scores – would become his lifetime work, and make him one of the foremost composers of the twentieth century.

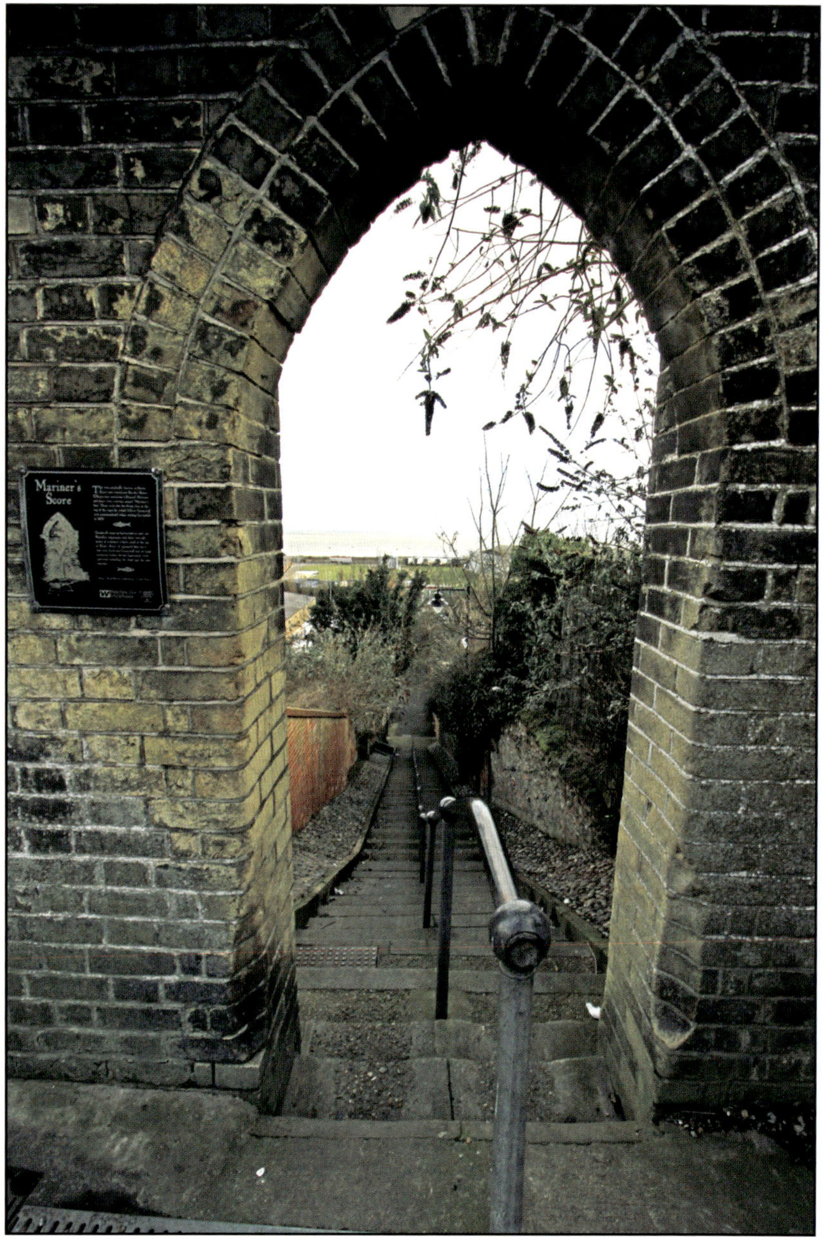

Mariners Score (above) was formerly known as Swan Score, named after the now demolished Swan Inn at the top, in which Oliver Cromwell stayed when hunting down Royalist supporters.

Oulton Broad – gateway to a boater's dream

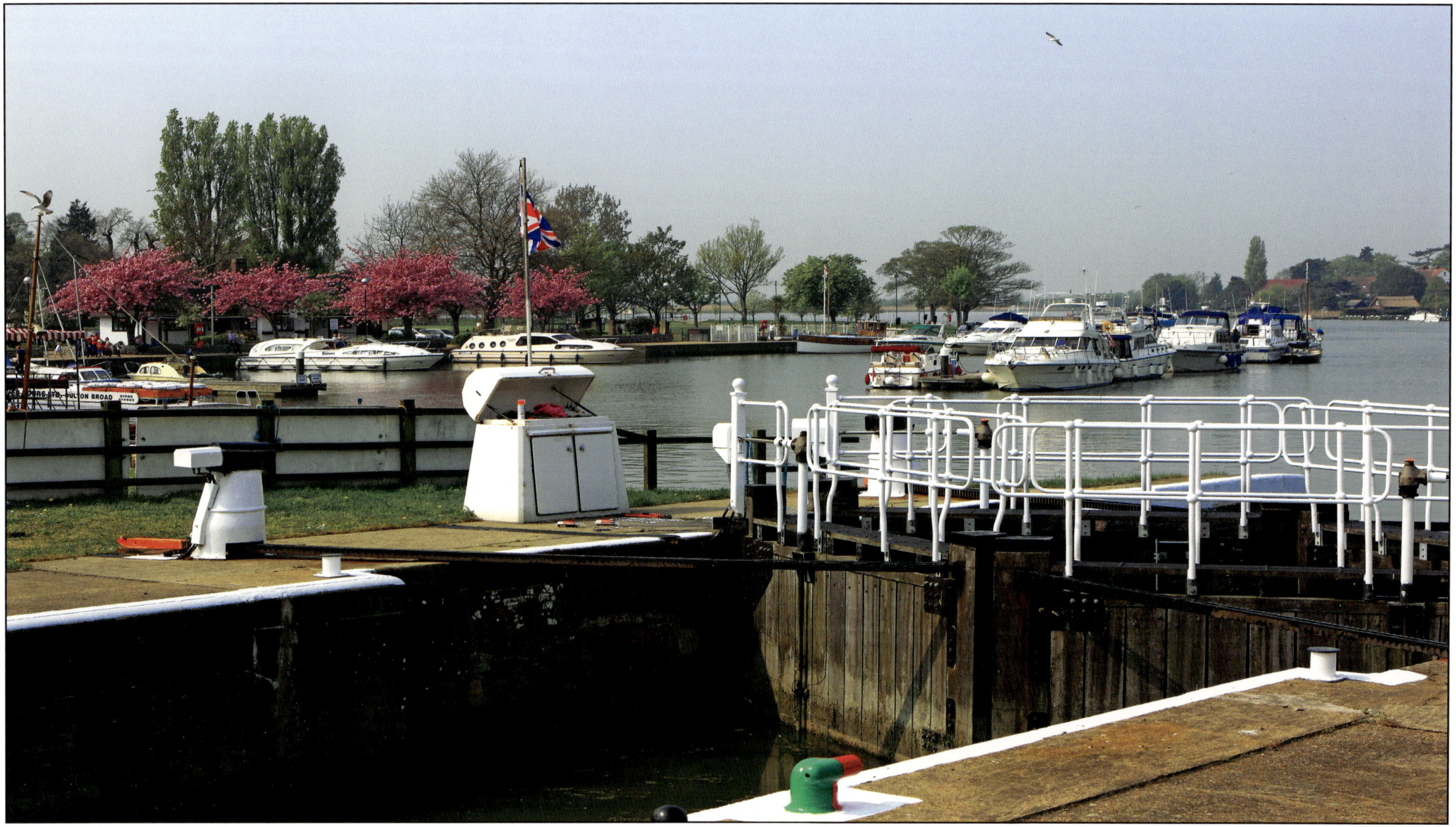

This lock gate at Oulton Broad, just on the western outskirts of Lowestoft, leads to the non-tidal holiday playground of the Broads. From here the placid waterways of the Suffolk and Norfolk Broads can be explored as 'skipper' of your own hired motor cruiser.

The end of the road!

South from Lowestoft and past the holiday and caravan parks of Kessingland, the shoreline becomes an undeveloped deserted coastline bordered by high cliffs and fields of light arable land, making it a coastal walker's paradise of peace and solitude. Not without good reason is development restricted along this coast.

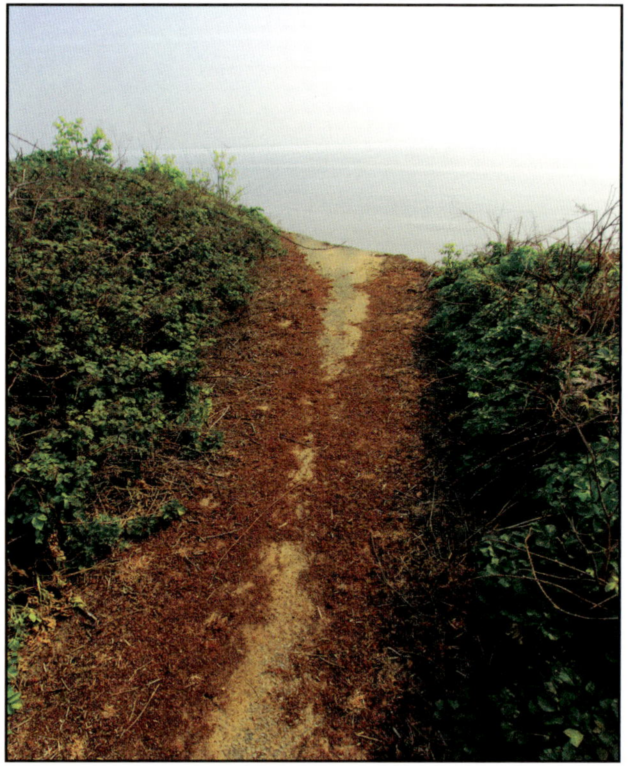

All twenty residents of Covehithe can only wait and dread the time when their properties, farms, and church fall victim to the ever-encroaching sea. Almost a third of a mile of land has been lost here during the past 150 years, and their cliff-top corn fields are being eroded at a faster rate now than ever before, under the merciless hammering received when North Sea storms and high tidal surges vent their fury on this vulnerable sandy coastline. The weed-covered road that once led to the beach now comes to an abrupt cliff-top stop – going nowhere (right). In the Middle Ages Covehithe was known as North Hales, and prospered during the reign of Edward I when a magnificent church was built to showcase its wealth (opposite page). Destroyed during the civil war, the current smaller church was rebuilt within the ruins in 1672, retaining the original tower. The 'downsizing rebuild' reflected the declining prosperity of the town.

As a county Suffolk is rich in grand churches, and coastal Suffolk is no exception. Early productions of Britten's operas were hosted in churches when no other venue was suitable.

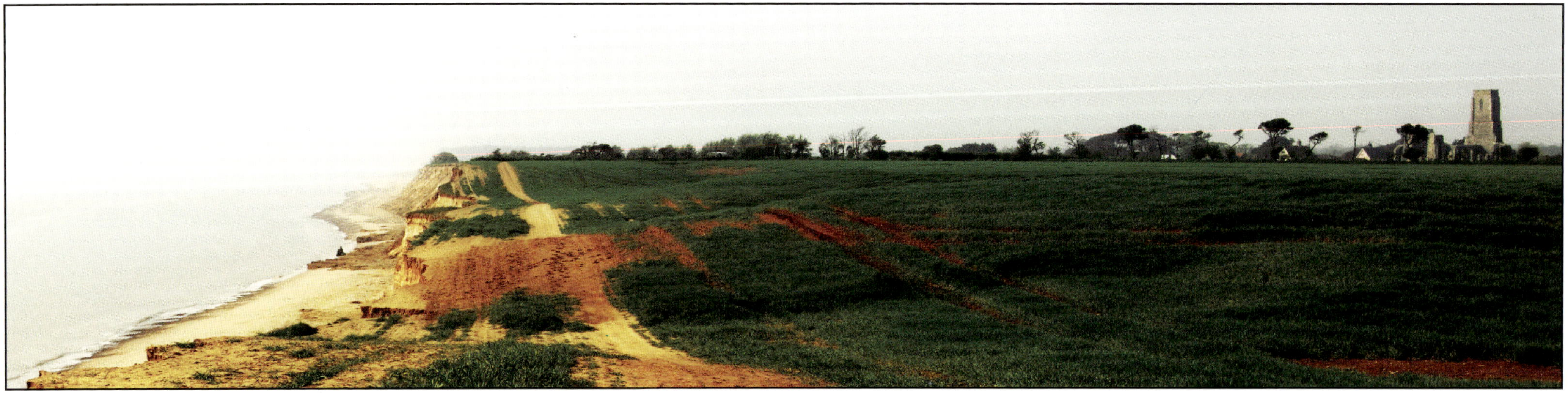

This picture clearly shows how arable land has been lost to erosion since this field was seeded with cereal crops only a few weeks before this picture was taken.
How long will it be before St Andrew's Church, Covehithe succumbs to the ravages of the North Sea?

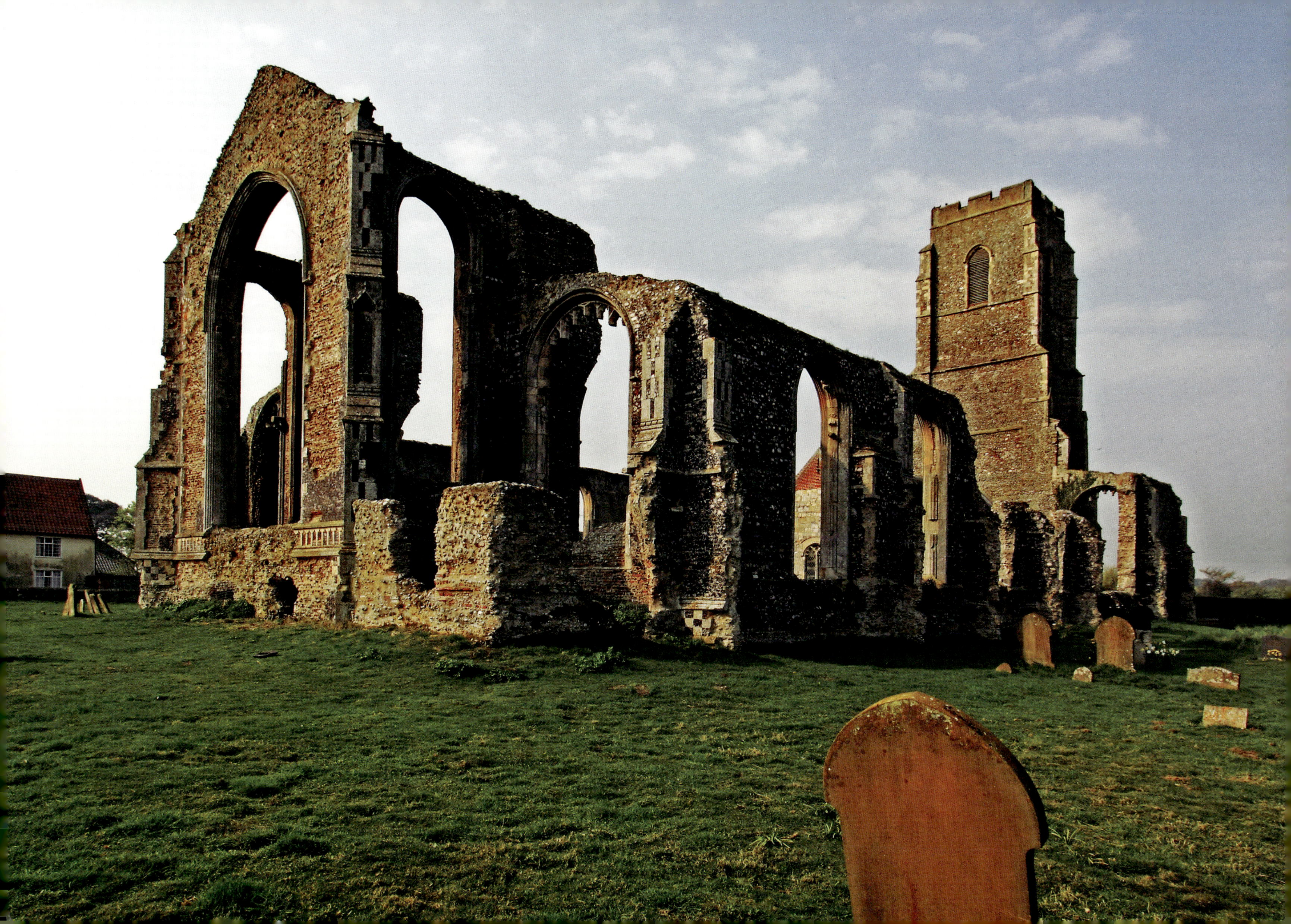

Southwold

Southwold conjures up a clichéd picture of an upmarket East Coast seaside town with gaily painted beach huts, a lighthouse, a famous brewery and one of Suffolk's finest churches. Yes – it's all of that, and much more. It is a place that speaks to people in different ways. It stands resolute on a low cliff top, manly defying everything that the North Sea can throw at it. Notwithstanding its hard-core robustness, I get a sense of femininity about the place – delicate, colourful, almost prissy in its architectural individuality – but make no mistake, it's bold in its atmospheric character. It is, in essence, a photographer's and artist's dream of a place.

The *Domesday Book* mentions it as being an important fishing port. It received its charter from Henry VII in 1489. A shingle bar gradually built up outside the outer harbour and prevented the town from developing its seafaring ambitions. A devastating fire in 1659 destroyed most of the town – the reason why no timbered buildings remain today – and damaged St Edmund's church. Some areas were never rebuilt; instead Southwold now benefits from unique open greens to the south of the town, bordered by very tasty houses, some originally built for wealthy sea captains.

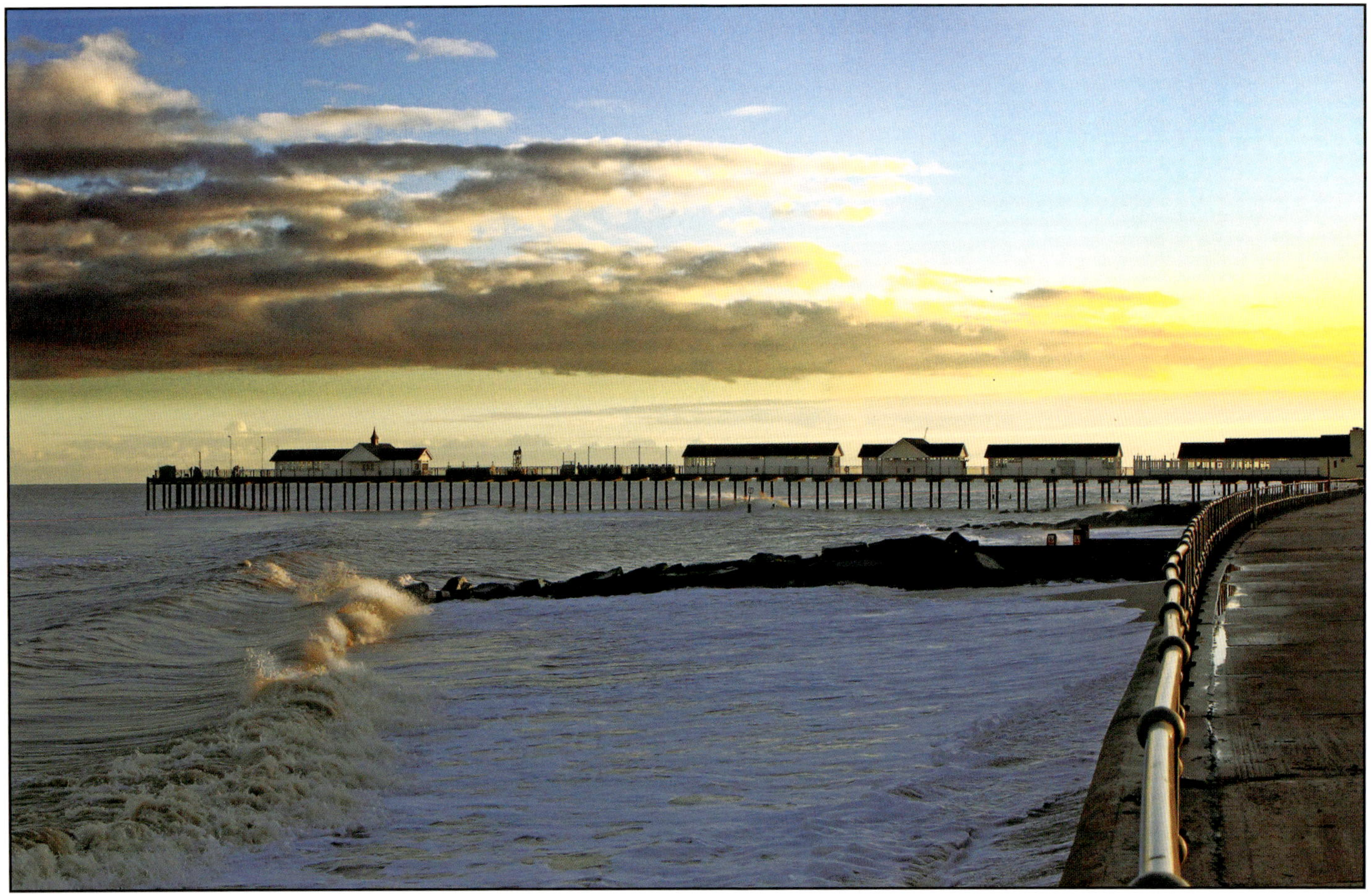

When you hear talk of beach huts changing hands for six-figure sums, you know we're not talking about your average bucket-and-spade resort, although it is a very popular family destination, with its award-winning sandy beach and all-weather pier entertainments. This is a place where the seriously wealthy have second homes. Keep an eye out for the glitterati – the chances are you will happen upon one during a visit. It's also a popular location for film and television producers. The writer Eric Blair, better known under his pen name of George Orwell, returned to live here with his parents (next door to where the fish and chip shop now is – look for the blue plaque) where he wrote his novel *A Clergyman's Daughter*.

Benjamin Britten had a mild flirtation with Southwold when he sounded out the town council to back a music festival here. This was just after the Second World War, and they were not impressed with the idea. A later approach made to Aldeburgh council proved to be much more fruitful for all concerned.

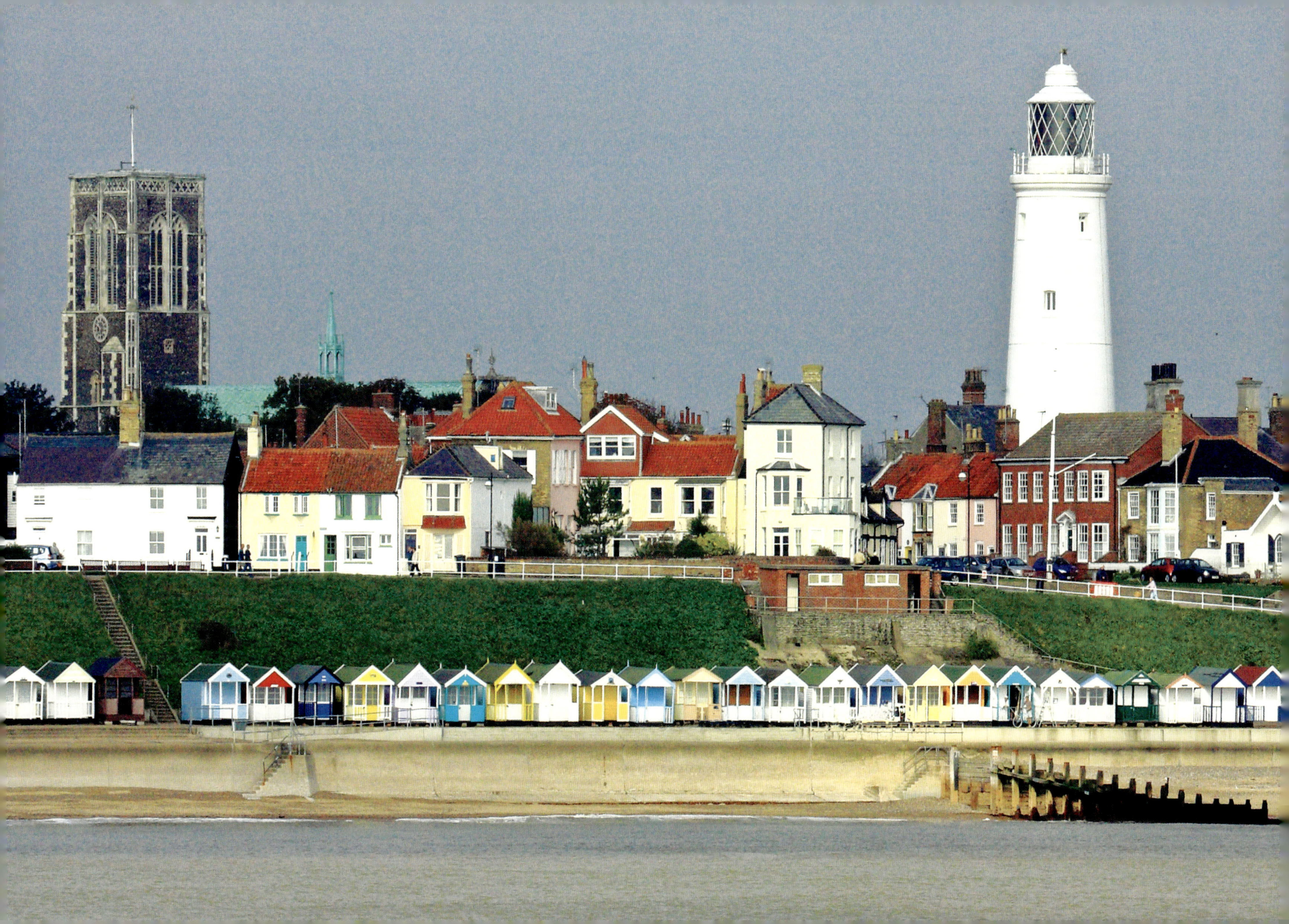

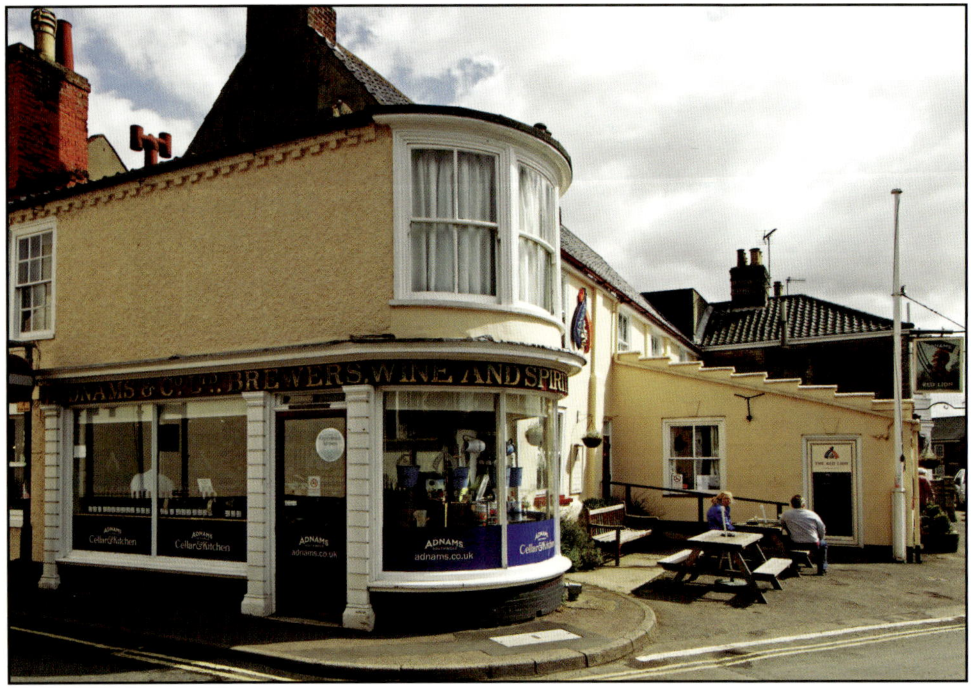
adnams.co.uk

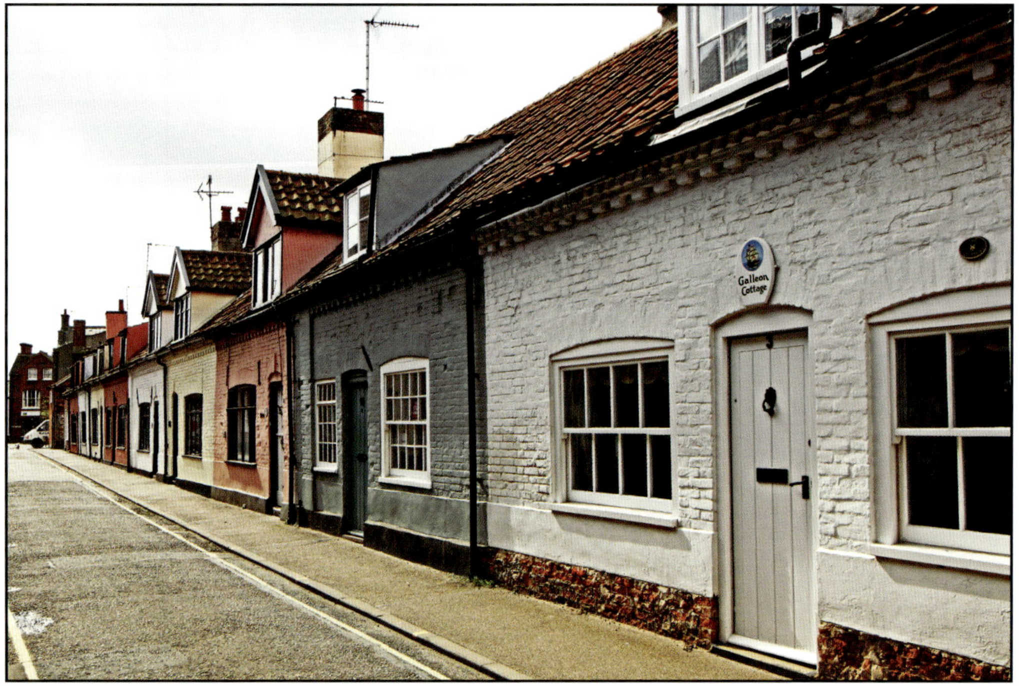
Galleon
Cottage

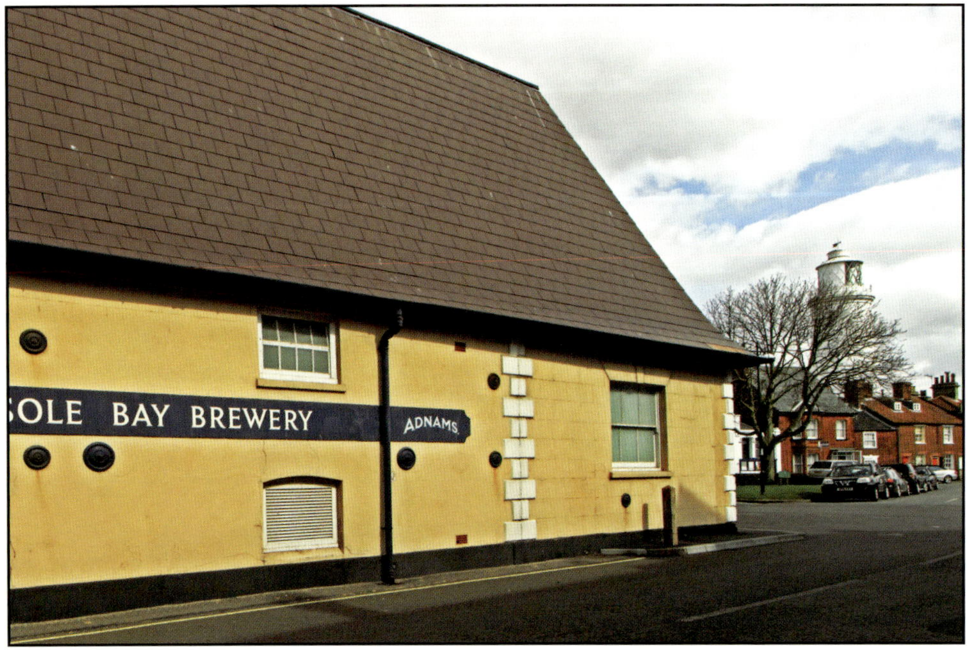
SOLE BAY BREWERY
ADNAMS

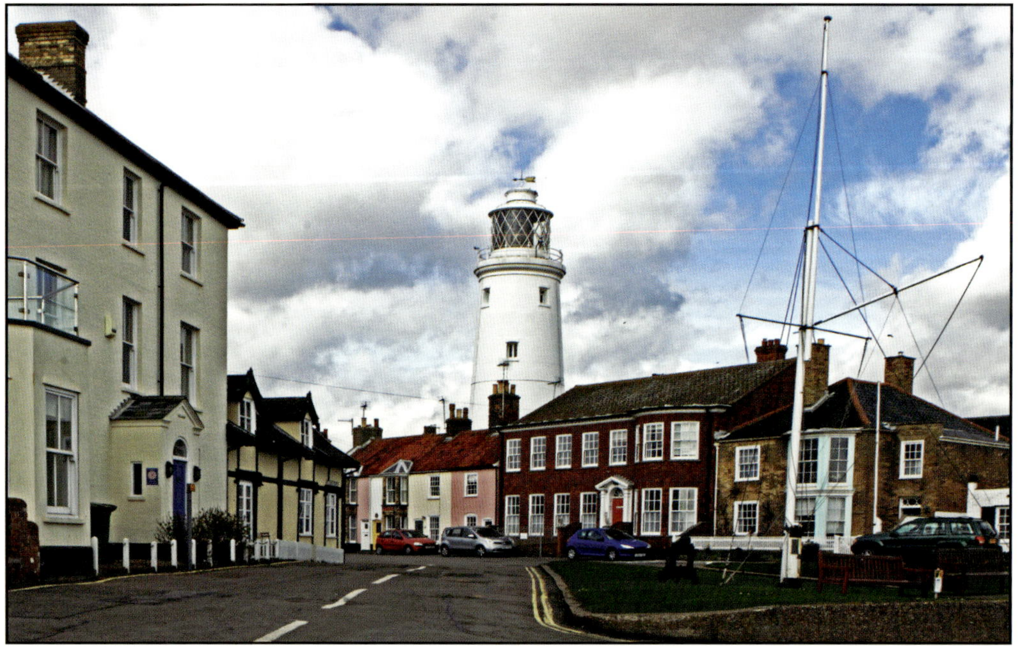

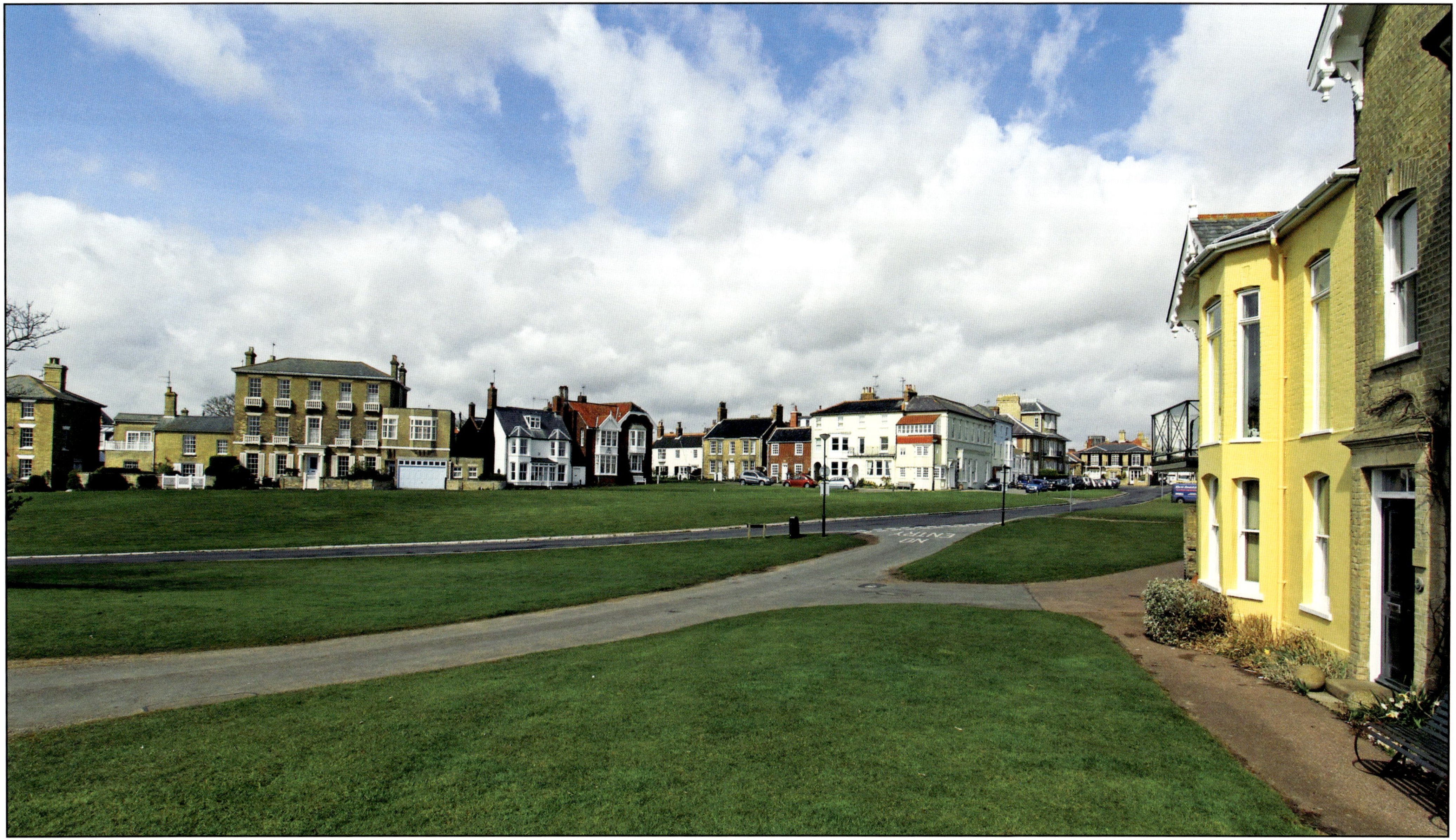

A glorious mélange of housing styles and architectural gems, of proportion and size, of openness and cosiness, all of which came together long before the advent of town planners. Southwold residents are fiercely proud of their town, although few born-and-bred residents can now afford even the smallest of terraced cottages due to highly inflated property prices in the old town – most are now holiday homes. The lighthouse, which can be seen for miles around, merges unobtrusively into the whole scene, as do Adnams brewing interests, evident everywhere in the town; it all just fits together harmoniously – and it works.

The casual visitor quickly passing by St Edmund's Church on the road into Southwold could be forgiven for taking only a cursory glance, thinking that it's just another beautiful Suffolk church.

Stop ... don't go past.

This is one of the loveliest of Suffolk churches, and deserves much closer examination, inside and out. Built in the fifteenth century at about the same time as other great Suffolk churches, this one is truly outstanding. Not only is the outside facade wonderfully proportioned: look more closely at the finest detail on the flushwork of knapped flint (flushwork is where the flint is laid flush with the wall) – it is an amazing example of the decorative skills of the stonemasons who built it.

Venture inside and it becomes even more breathtaking. For a start it's so light and airy. The original stained glass windows were taken care of by Mr Dowsing and his band of puritan vandals in 1644. Subsequent replacement dark Victorian stained glass windows were blown out by Mr Hitler's bombers. So we are left, fortuitously in my view, with a light interior that does full justice to the beautiful hammerbeam roof and painted ceiling, and one of the finest screens of any church in the county. Comprising three screens – a rood screen across the chancel arch and parclose screens across the north and south chancel aisles – they stretch from one side of the church to the other. Although they have been beautifully and sensitively restored they still retain their original thirty-six dado figures.

There is some speculation that these screens might originally have come from elsewhere – possibly Covehithe or Kessingland or nearby Walberswick – all churches that were downsized as their prosperity waned.

St Edmund's Church Southwold

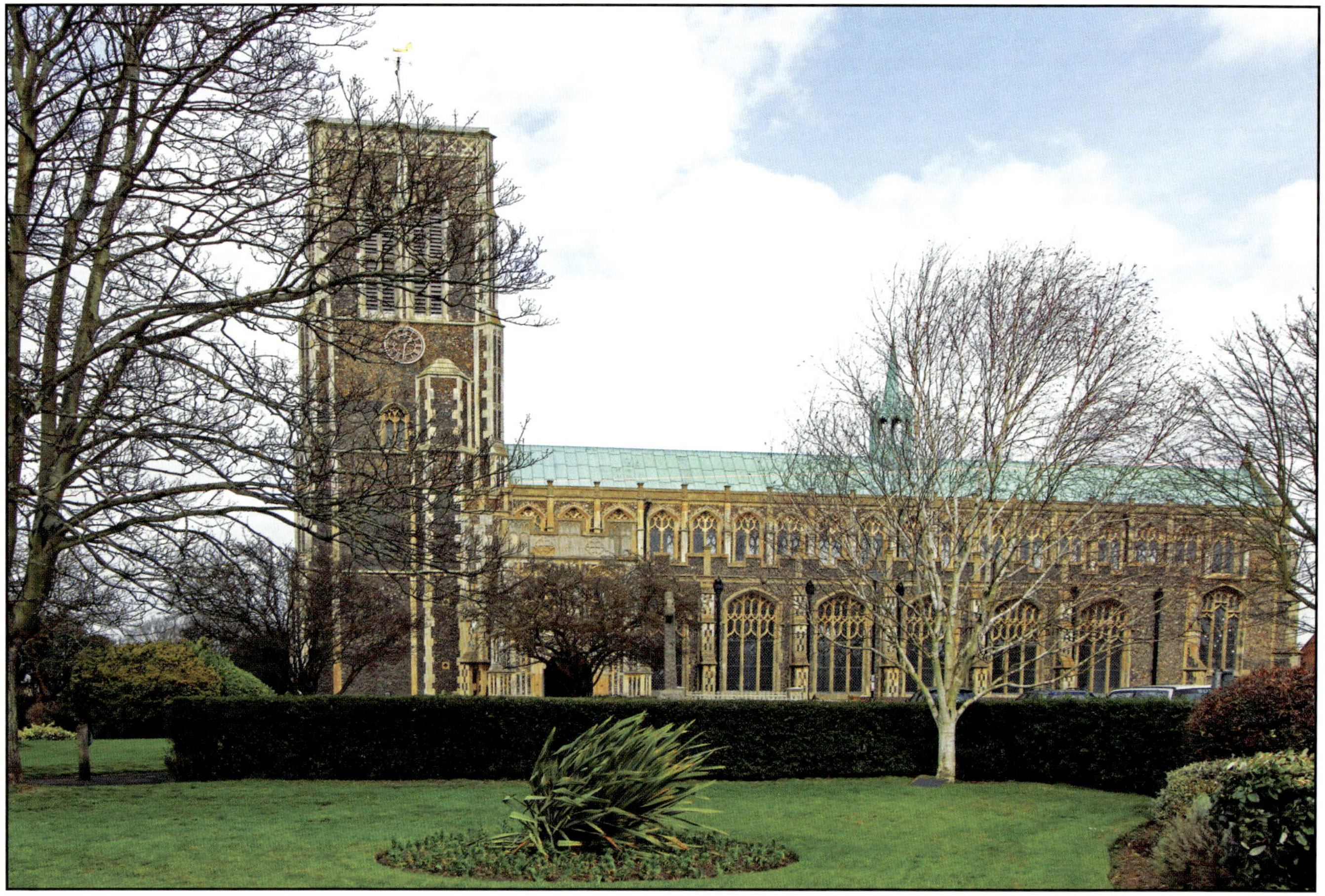

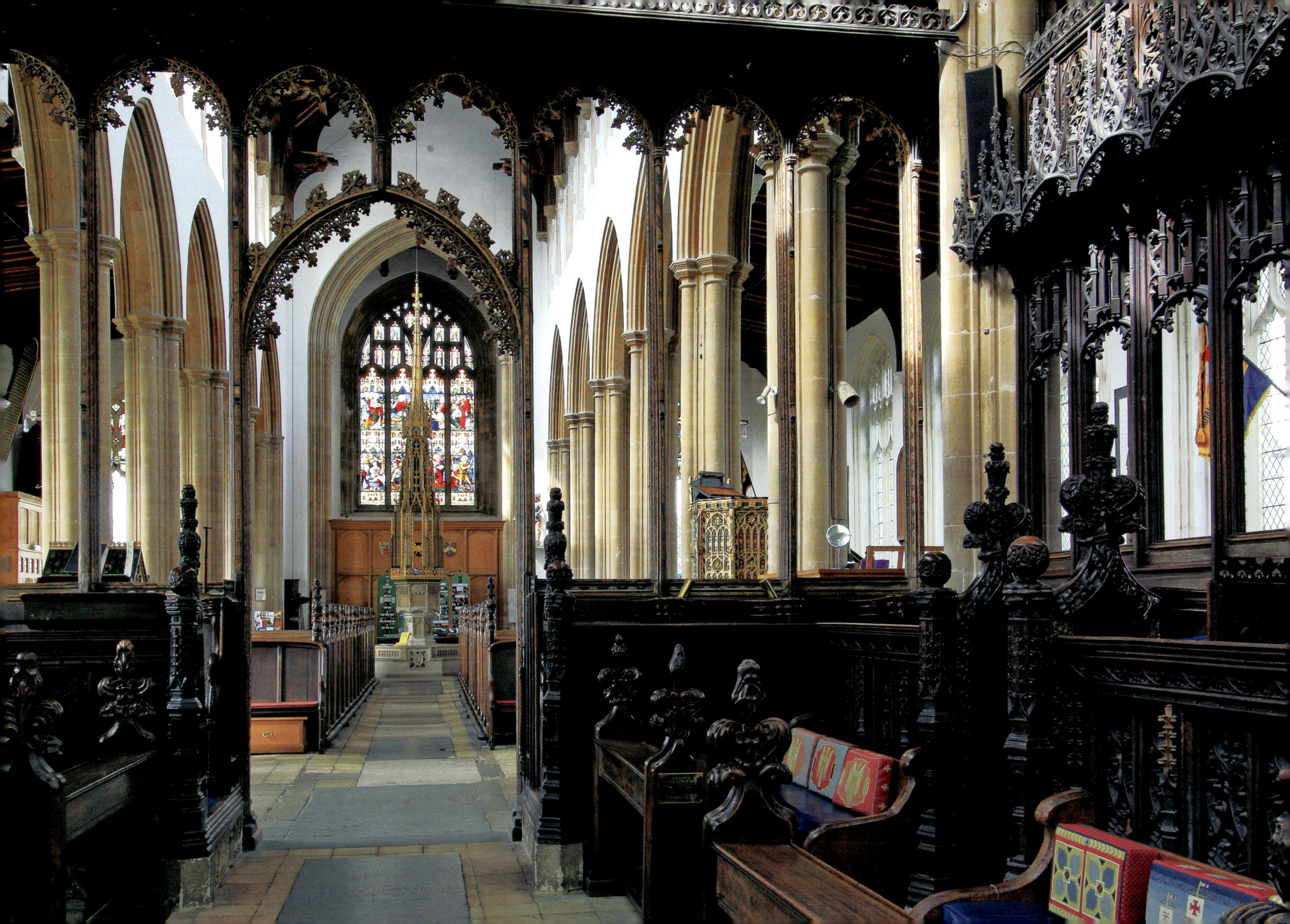

Suffolk craftsmanship at its very best

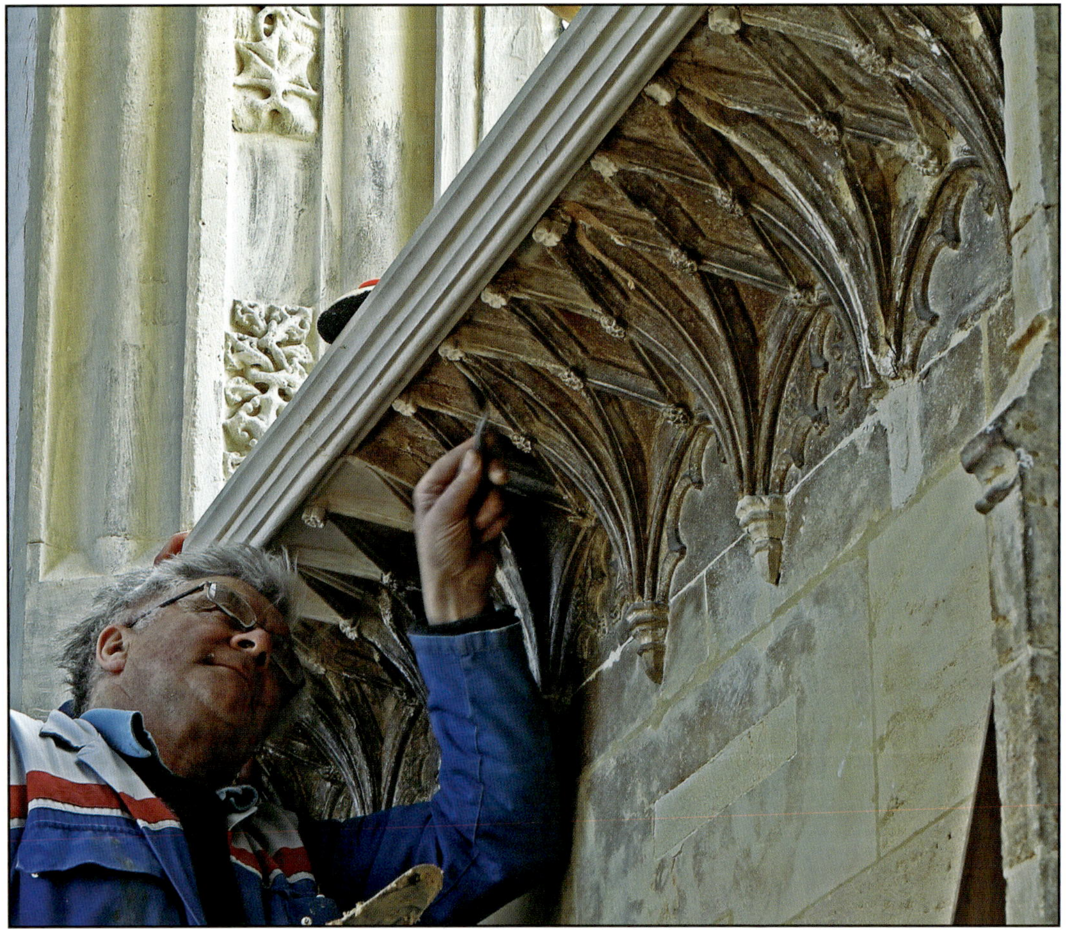

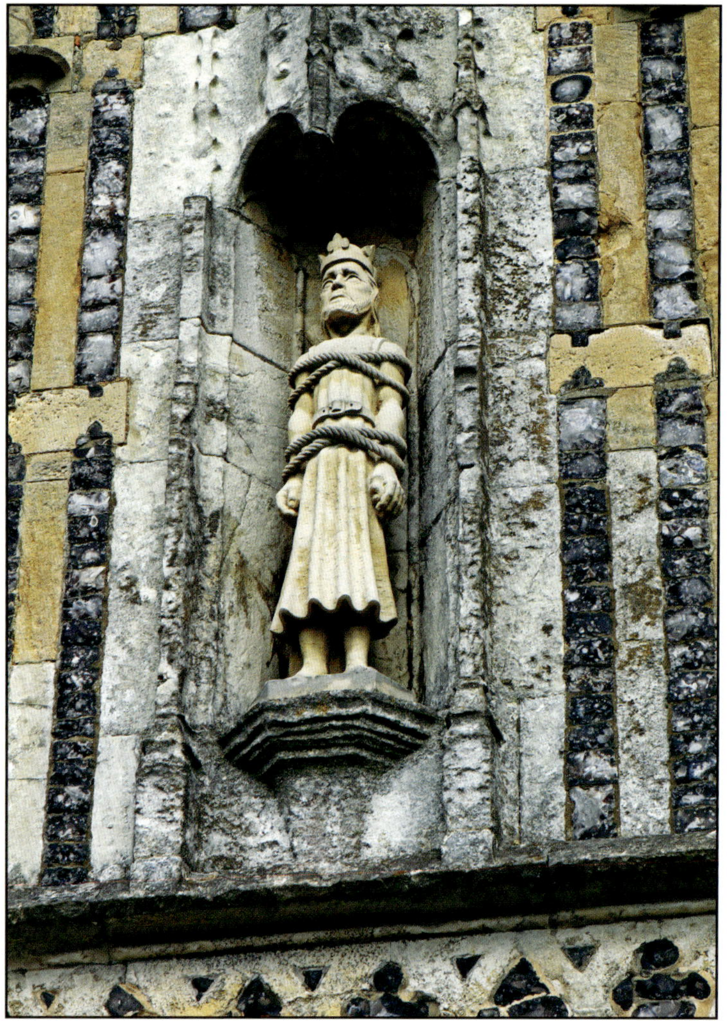

The church was named after St Edmund, who was crowned King of East Anglia in about AD 855. He was a great leader and Christian, who was murdered and martyred for persistently refusing to renounce his faith. Various legends surround his death, and many in East Anglia regard him as the true patron saint of England, debunking the mythical St George. The statue above the entrance porch of the church depicts St Edmund bound with rope, before he was shot through with arrows and beheaded. His feast day is held on 20th November, and to celebrate this day Southwold children have traditionally been given sticky buns.

Walking around St Edmund's church, superb craftsmanship just shouts at you. The skill of the woodworker's intricate carvings is matched only by those of the stonemason. Modern-day craftsmen continue that noble tradition. The magnificent hammerbeam roof is relatively modern, and repairs and renovations are an ongoing process to maintain this wonderful church for future generations to enjoy. The splendid screens are seen in more detail on the right.

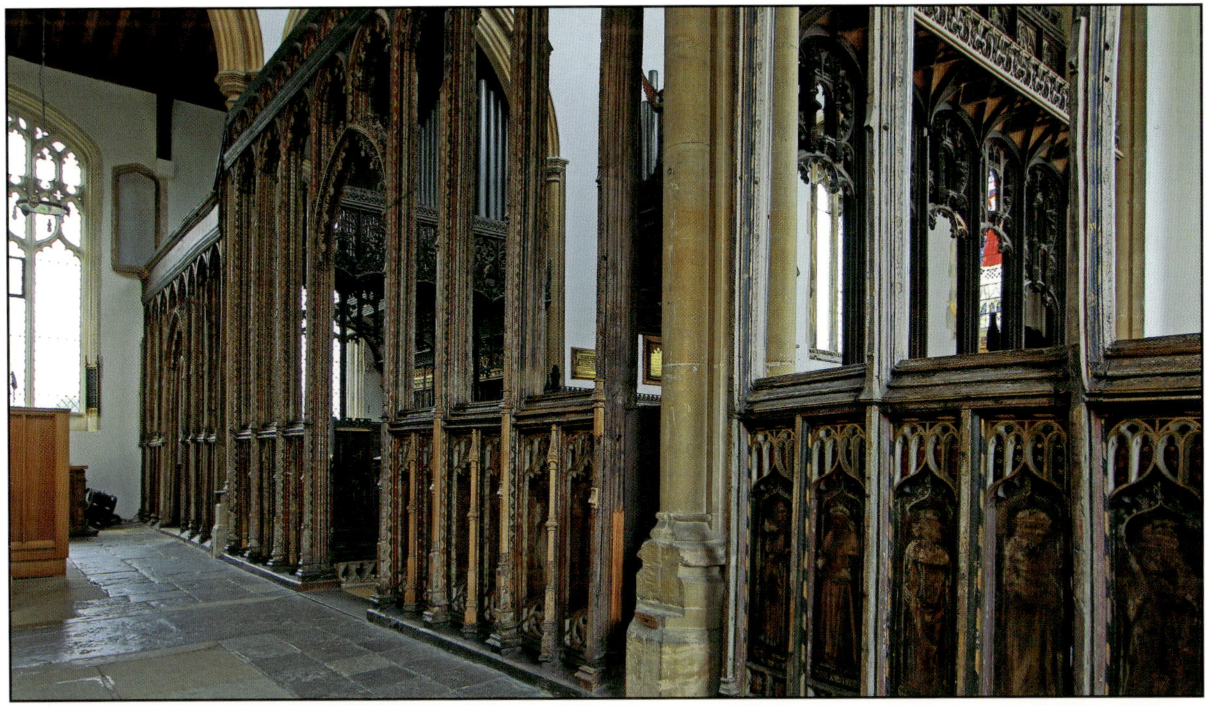

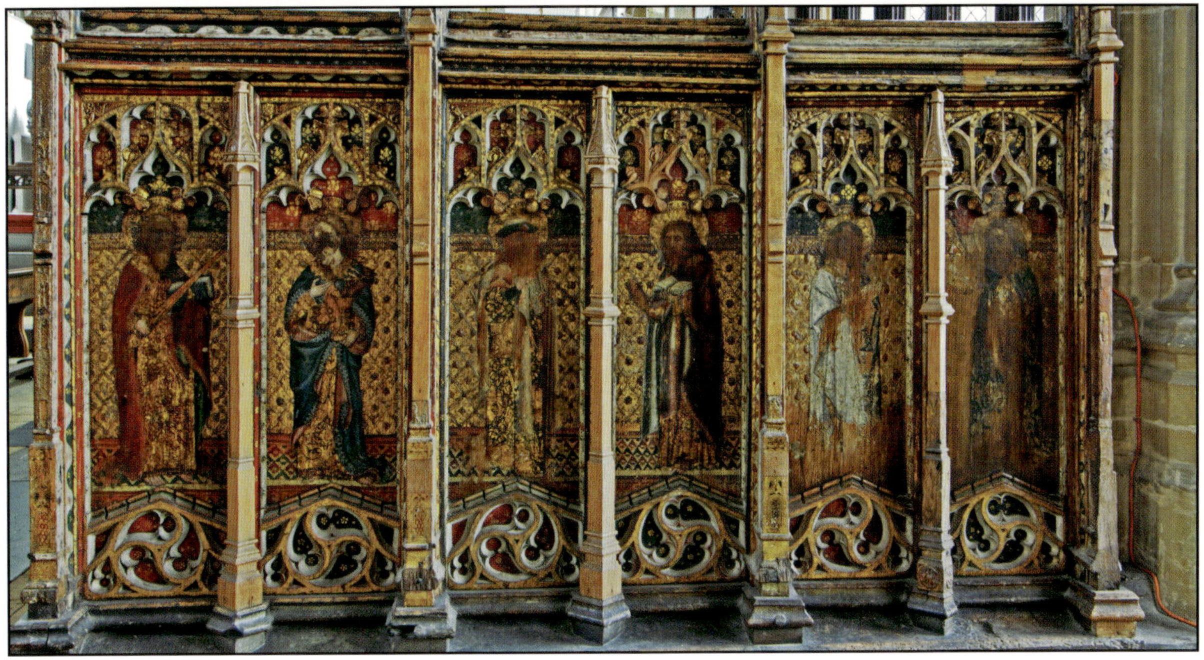

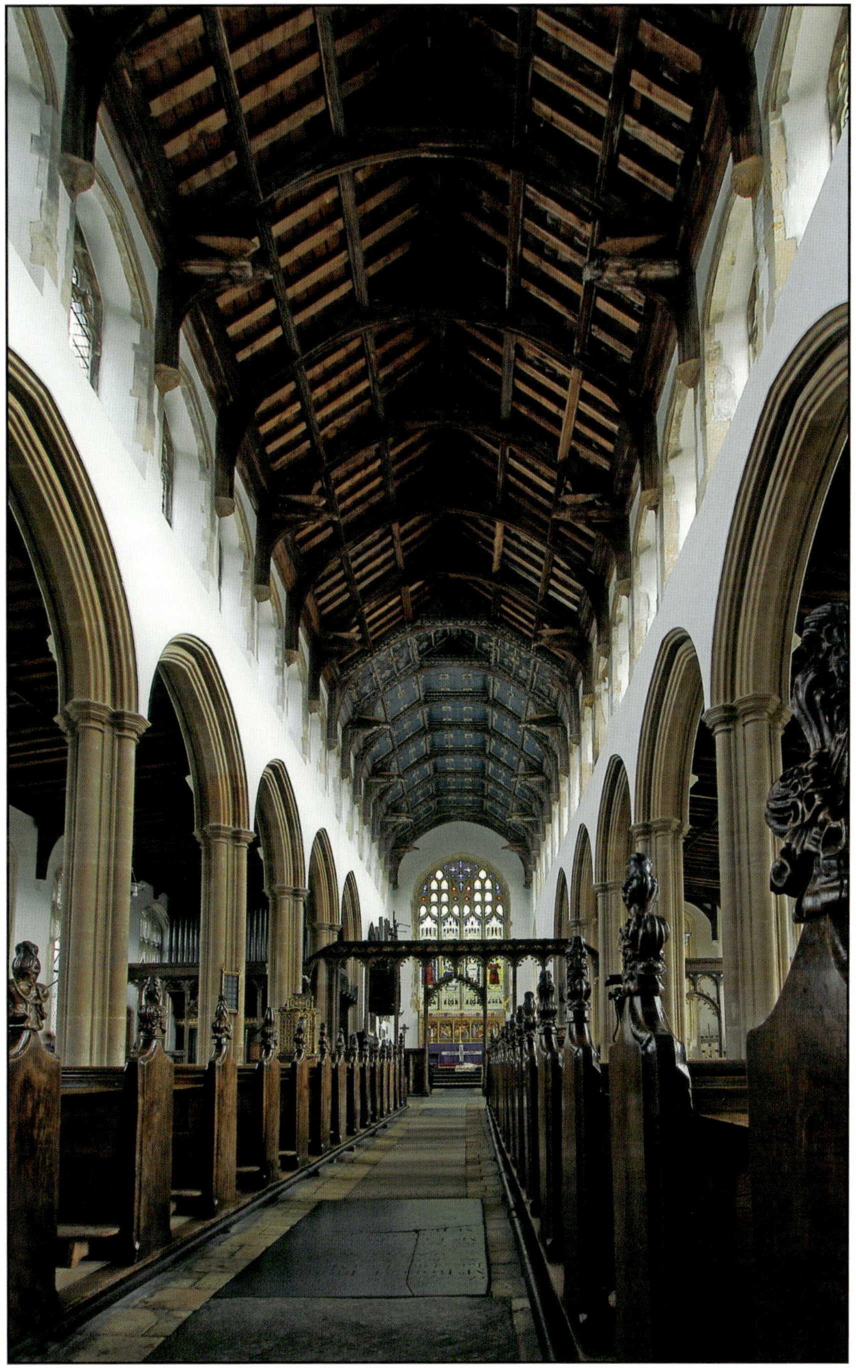

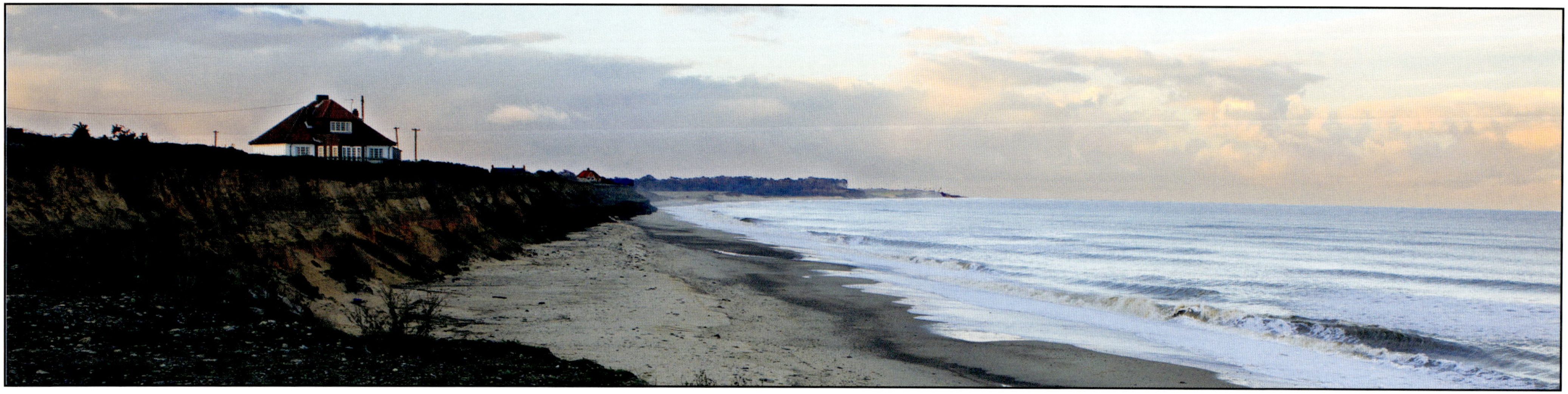

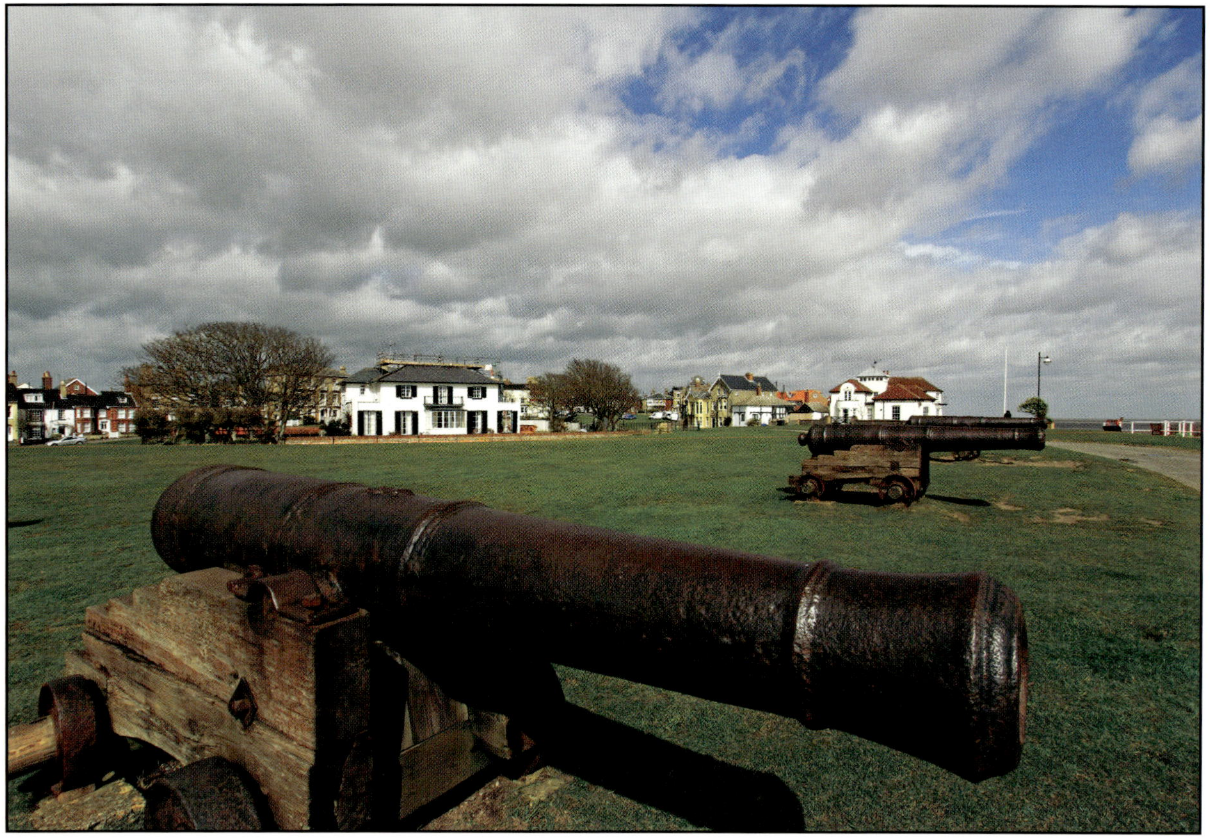

The Battle of Sole Bay

Like all Suffolk's coastal towns, Southwold has seen its share of sea battles. In the summer of 1672 the bloody naval battle of Sole Bay was played out within sight of Southwold, when a combined total of 151 ships and many thousands of sailors of a joint Anglo-French fleet battled against the Dutch for naval supremacy. With heavy losses on both sides, the conflict ended inconclusively, with many bodies being washed ashore onto surrounding beaches.

The ongoing battle with the sea continues at Easton Bavents at the north end of Southwold (above) where cliff erosion threatens property. Turn around 180 degrees (right page) and this is how close Southwold town is to this area of erosion.

Not even the eighteen-pounder cannons standing on Gun Green, put there to commemorate the Battle of Sole Bay, can offer any protection against the mighty North Sea. Fortunately for Southwold old town it stands on high ground and is protected by sturdy sea defences, unlike the harbour area to the south.

Undoubtedly Britten's music was influenced by the vicissitudes of the North Sea.

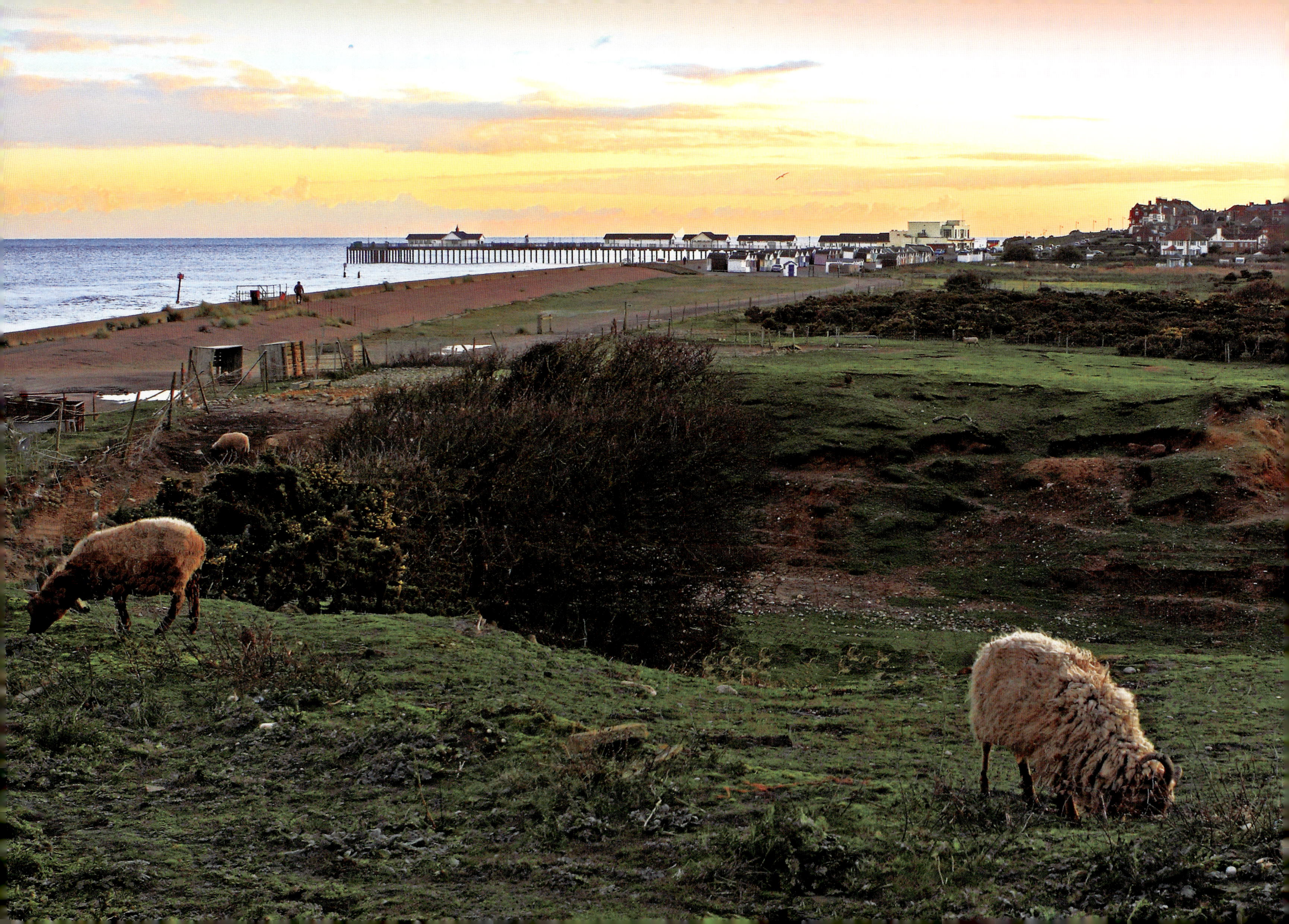

Southwold Harbour

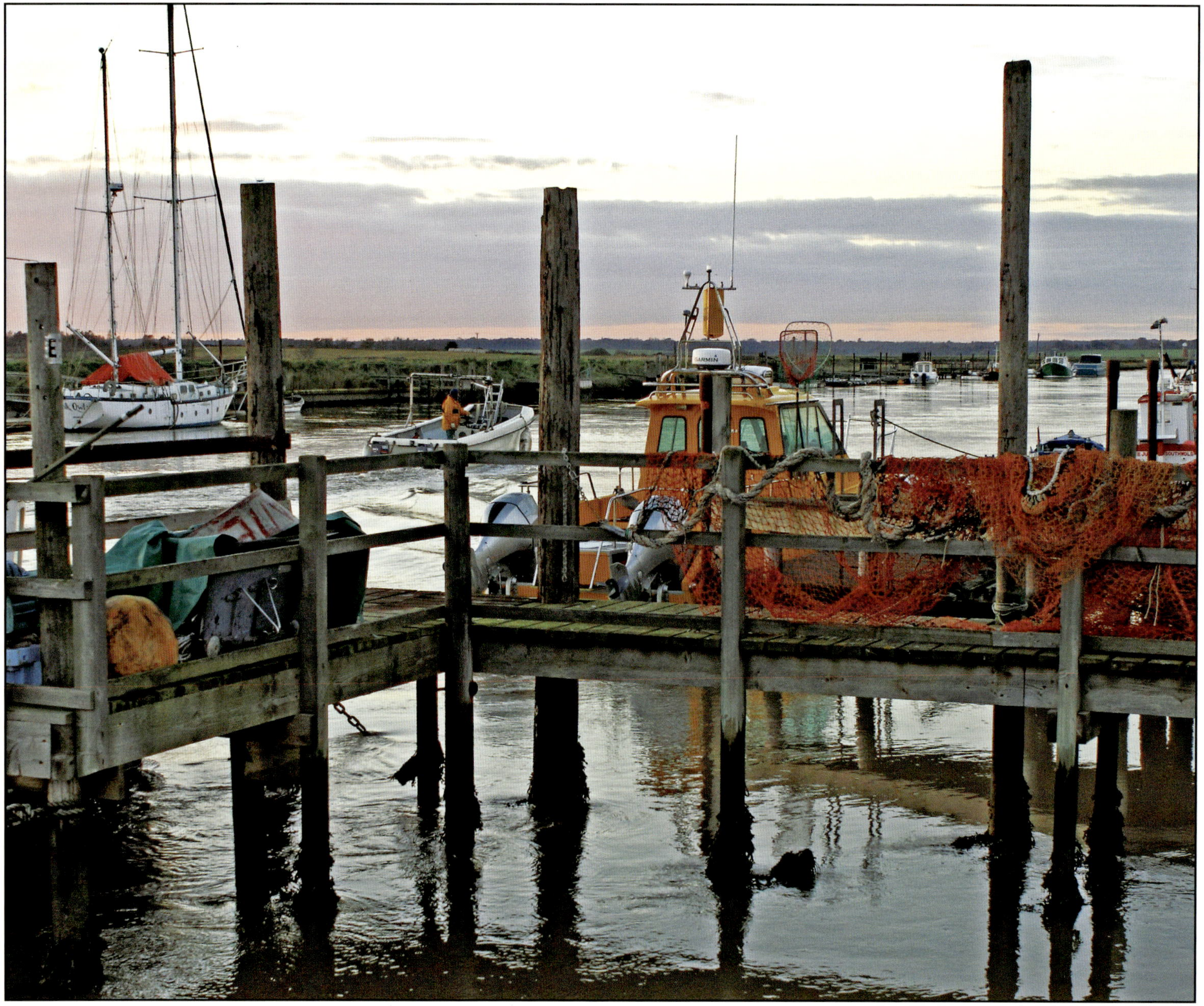

Southwold is virtually surrounded by water, making it almost an island. The harbour is at the mouth of the River Blyth, and a little way upstream Buss Creek encircles the higher land around the town. The notorious surge tides in 1953 caused flooding havoc in this low-lying creek region, and to the harbour. Some idea of how high the water came is dramatically illustrated at the Harbour Inn where markers on the outside wall indicate the height of the flood water – ten feet above normal high tide. This area still floods during exceptional high water.

The harbour river bank is a wonderful orderly mess of boats, wooden huts, jetties, buoys, fishing nets, and other paraphernalia used by fishermen, boat builders, yachtsmen, and others who live by the sea. Fish, straight out of the North Sea, don't come any fresher than when bought at one of the harbourside fishermen's huts.

The RNLI have a lifeboat station near the entrance to the harbour. Across the river is the village of Walberswick, which can be accessed here by a row-boat ferry during the summer season, or, further upstream, via a Bailey bridge for pedestrian use.

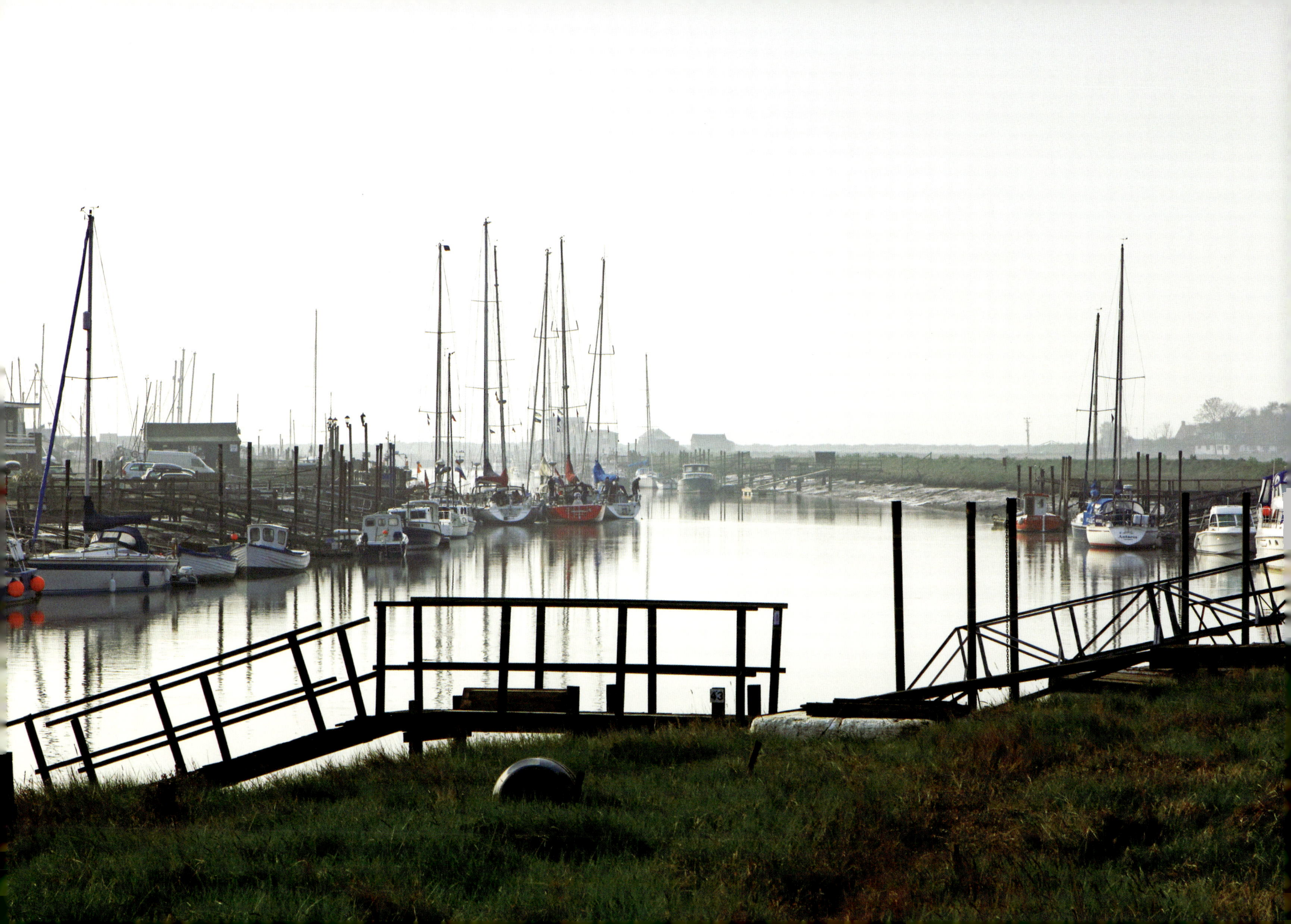
Antares
43

Blythburgh – an historic village with a big heart for music

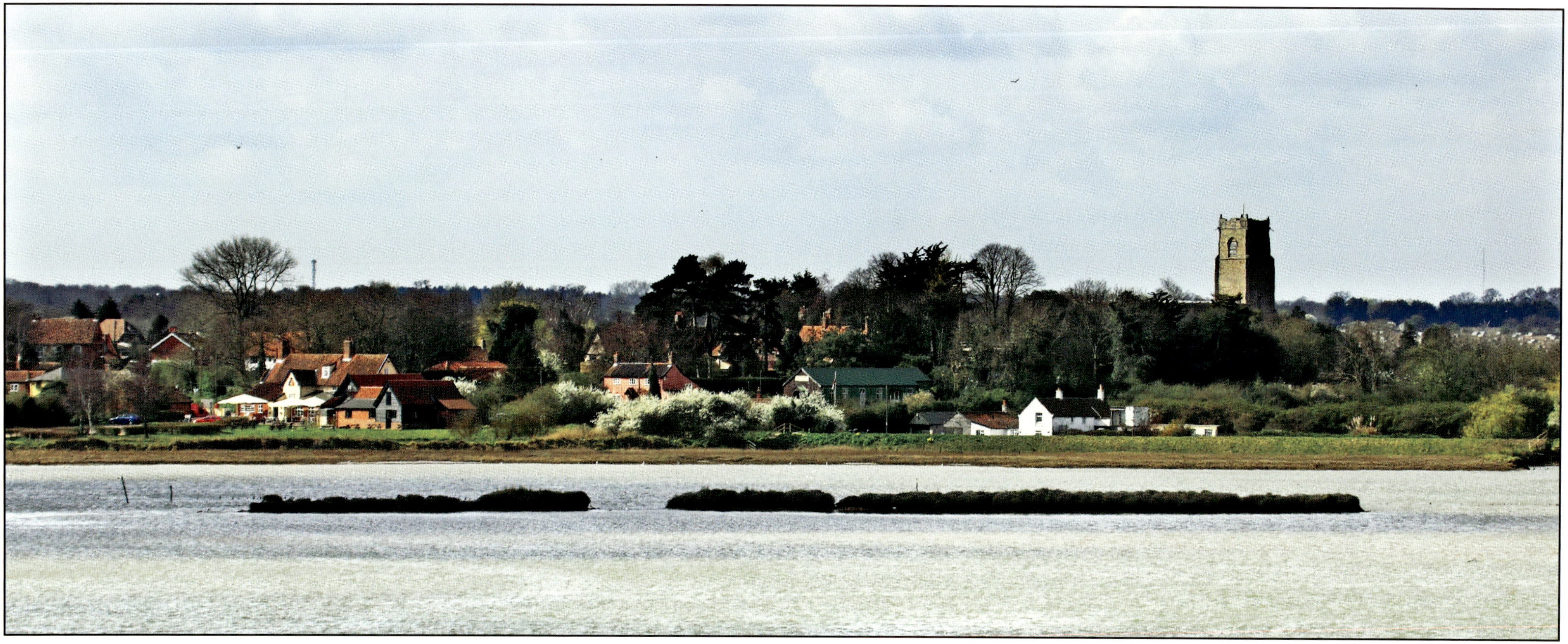

Blythburgh is four miles inland by road from Southwold – a road with lovely views of the River Blyth, which remains tidal until it reaches Blythburgh village. At high tide, a large lagoon – Blythburgh Water – opens up over the mud flats that were, before the river wall was breached, fertile farmers' fields. The busy A12 cuts this friendly village in two, a village that can boast a proud history as being one of the earliest Christian sites in East Anglia, having had a church here since AD 654.

The present fifteenth-century church – Holy Trinity – known as the 'Cathedral of the Marshes', has suffered a series of disasters, both man-made and natural. Having seen a period of wealth, and then general neglect due to rural poverty, it fell into a sad state of disrepair, and it wasn't until the late nineteenth century that restoration work was undertaken, bringing it back to more-or-less as it is now – one of Suffolk's most beautiful churches.

Benjamin Britten discovered the rich acoustic quality of this church, and used it as one of the Aldeburgh Festival main venues before the advent of the Snape Maltings Concert Hall. It is still occasionally used for musical events.

More recently music from a festival of another kind has rattled the church windows – The Latitude Festival – which is held annually at the nearby Henham Park half a mile away, where 35,000 or more people gather, and camp, to enjoy a weekend of pop and rock music and other open-air arts activities. This is one of the UK's major 'family friendly' festivals, and is a popular cultural event attracting fans from all parts of the country.

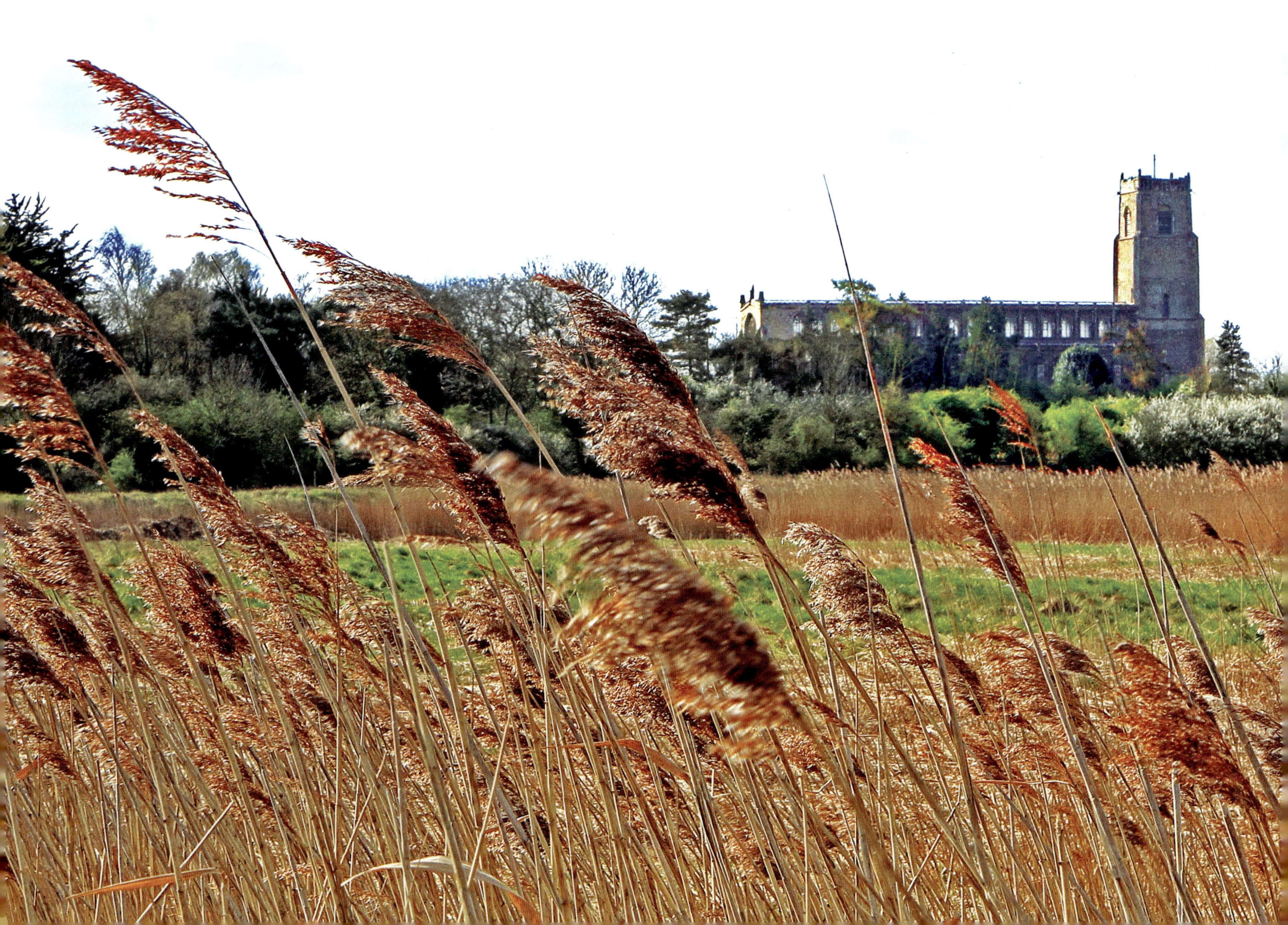

The Aldeburgh Festival's early reliance on churches

Blythburgh church was one of four churches in the area – Aldeburgh, Framlingham and Orford being the other three – that hosted concerts before the Snape Maltings Concert Hall was built. We are now entering the part of coastal Suffolk where the Aldeburgh Festival was conceived. Based in and around Aldeburgh, it was founded in 1948 by Benjamin Britten, his partner and singer Peter Pears, and the librettist Eric Crozier; the idea being to give a platform for Britten's music, and a home to their newly formed English Opera Group. From very small beginnings, and with limited financial resources, the festival productions became more ambitious, moving from small community halls to churches around the immediate area. These venues presented many logistical problems, but everyone pulled their weight and got involved. Stephen Reiss, who was the Festival general manager at that time, and I, together with anyone else who happened to be around, would frequently roll up our sleeves after final dress rehearsals and get stuck into moving chairs and scenery in preparation for that night's performance – there was a DIY 'making things happen' atmosphere in those formative times. Reiss was, in my opinion, the unsung hero of the Aldeburgh Festival – he was a talented administrator, and a virtual one-man managerial band who got things done. He was the person mainly responsible for suggesting, and acquiring, Snape Maltings as a concert hall site.

The early days of the Aldeburgh Festival were unique in that there was a special intimacy between the performers, conductor and the audience, a happy spin-off from the limitations the venues imposed.

These pictures were taken during a dress rehearsal when Britten conducted Mozart's opera Idomeneo in Blythburgh in 1969.

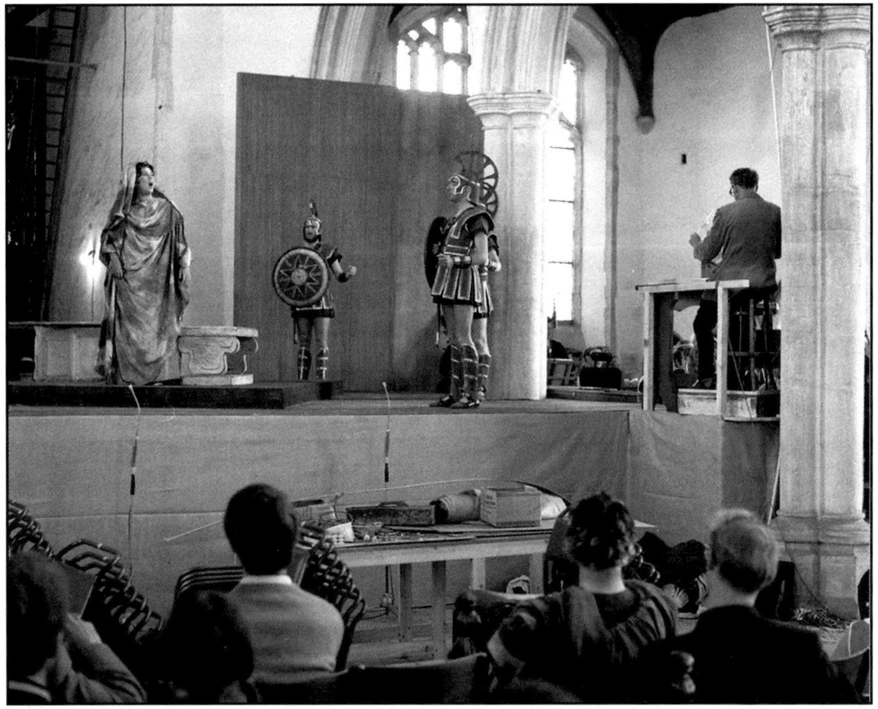

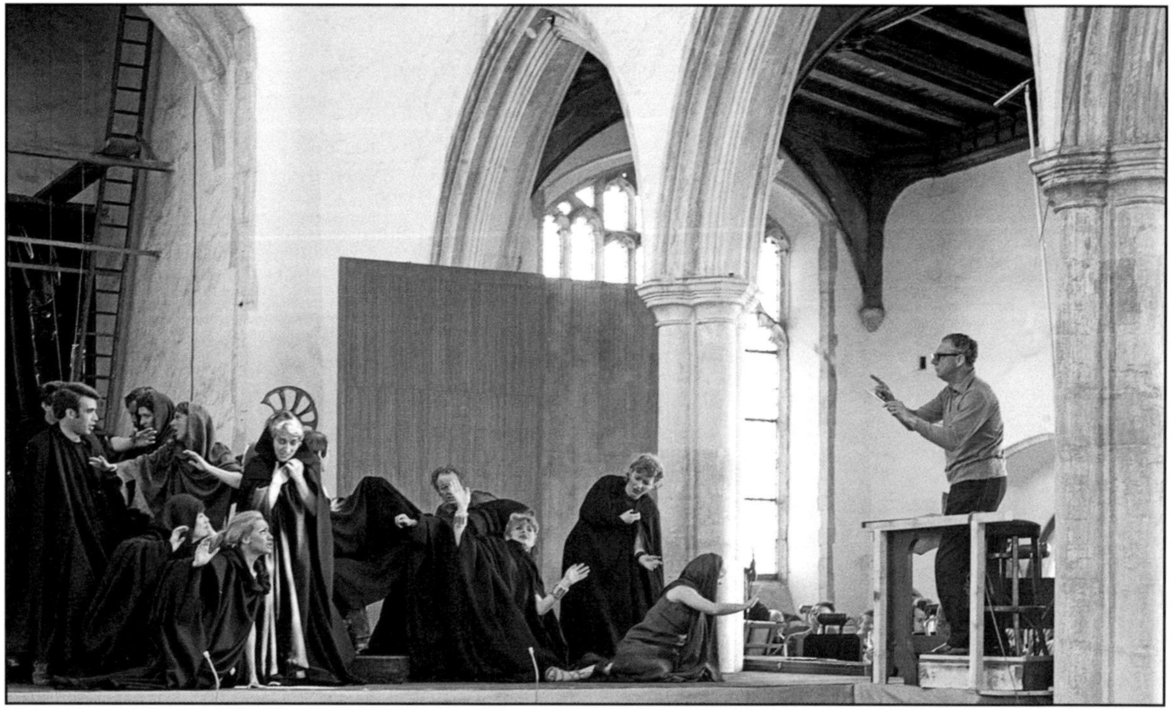

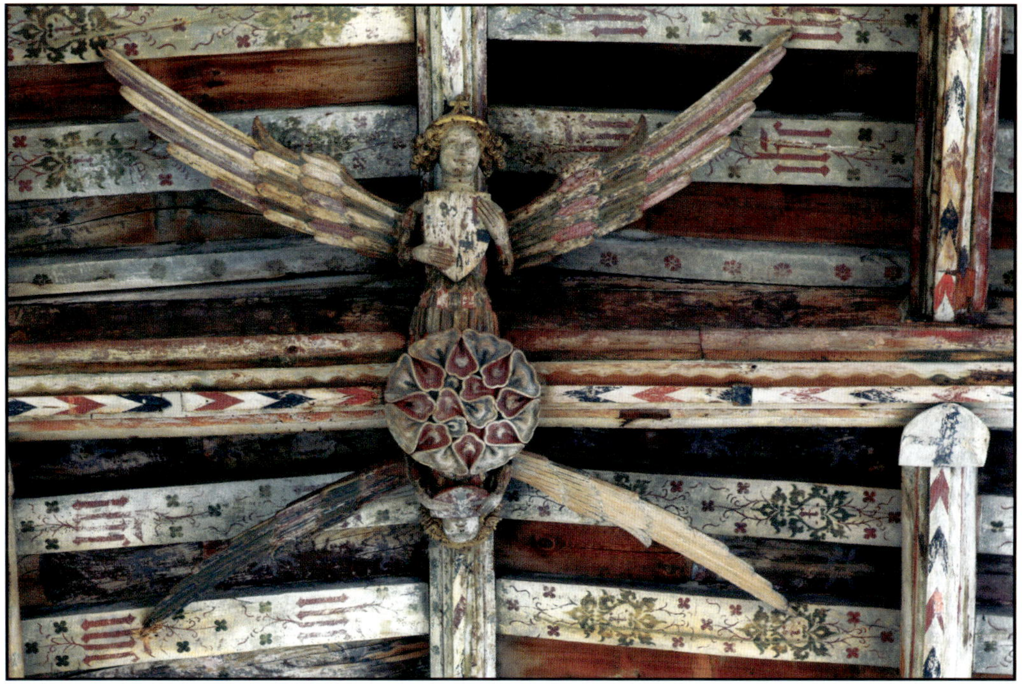

Britten enjoyed the atmosphere and acoustics of Blythburgh's Holy Trinity church, which gave added resonance to his music and to the voices of his singers.

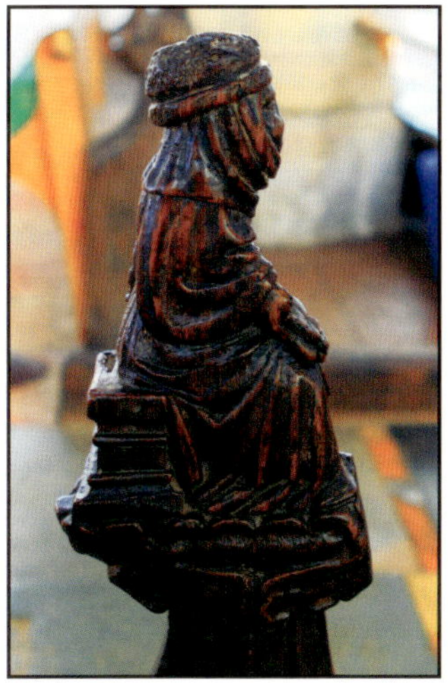

The church retains an earthy honesty about it, and is packed full of great medieval art. There is a fine sense of open space and light from windows high up in the clerestory, naturally illuminating the roof where twelve wooden winged angels stare down. Perhaps they looked down on Cromwell's men when they allegedly stabled their horses here: the rings on the stone pillars are said by some to be where they tied them. The bench ends and the choir stalls have beautiful carvings – just some of the many gems to discover on a visit to this most magnificent of all Suffolk churches.

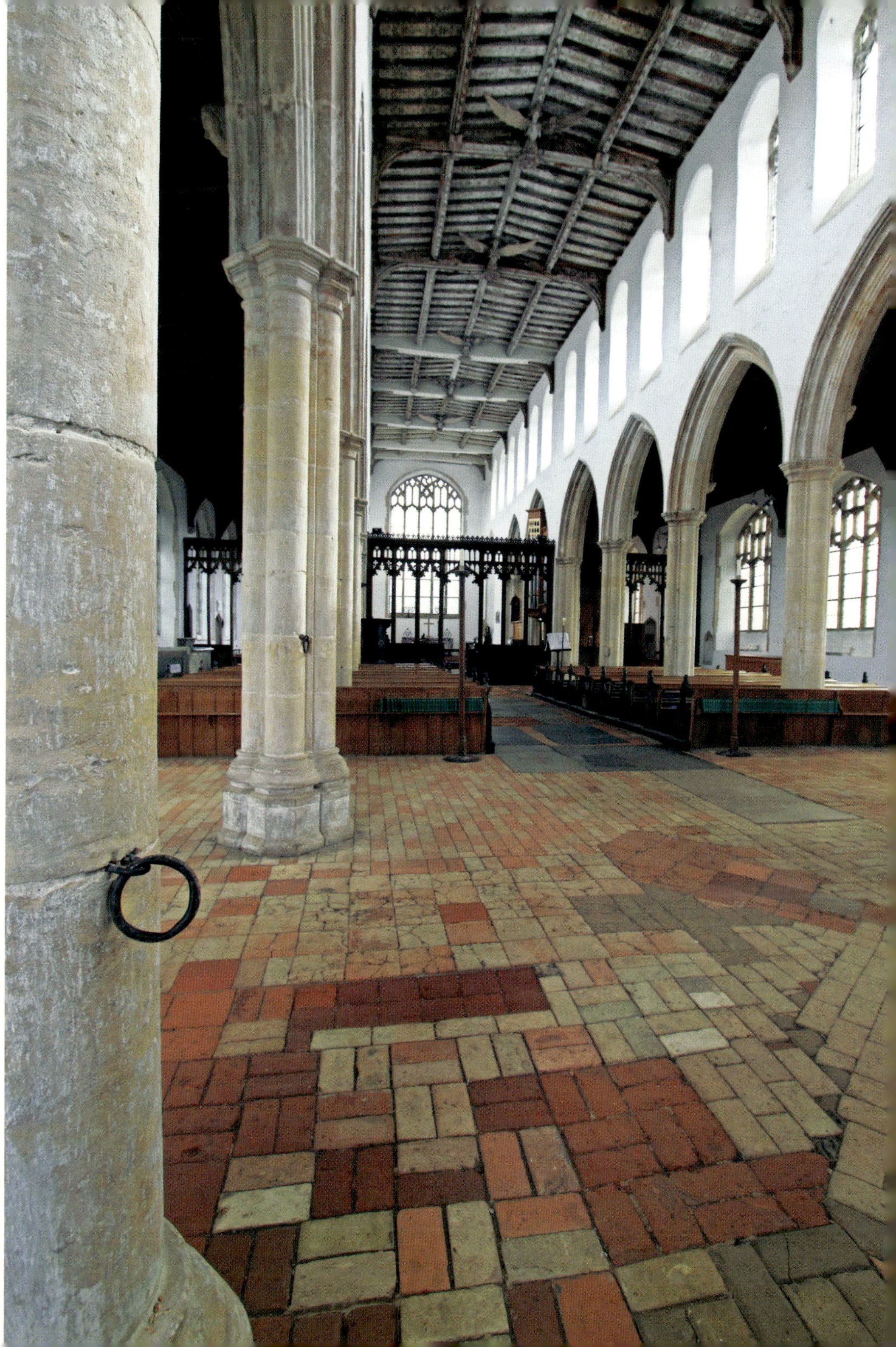

Dunwich

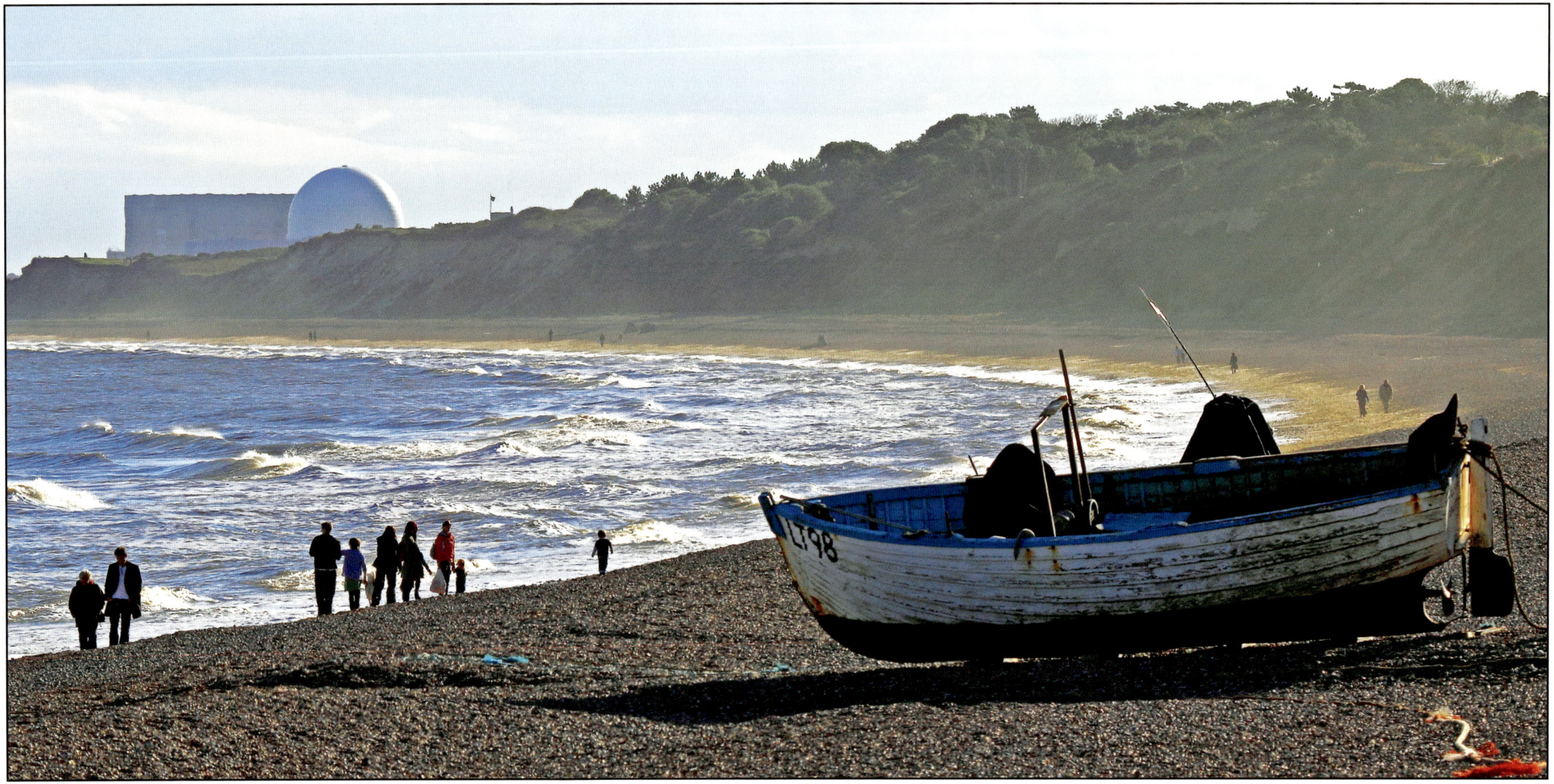

For the past 800 years Dunwich has been fighting a losing battle with the sea. Once a thriving city and harbour with eight churches, and the capital of East Anglia, it has been reduced to a small village tucked behind a perilously fragile shingle sea wall, and, like so much of this coastline, is in imminent danger of succumbing to the ever-encroaching North Sea. A lone fishing boat now occupies a place on the beach where a great city and its many churches once stood. Beyond the cliffs the skyline is dominated by the Sizewell Nuclear Power Stations. Perhaps the tragic maritime history of Dunwich was on Benjamin Britten's mind when he penned his opera, *Noye's Fludde*.

(Opposite page) A carpet of heather on Dunwich Heath, which, together with the former coastguard cottages, is now National Trust property.

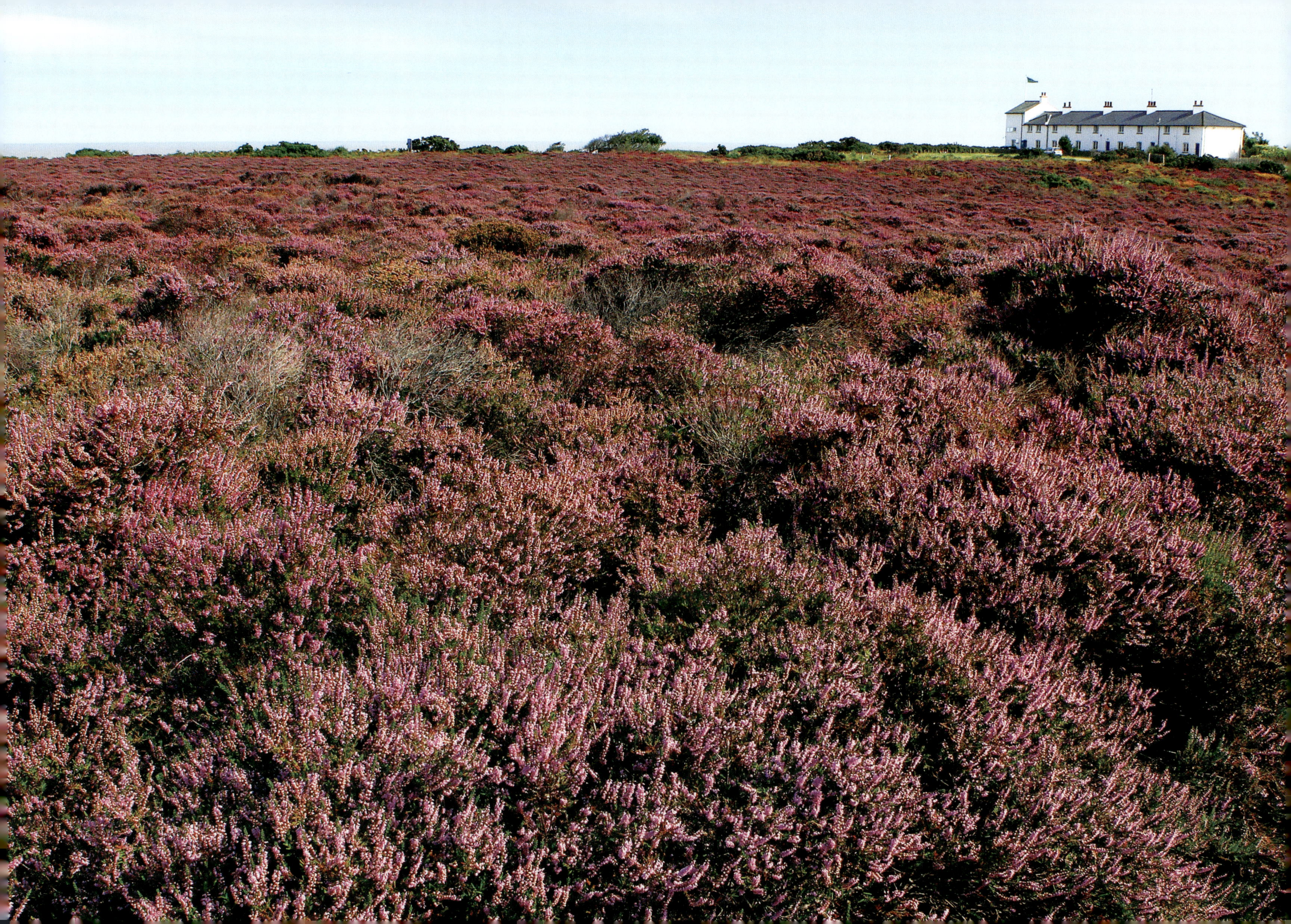

From a great city – to a small village

If evidence were needed of the destructive power of the North Sea, then Dunwich stands as proof positive of that fact.

In the eleventh century it was the tenth largest settlement in England, with one of the greatest ports on the east coast, serving the crusaders, and a major naval base. Before that it was a centre of religion where St Felix, the first Bishop of Dunwich, converted East Anglia to Christianity. Its many churches and religious houses were richly endowed with lands and income from tenants, and its citizens grew prosperous from shipbuilding, trade and fishing. Its population was half that of London, it was important enough to be represented by two members of parliament, and it had its own mint. That's how significant Dunwich once was.

The very same sea that provided such wealth to the city was also its downfall. The harbour gradually silted up and the sea clawed back land, reducing it over the centuries to what it is today – a small village with a pub, a few houses, and a popular fish and chip restaurant alongside the sea-front car park.

Visitors are reminded of that great past when exploring the ruins of the thirteenth-century walled Franciscan friary. The eastern part of the wall stands close to the eroding cliff edge. On the outskirts of the village the remains of the Chapel of the Leper Hospital are located in the churchyard of St James – the only remaining church in Dunwich, which was built alongside the ruins of the hospital in 1830.

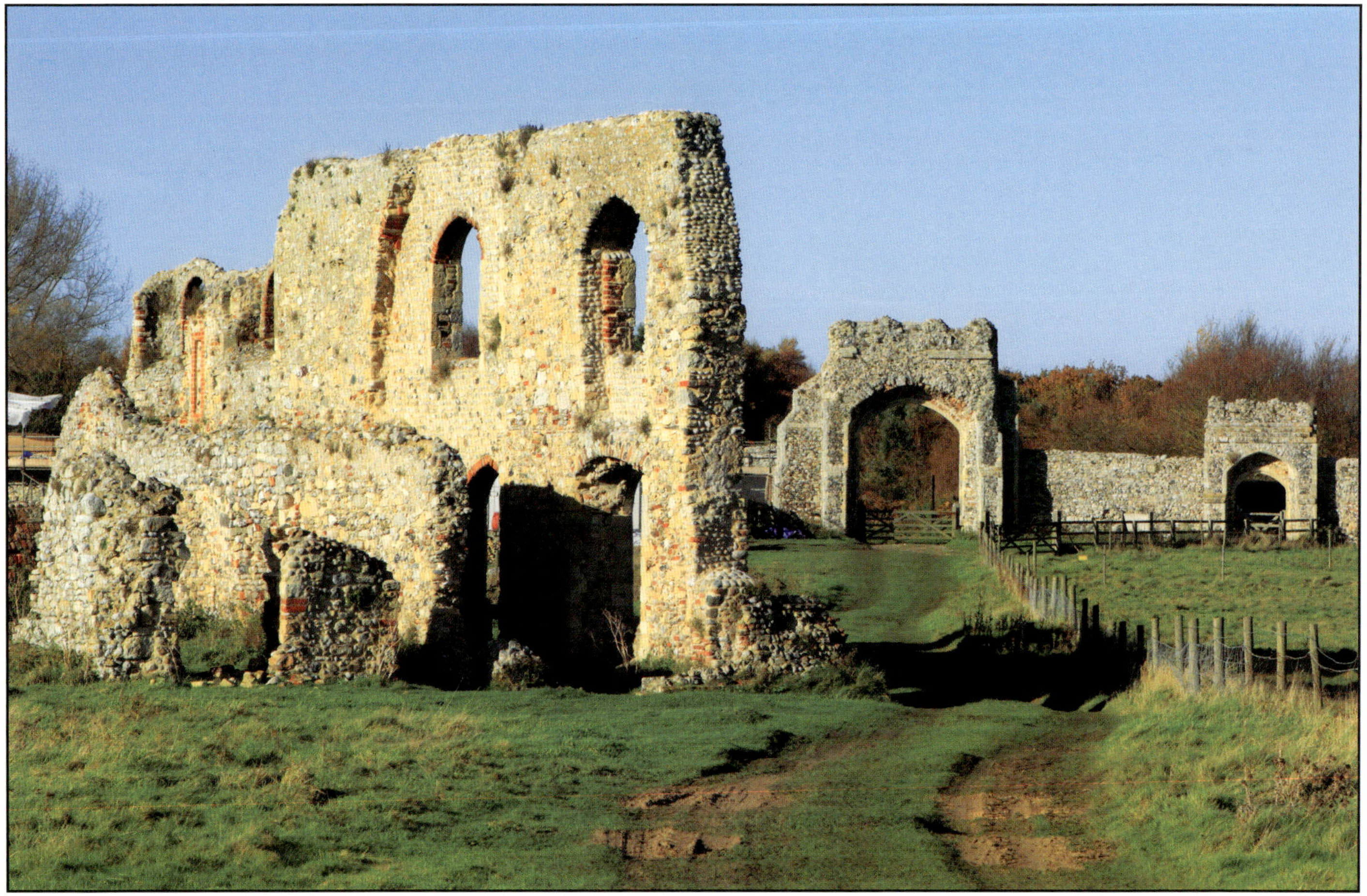

The friary was established here in 1289 just on the outside of the town boundary. Henry VIII closed all monasteries, and valuable building materials were stripped from them. The remains of Dunwich friary were converted into a house that was later used as a town hall and then a prison. In 1802 all the buildings were demolished except for what was left of the friary and the gated walls (above).

(Right) The ruins of the Leper Hospital, built over 800 years ago, was originally located well outside the town. Lepers were considered incurable and a health hazard to the rest of the population, and most spent their life in isolation hospitals cared for by charitable institutions. The building was eventually abandoned in the early 1800s.

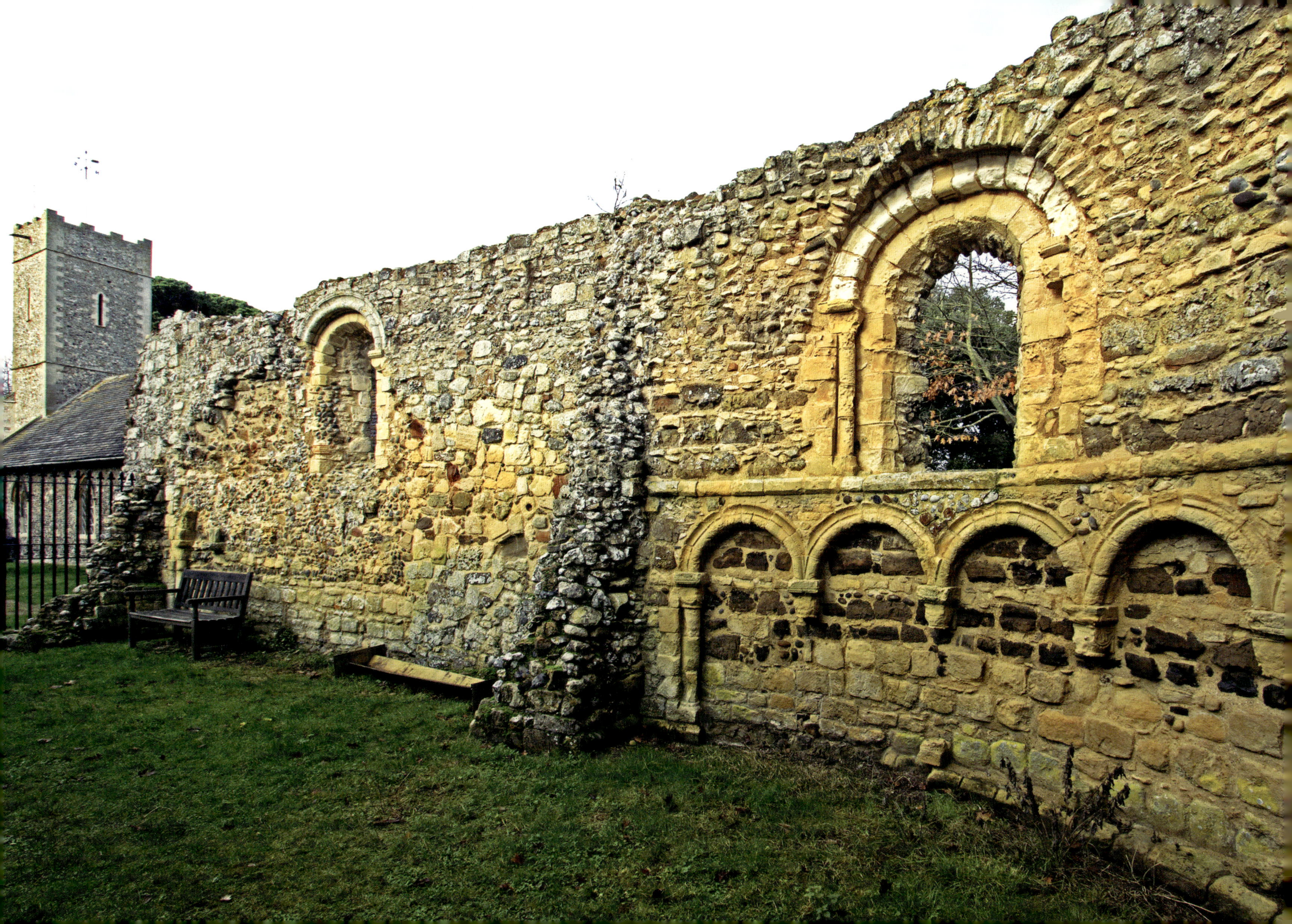

Minsmere

As part of coastal defences during the Second World War, the marshland was flooded at Minsmere to prevent it from becoming a possible site for invasion. Wildlife soon adopted this wetland. In 1947 the Royal Society for the Protection of Birds (RSPB) took over management of the site, and it is now one of the premier wildlife reserves in the country, and lives happily cheek-by-jowl with its near neighbour Sizewell Nuclear Power Station. Originally only a bird reserve, it is now home to all kinds of wildlife, but birds are what it's famous for, including rarities such as avocets, bitterns, marsh harriers and many winter migrant wading birds from northern climes. Purpose-built hides (below) afford bird-watchers excellent views of the wetland 'scrapes' and their avian occupants.

The remains of a small chapel (bottom right) on the edge of the reserve date back to 1182 – part of the wider precinct of Leiston Abbey. As an ancient monument it is a listed building – ironically, so is the second world war pillbox that was built inside it as part of coastal war defences.

The reserve is open all year round, and for the many thousands of wildlife enthusiasts who arrive on site every year, there is a visitor centre with a restaurant and shops.

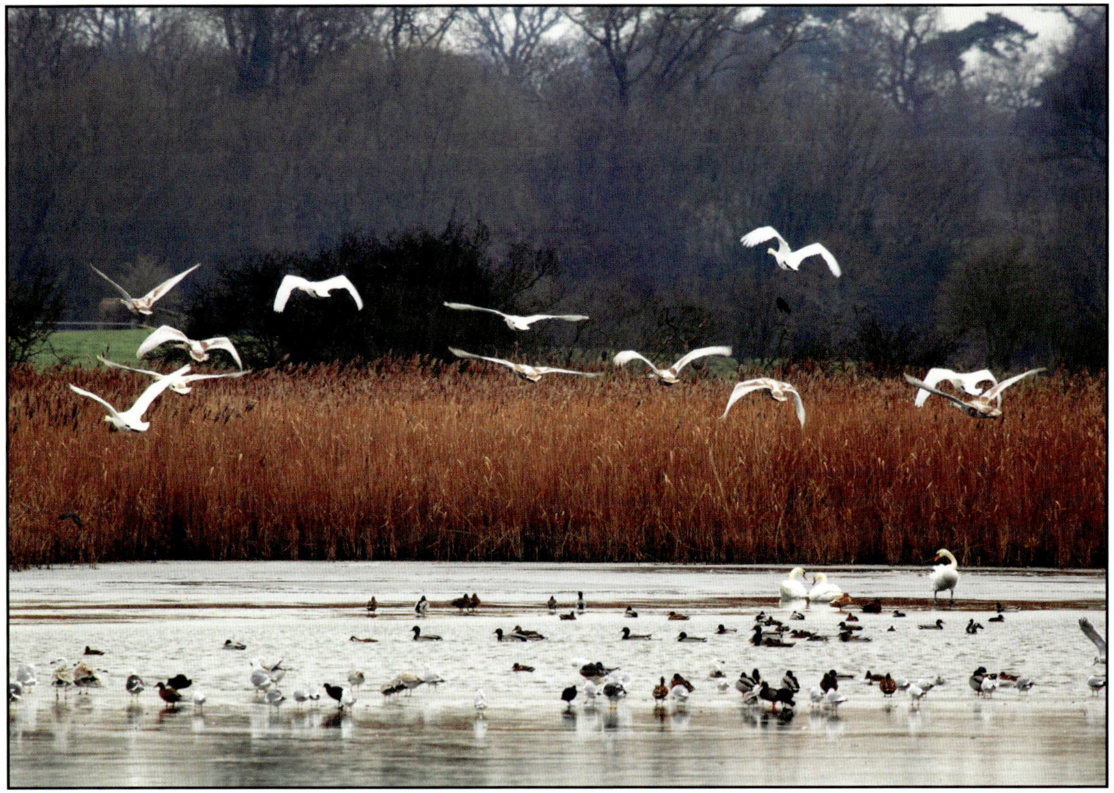

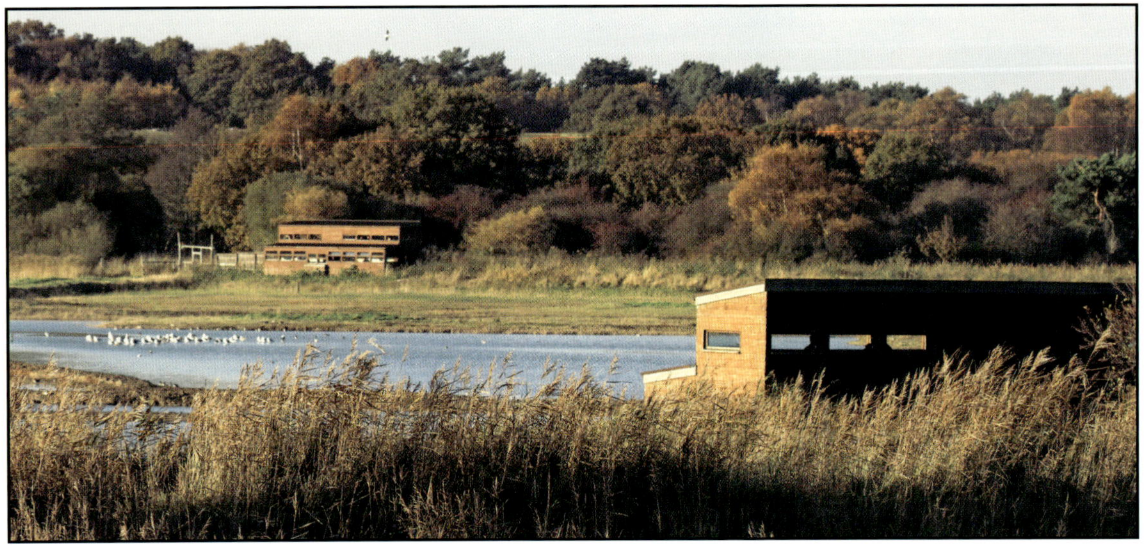

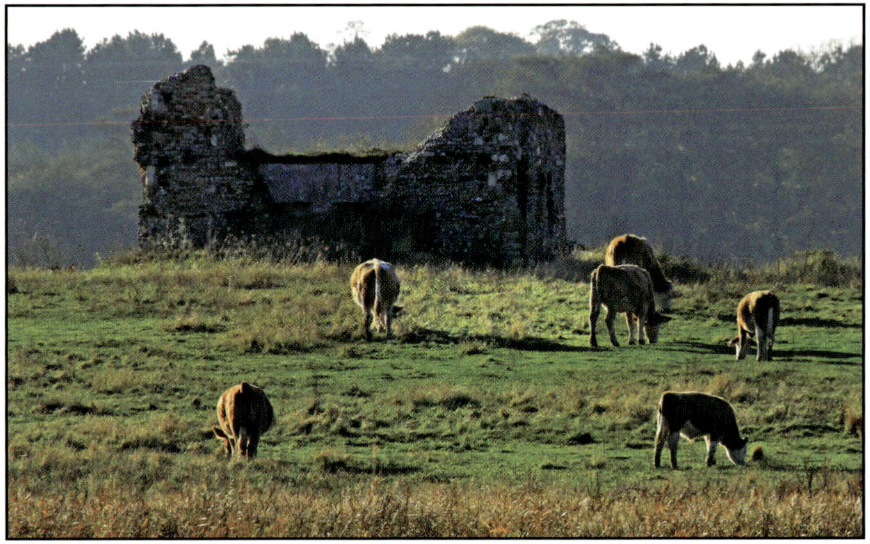

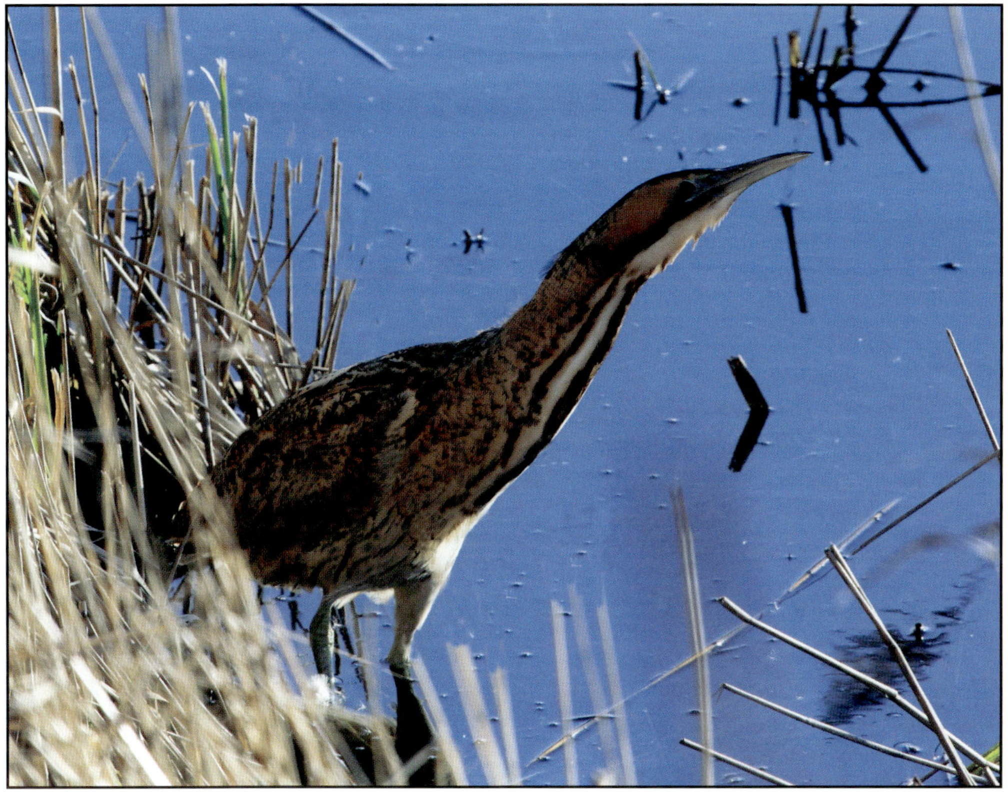

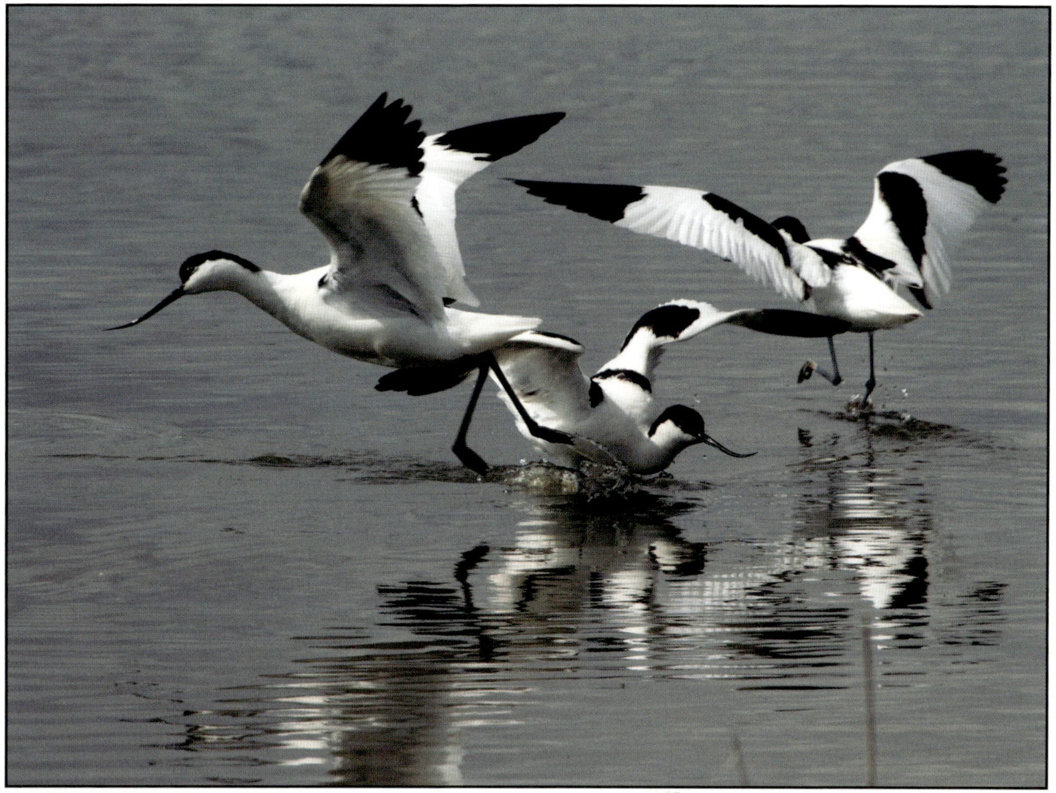

Very shortly after Minsmere was adopted by the RSPB, avocets (top right) started to arrive on these shores and breed here and at Havergate Island near Orford – the first time in the UK for over half a century. Now they are year-round residents, with colonies to be found on all Suffolk rivers. Bitterns (above) can be heard 'booming' in the springtime. Red deer start their rutting season in the autumn, and everyone's favourite, the kingfisher can be seen here all year round. Minsmere's bird-watching hides give photographers an ideal platform for taking stunning photographs. Benjamin Britten was very knowledgable about birdlife.

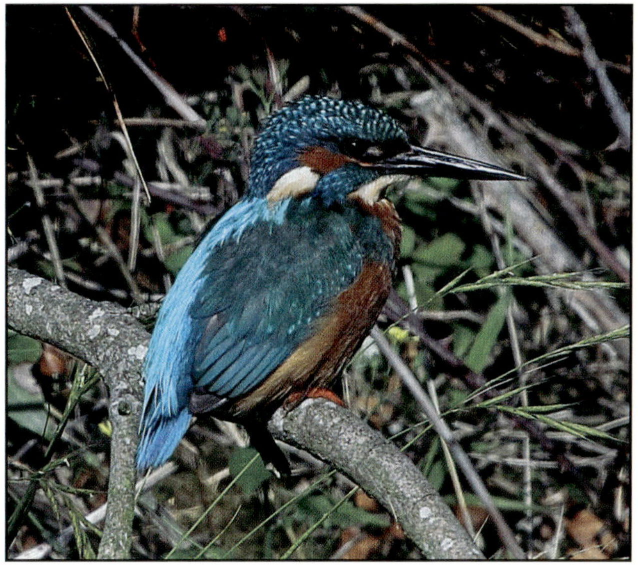

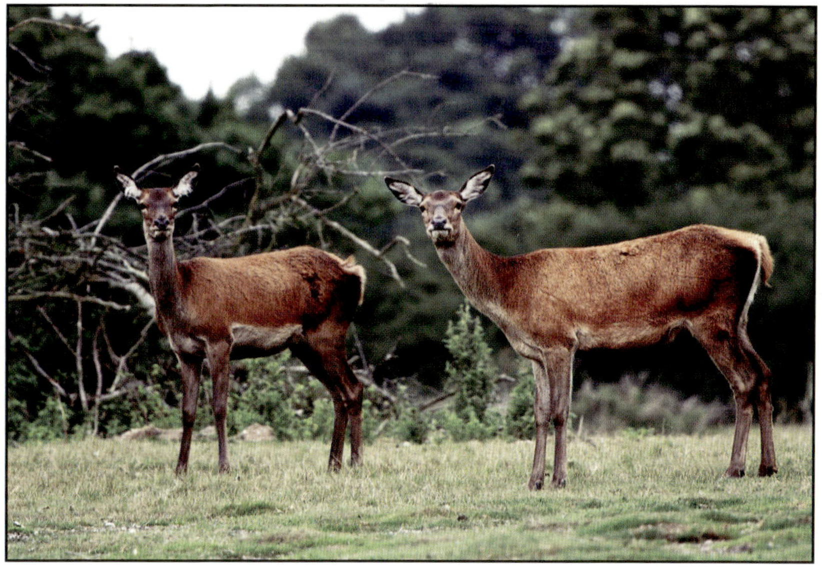

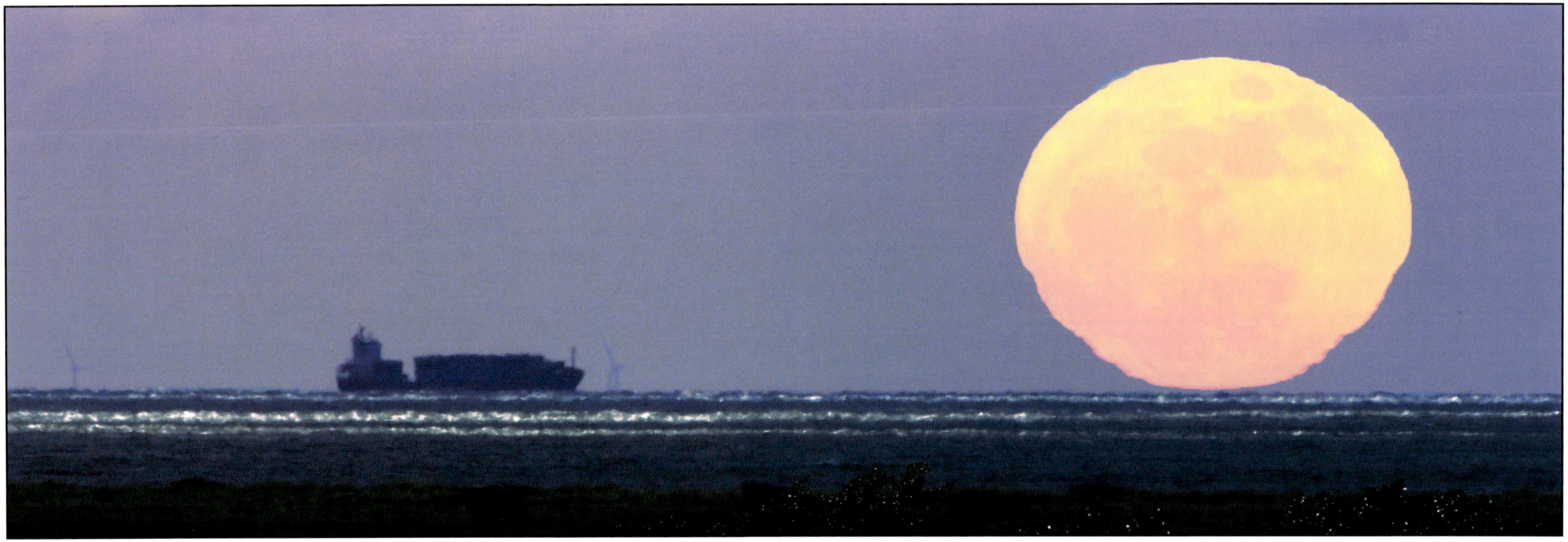

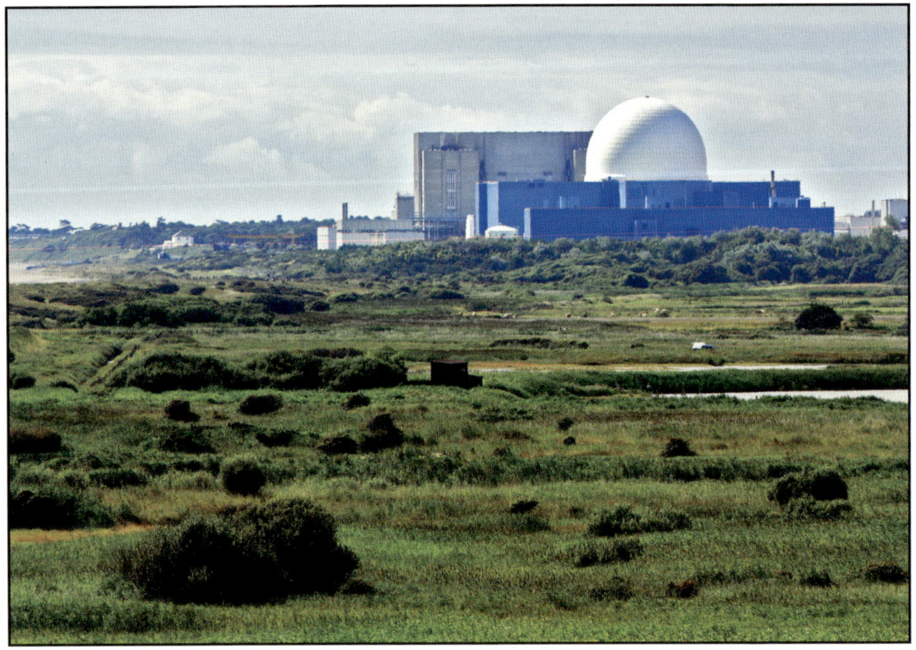

The 'power coast'

With the advent of the industrial revolution in the eighteenth century, man's thirst for ever more power to drive industry has been insatiable. Our Suffolk coast has done more than its fair share to harness power sources. Love or hate them, nuclear power stations at Sizewell have safely provided carbon-free electricity since the first 'A' station was commissioned in 1966: Sizewell 'B' came on stream in 1995 and now produces 3% of the country's electricity (photo left as seen from Minsmere Nature Reserve). Plans to build another station – Sizewell 'C' – are in the consultation phase as we go to press. This 1600 megawatt twin-reactor power station would supply 13% of the country's electricity.

Two of the many wind turbines on the Outer Gabbard windfarm – the world's largest offshore windfarm – are just visible on the horizon fore and aft of the ship in the above telephoto shot taken from Dunwich on the occasion of the 'supermoon' in March 2011. The Outer Gabbard can generate 500 megawatts of wind-powered electricity.

The nearby town of Leiston was famous for producing steam-powered vehicles in the late nineteenth century at the engineering works of Richard Garrett.

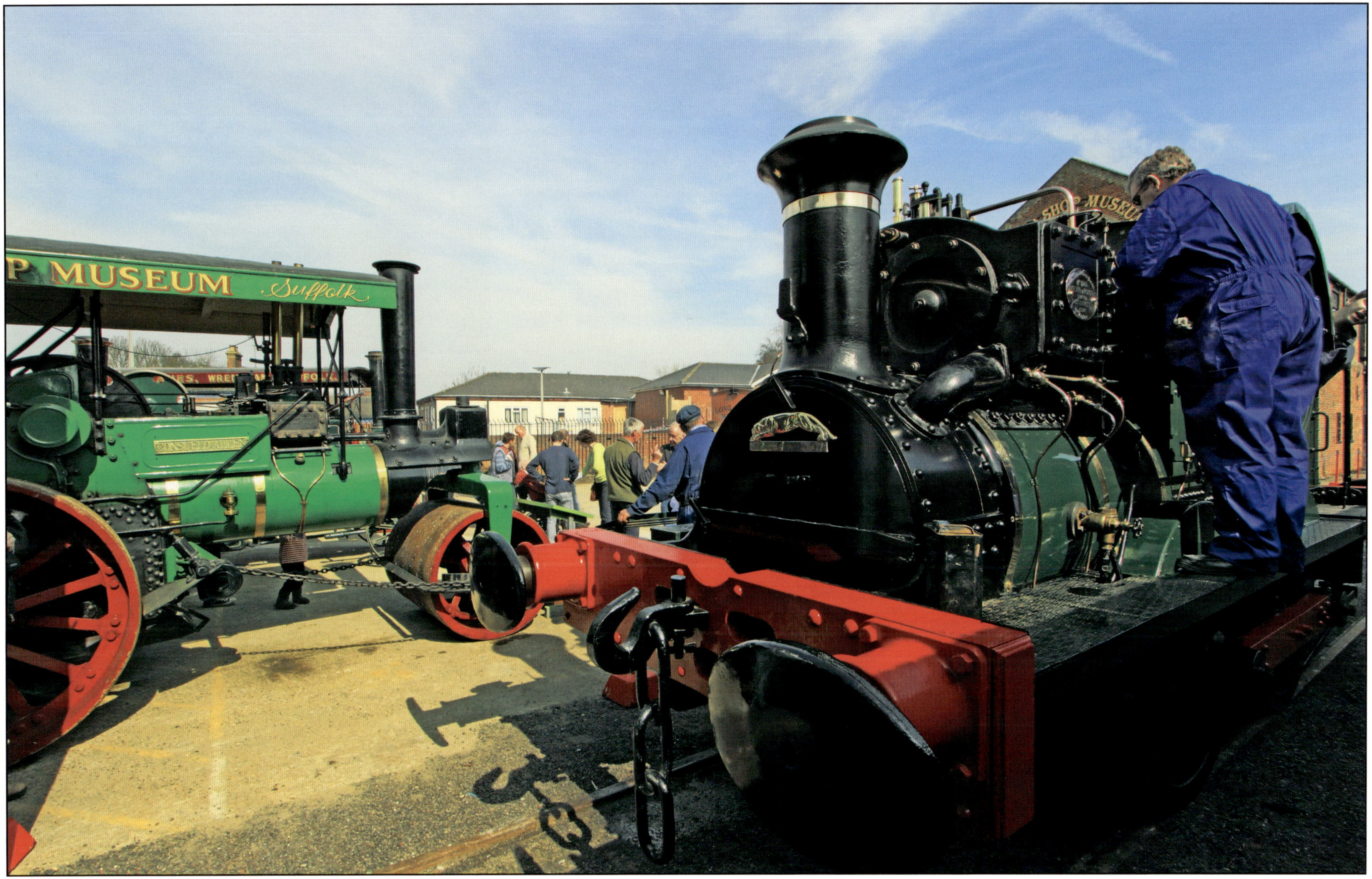

The Long Shop Museum at Leiston has a great collection of steam-powered engines of various kinds. The long shop was one of the first 'industrial production lines'.

Leiston: the Garrett Dynasty

Without the Garrett family of Leiston, Snape Maltings Concert Hall wouldn't exist – more about that later. Leiston is unique: a small Suffolk coastal town with a character all of its own, and with a history going back centuries. Leiston Abbey (right) was built here in the fourteenth century from building materials salvaged from the original abbey site at Minsmere. The Abbey House is now the Pro Corda music school for young people. It was during the nineteenth and twentieth centuries that the town really came into prominence, a period dominated by the engineering works of Richard Garrett & Sons – a family with great entrepreneurial foresight who built, on the site of a former blacksmith's shop in the middle of the Suffolk countryside, a large engineering factory to serve the needs of agriculture. They produced, among many other things, famous steam-driven traction engines, and pioneered one of the first 'flow line' production units in the world – the 'Long Shop' (opposite right). Saved from dereliction by enthusiasts, the Long Shop is now preserved as a museum, and is a fine tribute to the town's great industrial past: special open 'steam days' are held when lovingly restored steam engines are fired up to pay homage to the age of steam power.

During both world wars 'the works' (as it was known locally) produced munitions for the war effort, and the nearby Leiston Airfield was home in the last war to the American 357th Fighter Group, from where famous American test pilot and fighter ace, Chuck Yeager, flew. He went on to become the first man to fly faster than sound.

The townspeople, who relied solely upon Garrett's for their livelihood, had traditionally been very subservient to the Garrett family dynasty. Just before the outbreak of the Second World War – a time of great unemployment in the town – things changed when the 'workers' elected a communist councillor – the first in Suffolk – to give them a voice and represent them on the council. Paxton Chadwick, a well-known artist, went on to become a most respected town councillor and its first communist chairman. He was also a part-time teacher at Leiston's internationally famous Summerhill School, the first school of its kind in the 'free school movement' established by the pioneering educationalist A. S. Neill, and still housed in the former mansion of Richard Garrett.

Leiston is not a picturesque town, but its people have made it a town of great historical significance, where dignified and skilled workmen occupied its houses. The Garrett engineering factory has long since closed but today small industrial units set up on the site of the former 'top works' continue the proud tradition of manufacturing. The town is now overlooked by the Sizewell nuclear power stations – the largest employer in the area (right).

The oldest purpose-built cinema in Suffolk, the Leiston Film Theatre – a town-centre building with a mock Tudor frontage – was saved from closure in the 1960s when the town council bought it, and is now run by a supporters' club.

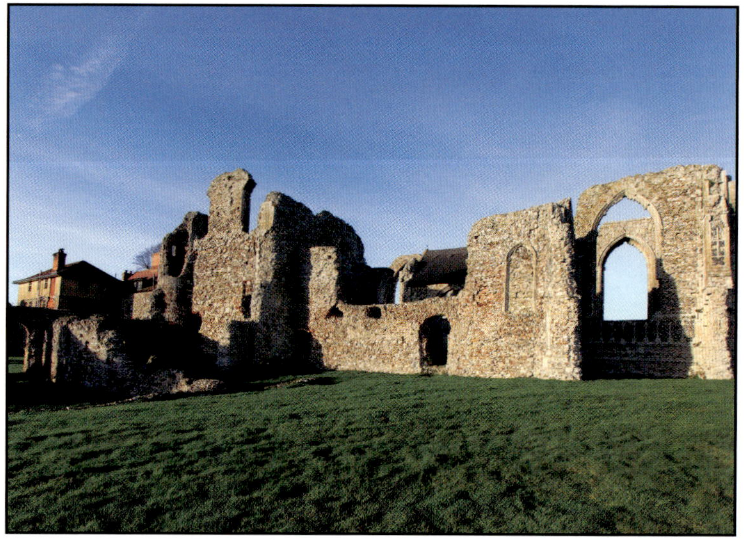

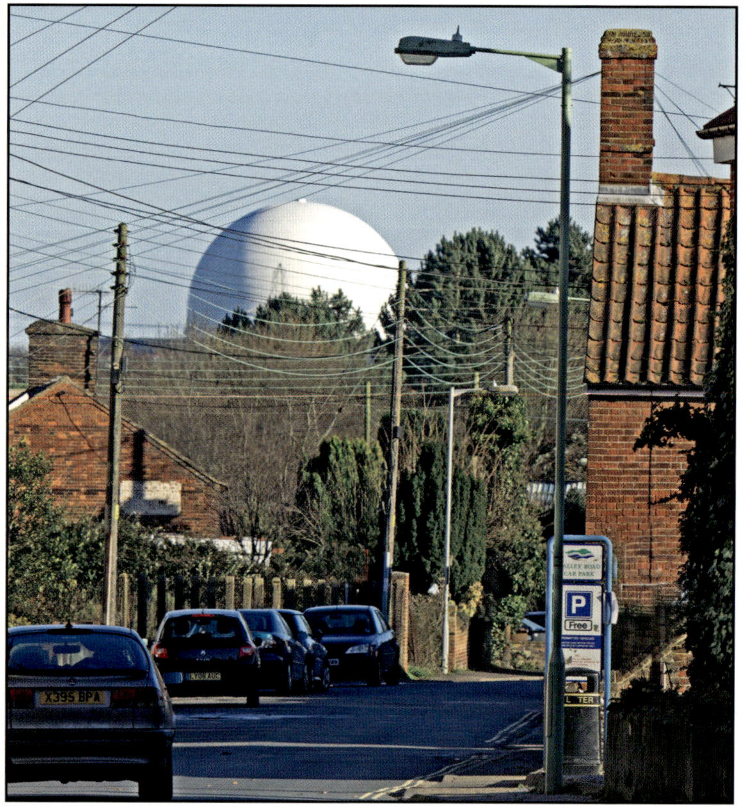

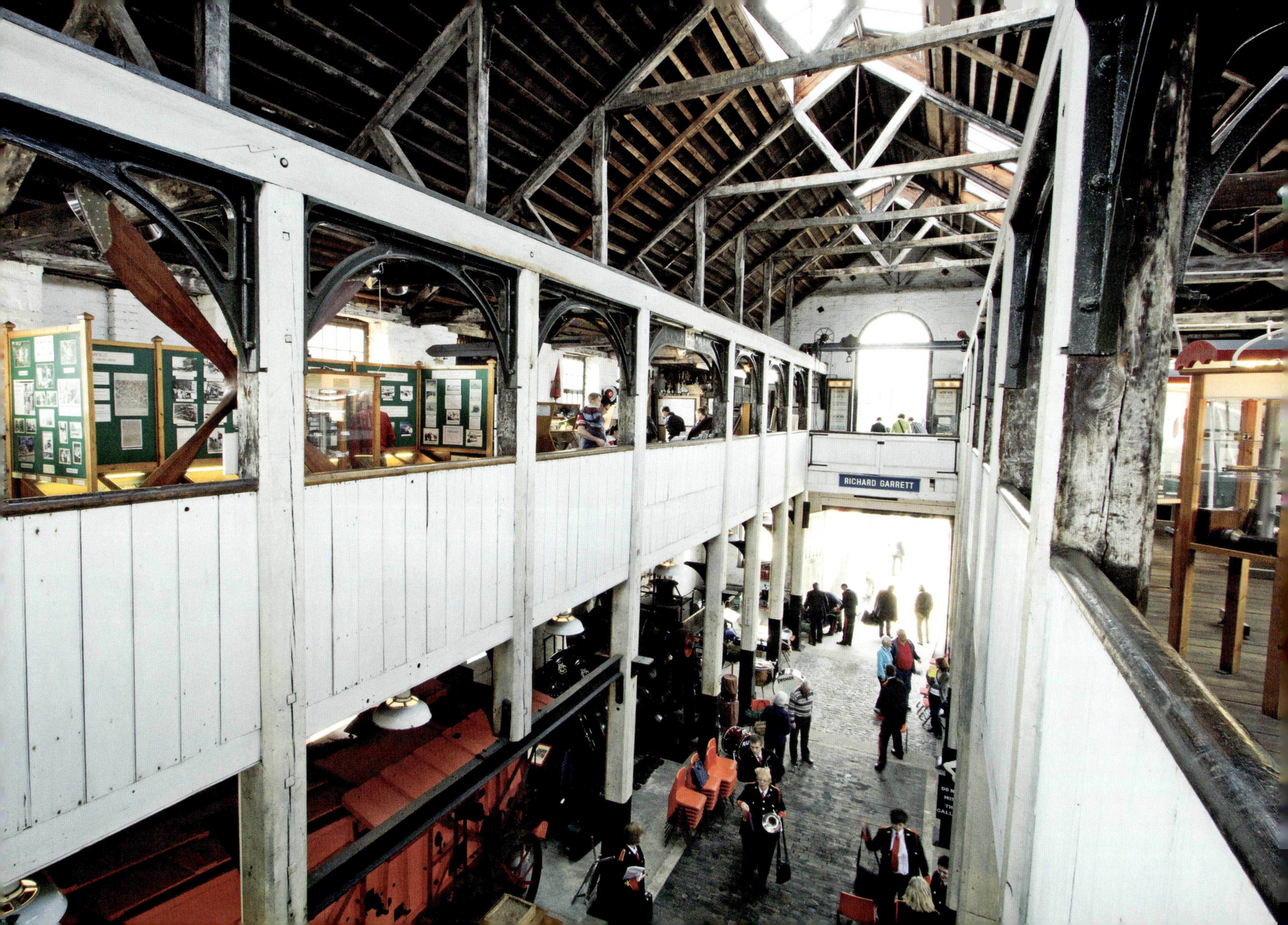
RICHARD GARRETT

The Suffolk villages and towns that Britten loved

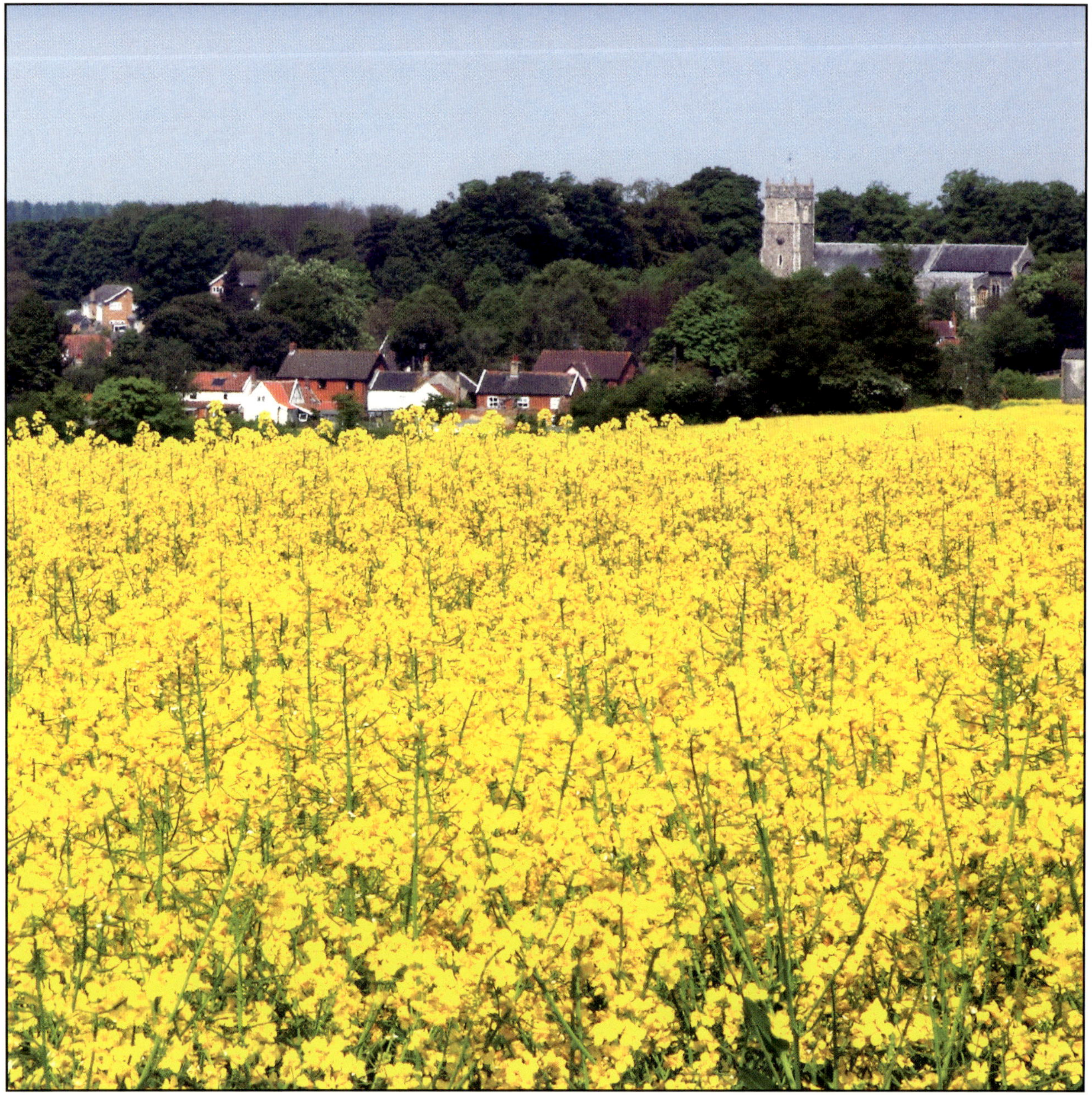

The Suffolk Heritage Coast, to keep at its most simple, is that part of Suffolk east of the A12 road. One of the main reasons this coastline has remained relatively unspoiled is due to its geographical isolation from major road networks – you have to come off the A12 at various places along its route to explore this region fully; there is no coastal road linking one place to another. For those who do venture off the main road, there is much to delight the senses.

Agriculture has always made a major contribution to this landscape, with cereal, potatoes, oilseed rape, and sugar beet being the main crops these days, with the occasional pig or dairy farm making up the rest. Agriculture is now big business here, but that was not always the case. Suffolk was traditionally a group of small farmers eking out a living as best they could by selling produce at farmers' auctions, markets and corn exchanges. Small farms remain uneconomic, and most have been bought up by the 'big boys'. Massive farm machinery has replaced the traditional farm worker, and the socioeconomics of the Suffolk countryside have changed beyond all recognition. Age-old farmhouses and workers' cottages, most of them previously in need of modernisation, now house the urban wealthy who commute daily to work, or have them as second or retirement homes, all of whom have lavished the kind of money on them that could scarecly have been dreamt about by their former residents.

The result of all this is we now have picture-postcard villages. Some are still lucky in having a village shop and post office, pub and a school, others have not fared so well. Nostalgic thoughts about the simple things of life we all enjoyed as children in the countryside must remain just that – nostalgic memories. The reality is that this part of Suffolk is above average in the income stakes, people are healthier, happier, and, given the choice, probably wouldn't choose to live anywhere else.

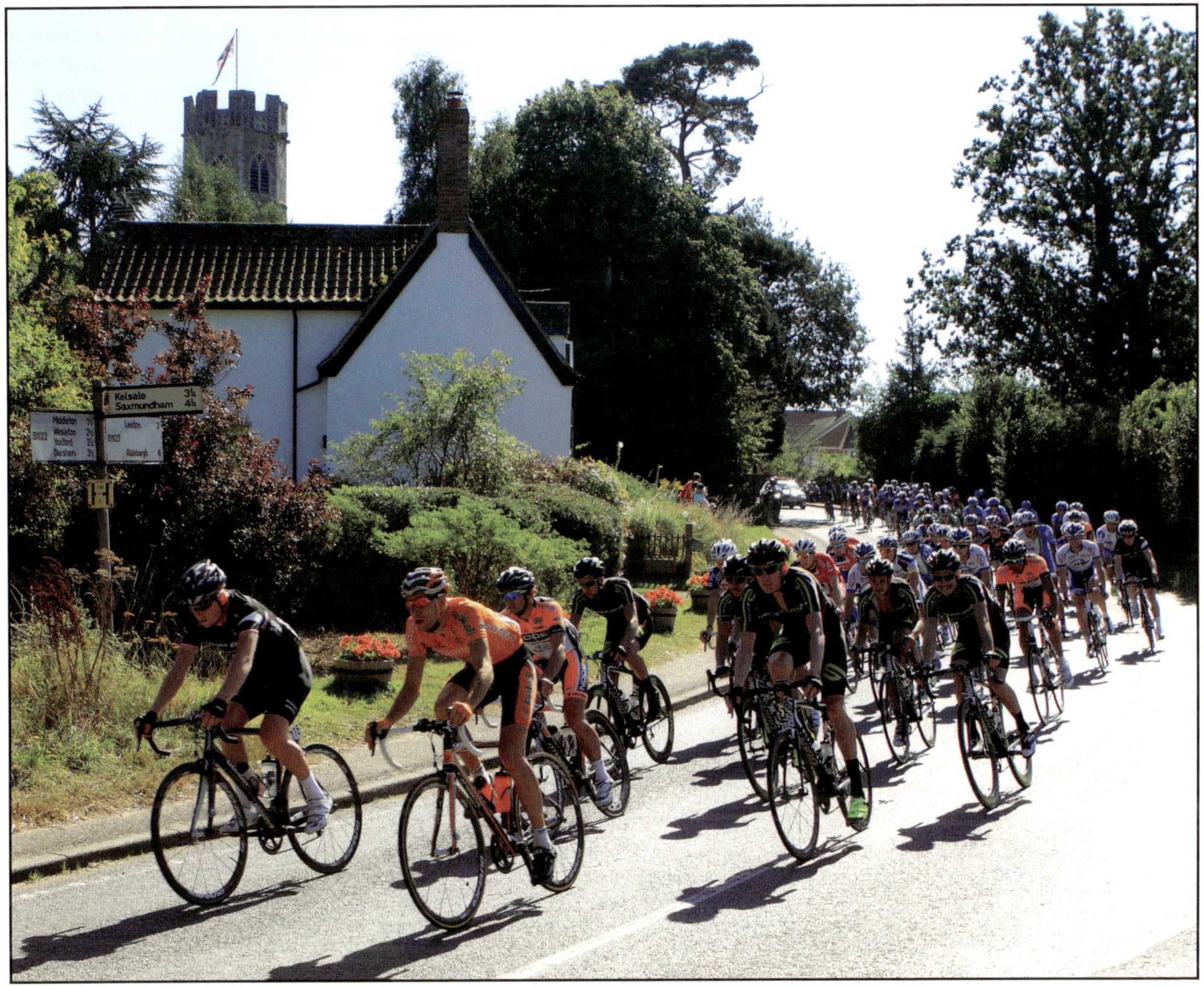

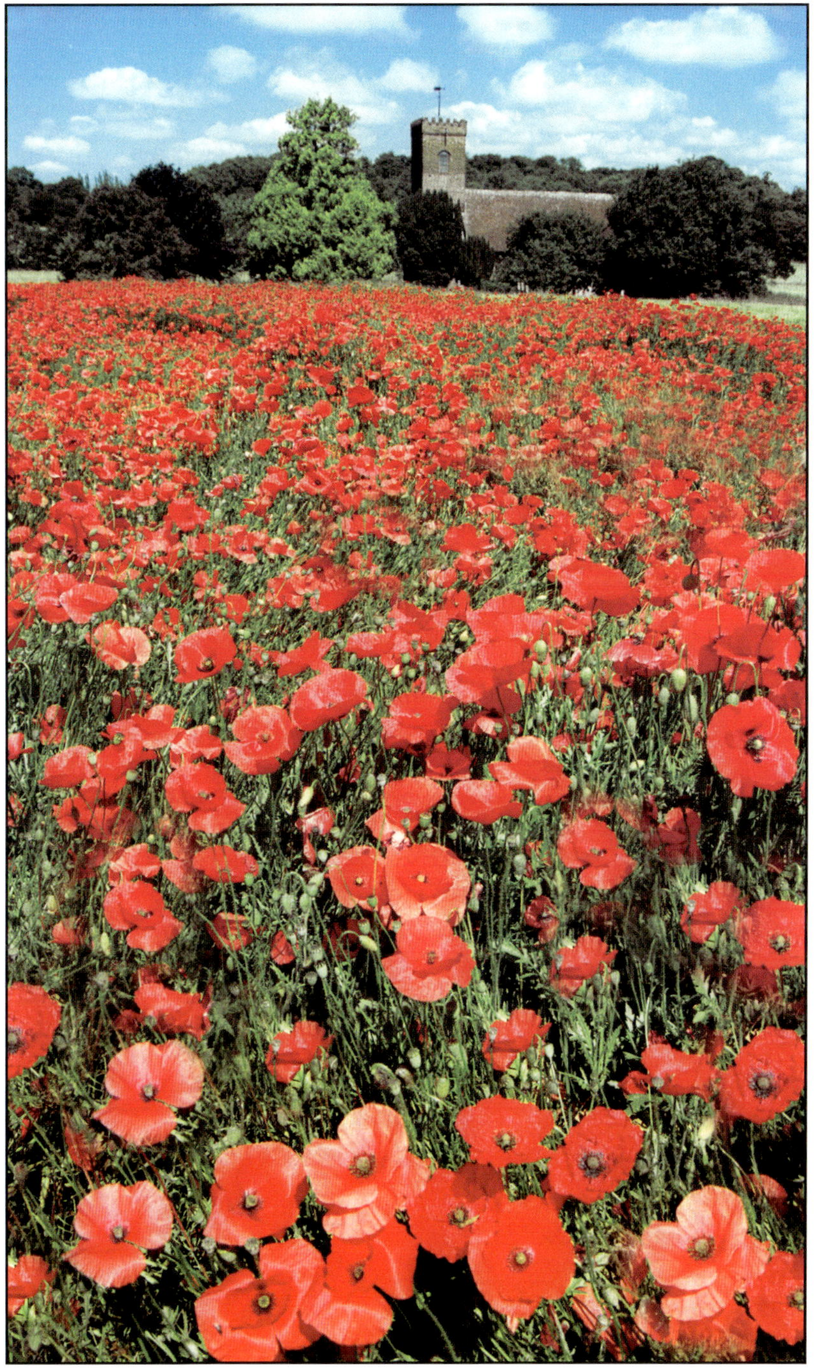

The attractive roads through the villages along the Suffolk Heritage Coast proved an ideal route for the first day of the 2012 Tour of Britain cycle race. The peleton is seen coming through Theberton village, not a stone's throw away from where the German Zeppelin airship L48 was shot down in the First World War by a plane from Orfordness. Part of the Zeppelin's framework is displayed in St Peter's Church porch.

(Opposite page) When fields of oilseed rape are in bloom during spring, the yellow illuminance from vast swathes of the crop is almost blinding. A less welcome crop is a carpet of brilliant red poppies. The two churches shown in these pictures are Kelsale and Carlton respectively, near Saxmundham.

Westleton

There was once a miller's windmill dominating the high ground on the sweeping expanse of Westleton Green. The only artifact remaining of the mill to celebrate the village's former proud agricultural past is the millstone, now situated at the base of the village sign on the green. The local garage carries on the agricultural tradition by specialising in the repair and maintenance of modern high-tech agricultural machinery, where monster tractors more often than not can be seen parked outside the premises awaiting attention.

The school, housed in an attractive building in the centre of the village, closed in 1967 after 125 years, due to insufficient numbers of children living in the locality. The redundant building was purchased by the residents and is now used as the village hall.

The church of St Peter (right), is unusual in that it has a thatched roof, and no tower. The church dates back to 1340, originally built complete with a tower. That collapsed in 1770 reducing it to a mere stump. Even that suffered a sad demise when a Second World War landmine fell close by rendering it unsafe, and it was subsequently dismantled.

The Crown Inn (top left), an historic coaching inn dating back to the twelfth century and now a popular hotel and eatery, had the distinction in April 2012 to have the second-in-line to the throne as one of their guests. Prince William and the Duchess of Cambridge stayed here after attending a friend's wedding in the locality.

Each August the spacious green at the heart of the village hosts the annual Barrel Fair, a popular and unusual event that attracts crowds from far and wide to watch locals and visitors of all ages competing against each other to see who can be the first to roll beer barrels up and down the green using only wooden staves (top right).

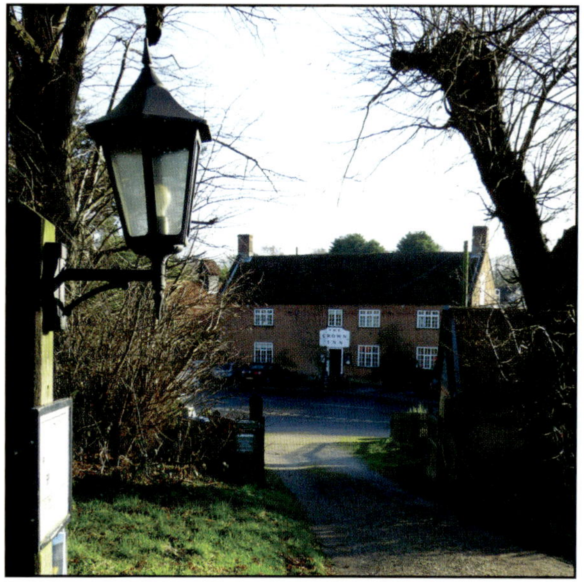

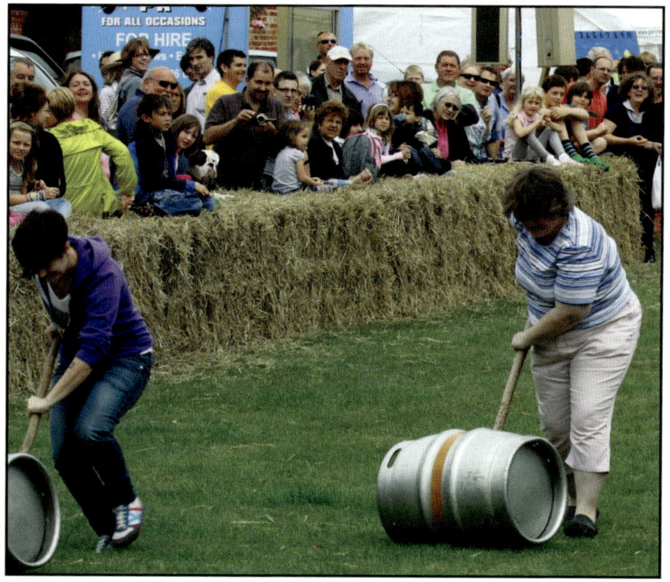

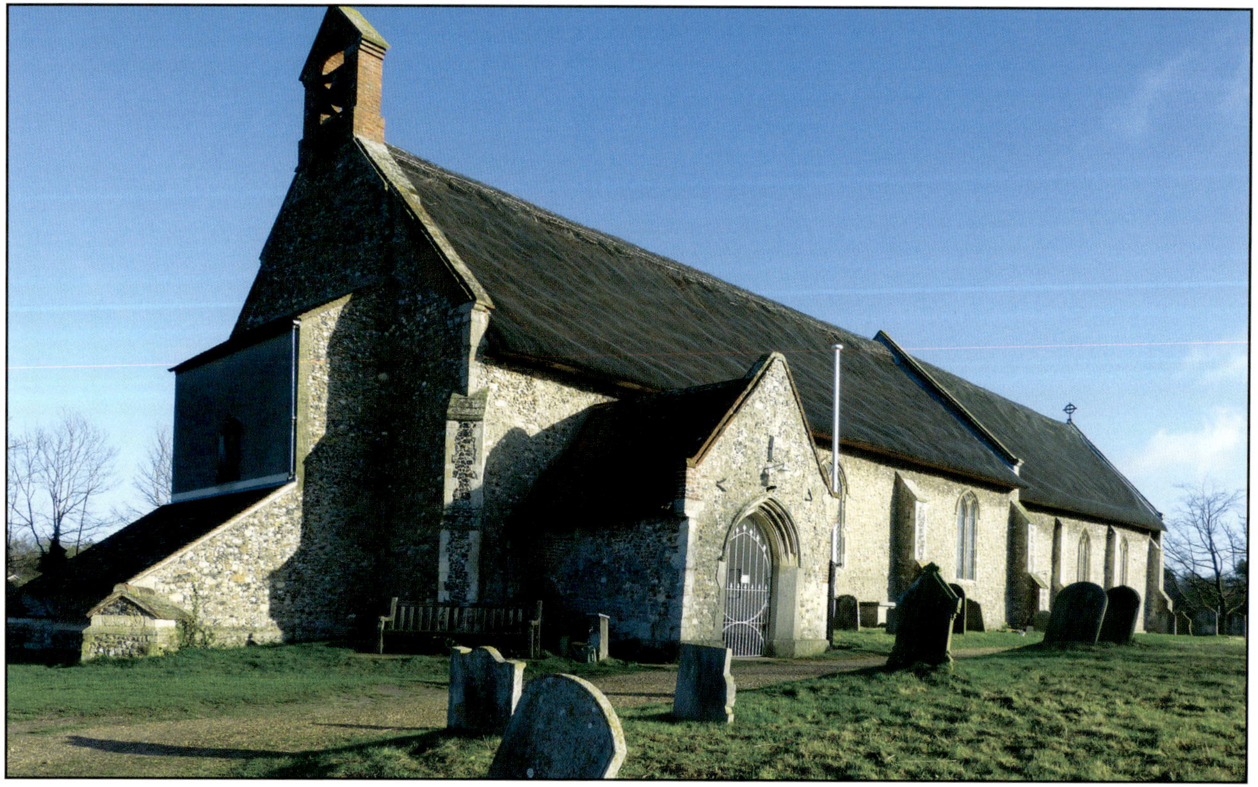

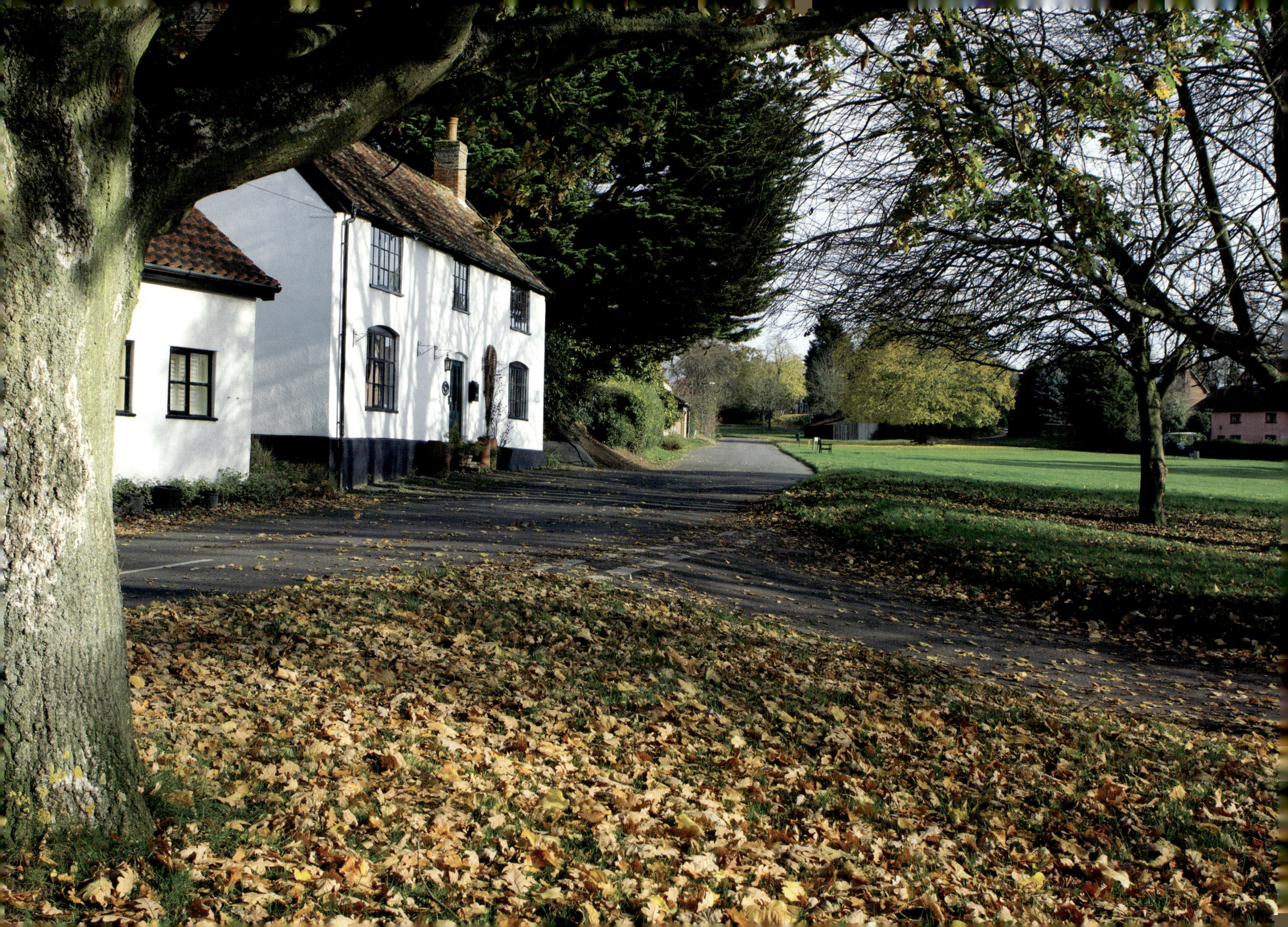

Saxmundham

Set in the heart of the Suffolk Heritage Coast, Saxmundham – known locally as Sax – has been a market town since 1272 when it was granted a charter during the reign of Edward II. A market is still held here every Wednesday (right). Until 1977 all the farmers in the area congregated here for the 'live and dead stock market' held on land that is now occupied by the Waitrose supermarket. Local pubs had special licensing dispensation on market days, giving them all-day opening hours (licensed premises opening hours were restricted by law then), making the town the centre of convivial and sometimes raucous social activity for agricultural workers for miles around.

Commerce and communication have been the mainstay for Saxmundham for generations. Straddling the old A12 road, coaching inns and hostelries gave respite to weary travellers (and still do), being then a convenient staging post between Lowestoft and Ipswich. The railway station was opened in 1859.

The popularity of Saxmundham as a shopping centre increased with the arrival of two major supermarkets – Waitrose and Tesco – having been built on opposing sides of the road on a previously run-down area just off the High Street. Careful siting and appropriate planning of these two shopping giants have sensitively juxtaposed the old with the new. The White Hart coaching inn stables (right) in Fromus Square serve as a reminder to passing supermarket shoppers of the town's place in history. The large retail developments have brought a renewed commercial vibrancy to the town, benefitting the other speciality shops and restoring Saxmundham as a popular shopping hub for the surrounding area.

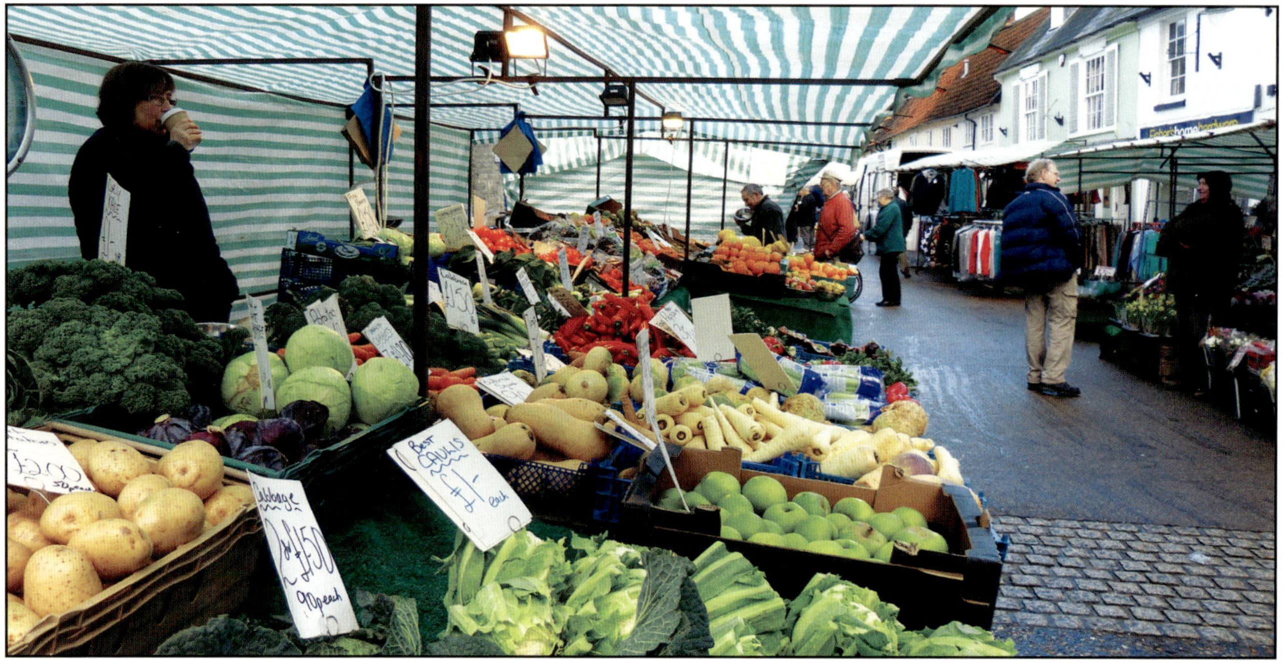

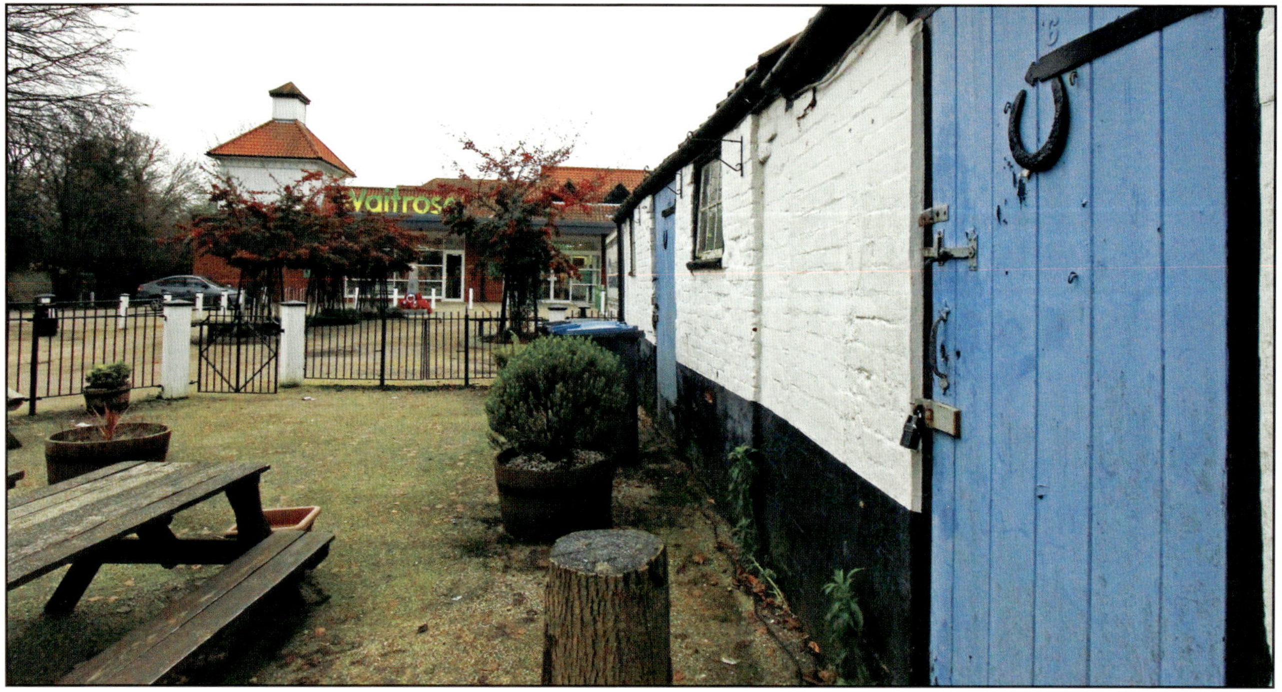

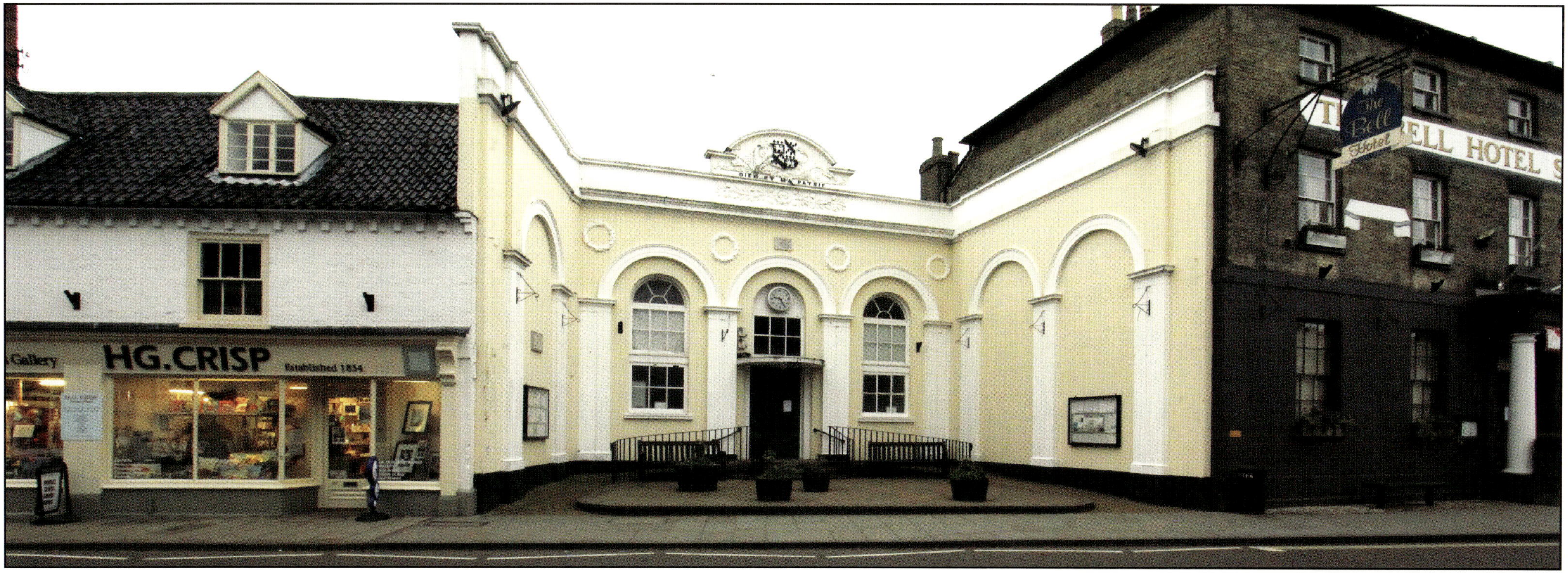

The High Street running through the centre of the town has a unique collection of period buildings and shops, giving the town an almost Dickensian feel, some have glazed bow windows and another has been a jewellers shop since 1769, and remains almost unchanged inside and out with wooden window shutters that are put up at at night. Many of the shops date back to the Tudor era with Victorian facades added later.

The whole of the street is designated a conservation area. The Market Hall (above) is one of the most distinctive-looking buildings with its neoclassical frontage. It was built in 1846 as a corn exchange. The Bell Hotel dates from about the same time, but occupies a site that has been an inn for centuries.

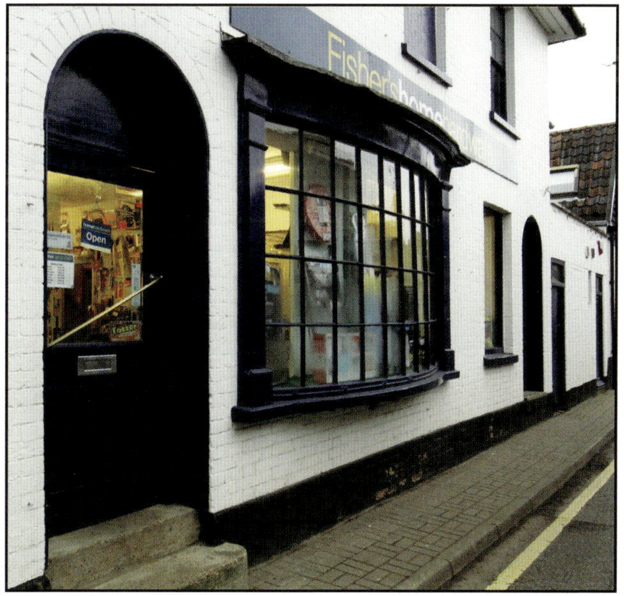

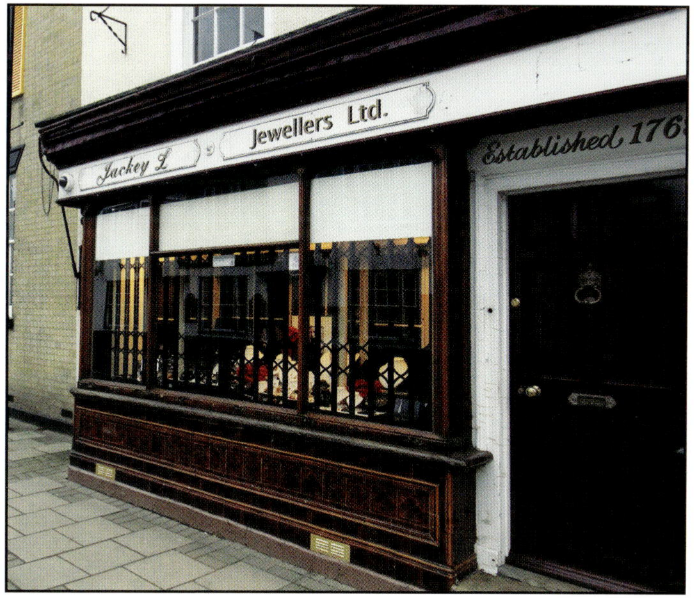

Thorpeness

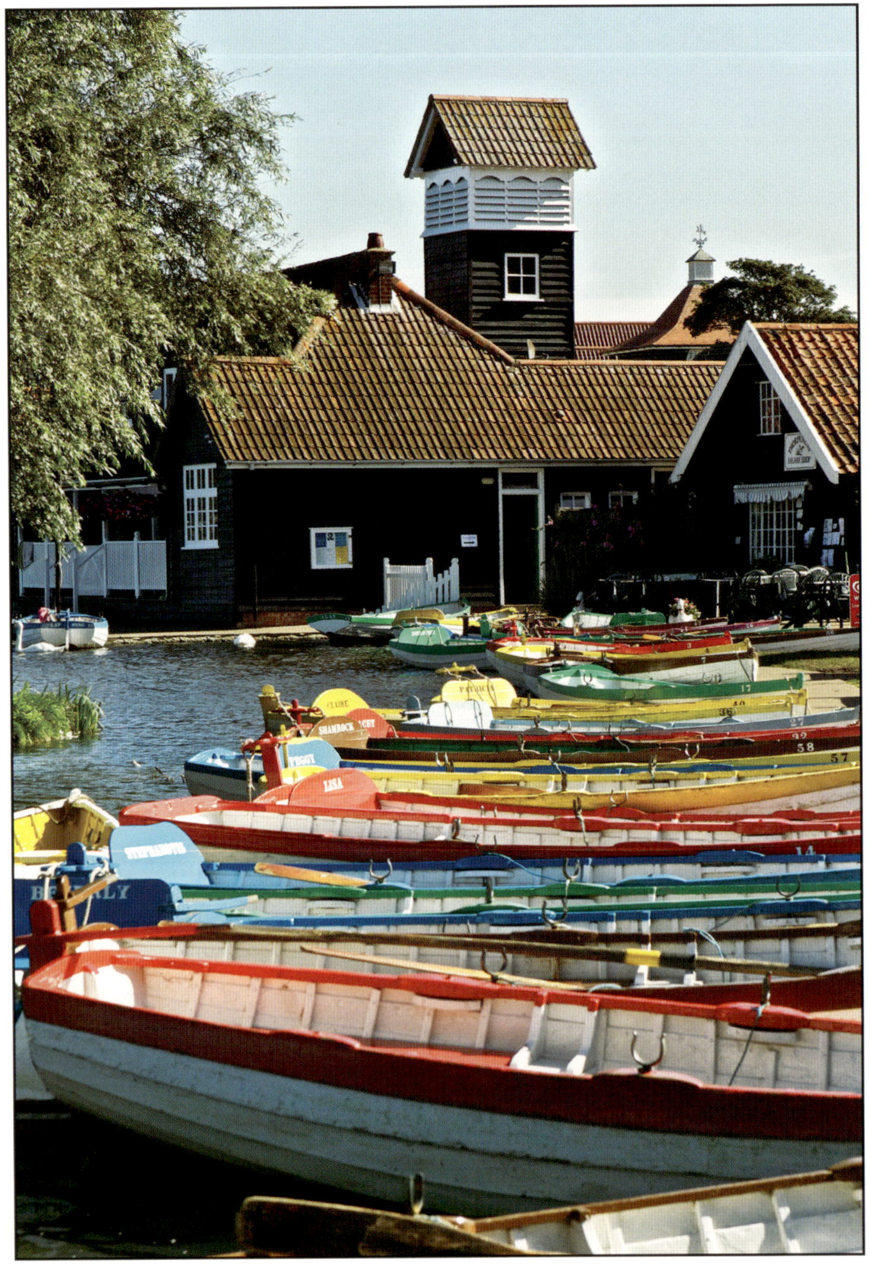

Back to the coast and a short coastal walk from Sizewell, and within sight of Aldeburgh, brings us to the former smugglers' hideout village of Thorpeness. In 1910, local landowner Stuart Ogilvie developed Thorpeness into an up-market fantasy holiday village, making it possibly the first leisure theme park in the country – long before Billy Butlin set up his camps. Wooden holiday homes were built in mock Jacobean and Tudor styles, a boating lake was excavated – the Meare – and the water tower was made to look like a house up in the clouds. A redundant windmill was transported from the nearby village of Aldringham to pump water to supply the houses, and an eighteen-hole golf course was established.

Once popular with the colonial community on long leave from overseas appointments, this was, and still is, a great fun place for visitors, although most of the property is now in private hands. Nearly all of the carefully maintained boats (below) used on the Meare today date from the time when it was first opened – a hundred or more years ago. Several generations of visitors would have rowed, sailed or punted these very same craft, with the same names, around the Meare in search of adventure in this Peter Pan-like fantasy world. J M Barrie, who wrote the *Peter Pan* books, was a friend of the Ogilvies.

Benjamin Britten was fond of Thorpeness and attended small open-air musical gatherings around the Meare.

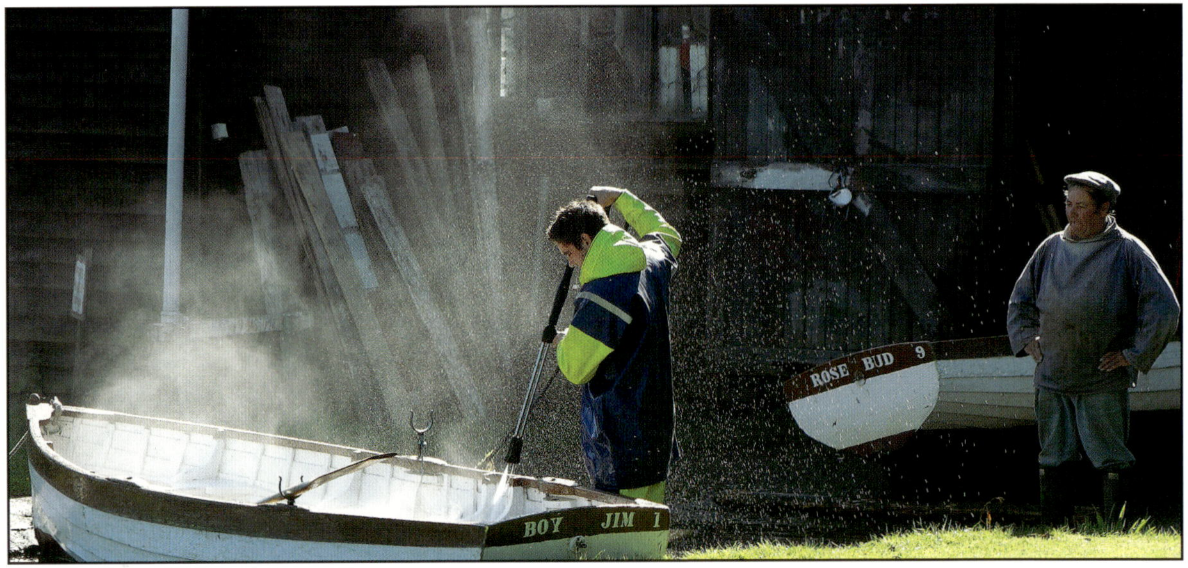

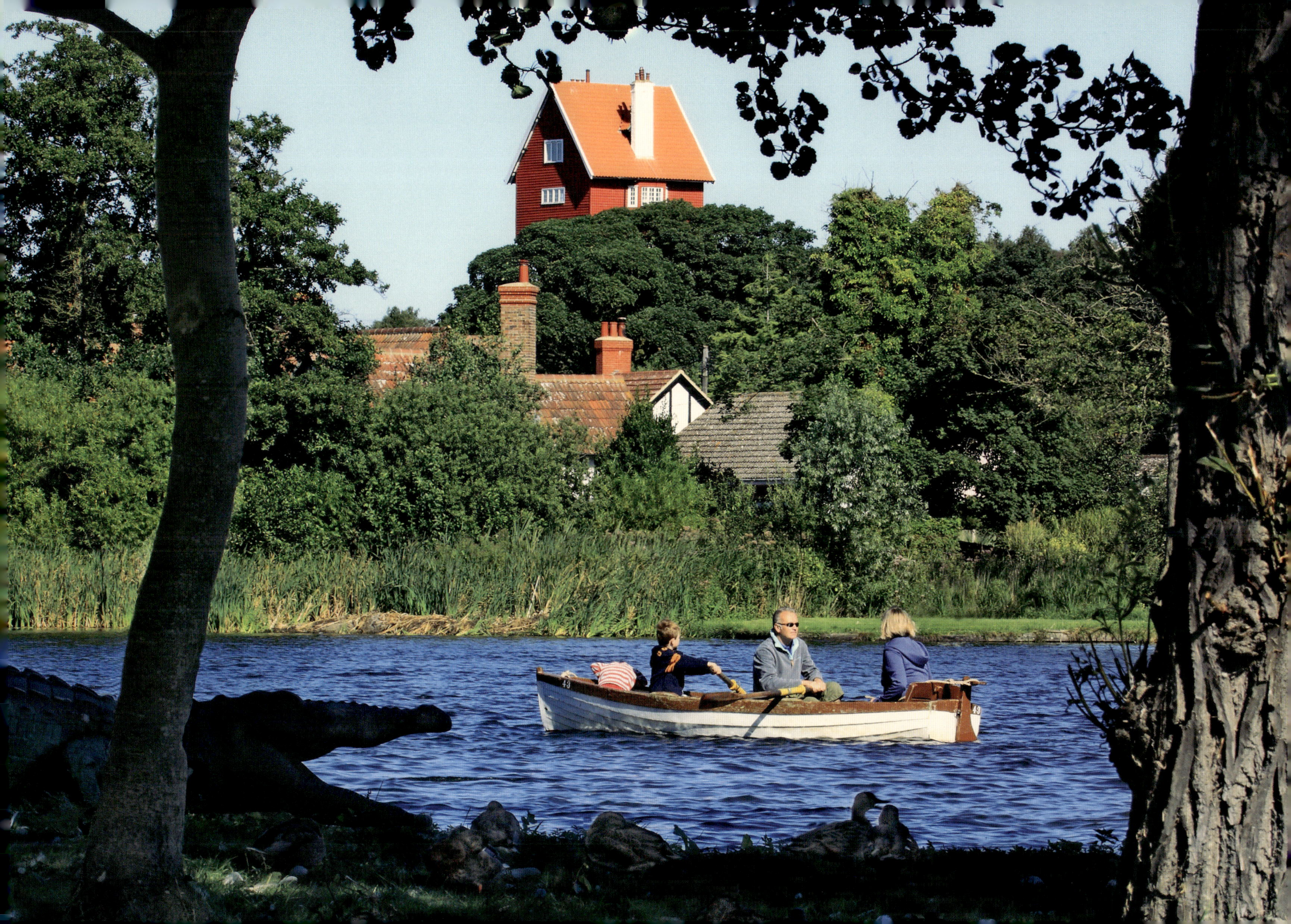

Britten's Aldeburgh

The stony beach from Thorpeness to Aldeburgh was familiar territory for Benjamin Britten who frequently walked his dogs here.

Suffolk artist Maggi Hambling's impressive sculpture the *Scallop* stands, controversially, on the beach approaching Aldeburgh. Pierced around the outer rim are the words 'I hear those voices that will not be drowned' from Britten's critically acclaimed opera *Peter Grimes*, a work adapted from Aldeburgh-born poet George Crabbe's *The Borough*, a dramatic tale of fishermen's lives set in a fictional fishing village, widely thought to be based on Aldeburgh.

The stainless steel *Scallop* is now one of the best-known sculptures in Britain. I like it; it says everything I need to know about Aldeburgh and its surrounds.

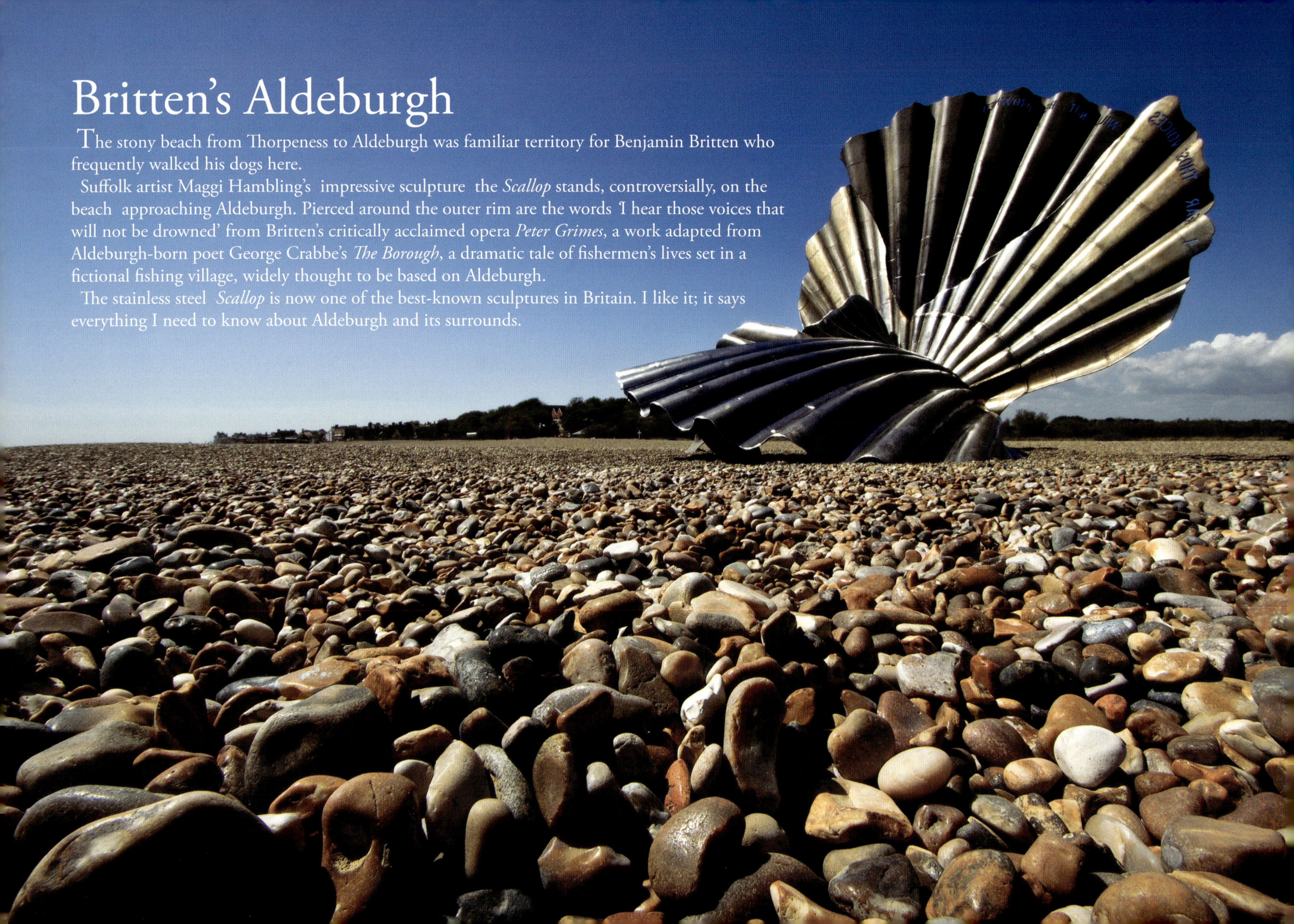

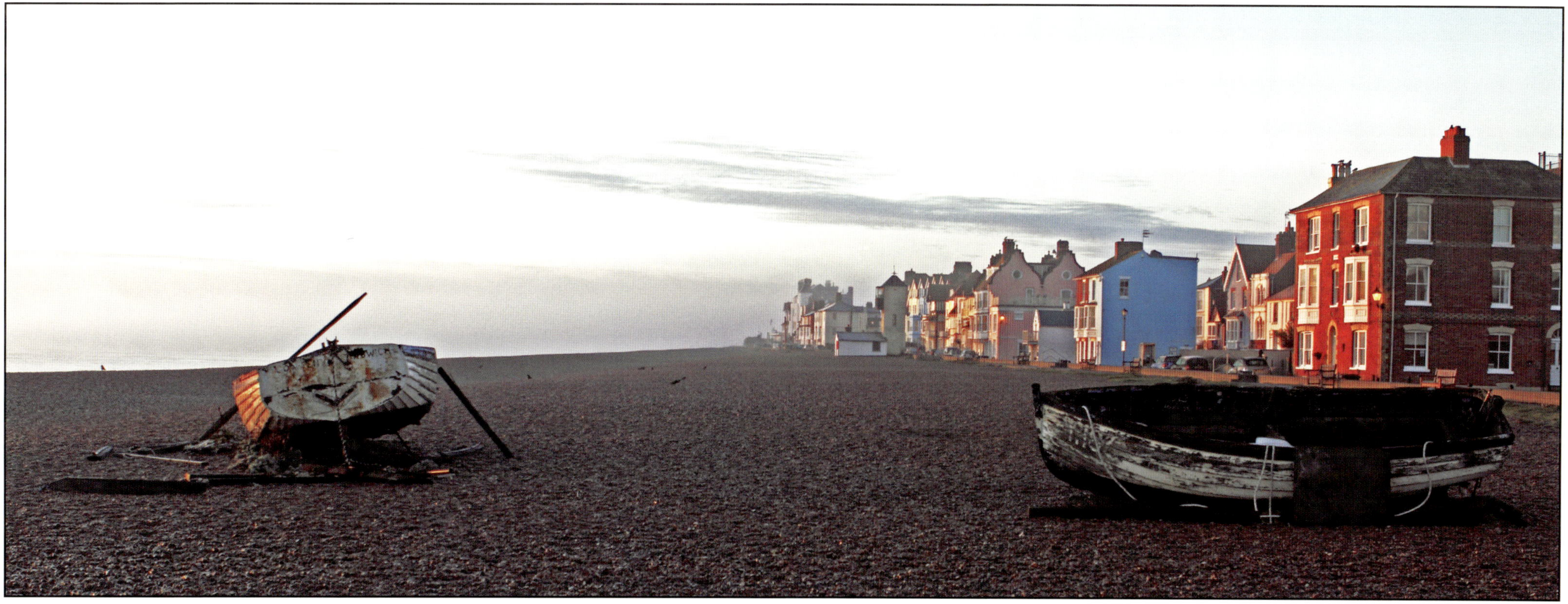

In 1947 Benjamin Britten and his partner Peter Pears moved from the Old Mill, Snape, to live in Aldeburgh, on Crag Path, in a house overlooking the beach and sea – with views that would have conjured up nostalgic memories of his childhood home in Lowestoft. He was passionately fond of the Suffolk coast in all its moods, and had a great kinship with the local people – he shared coastal dramas with them when his house was flooded in 1953.

I feel sure that the *Scallop* would have met with his approval. Firstly the subject matter would have appealed; secondly, the artist and the craftsmen who fabricated it – J T Pegg and Sons – are all Suffolk born and bred.

When he asked me to do his photography, being a local lad would have gone in my favour. I enjoyed working with him: he was always helpful, easy to work with, responsive, and very generous in both words and kind.

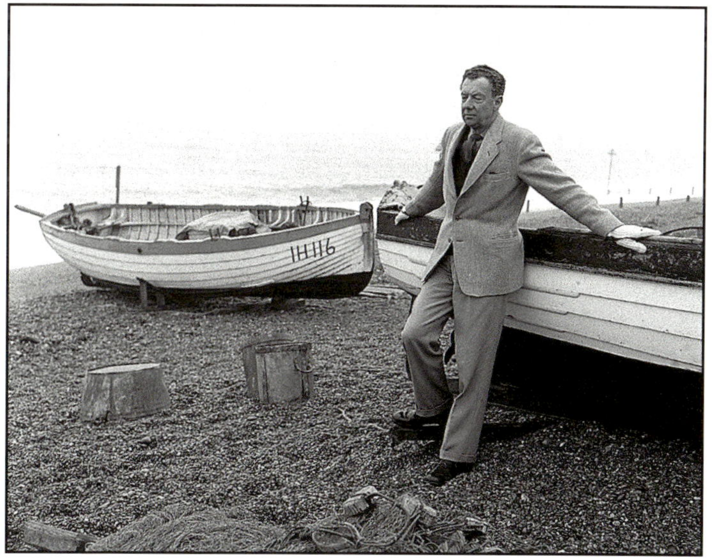

'I envy artists and photographers, they can capture mood and atmosphere with the click of a shutter, or with a simple brush stroke,' he once told me. However, Imogen Holst, daughter of Gustav Holst and Ben's music assistant, often remarked that she had difficulty in keeping up with the speed of his composing.

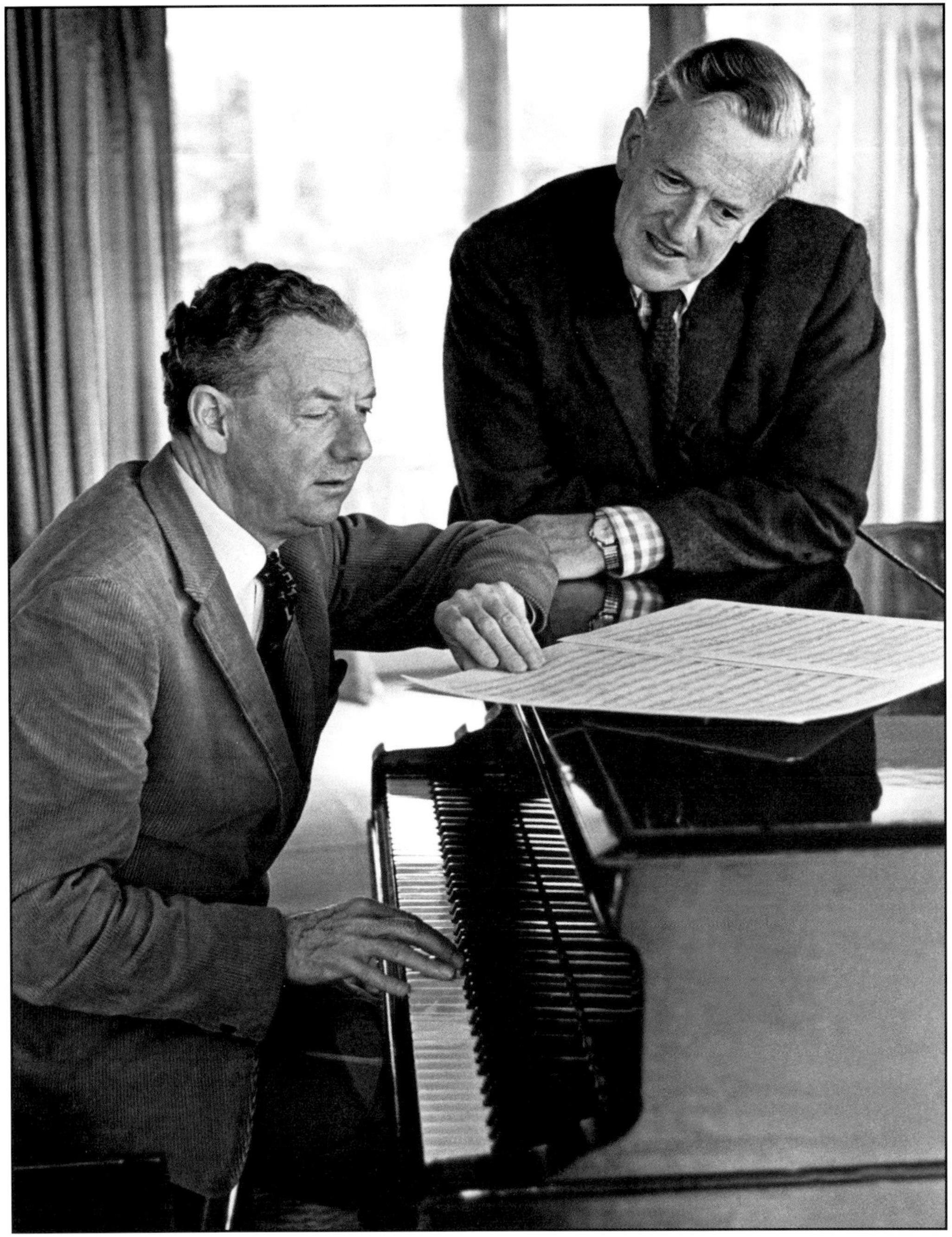

Ben and Peter looking at a music score together in the library of Red House.

Red House – home and office

Benjamin Britten and Peter Pears moved from their seafront house on Crag Path in 1957, to a former farmhouse on the outskirts of Aldeburgh. They felt the need for more space, and a bit more privacy than Crag House afforded them.

This was where much of Britten's music was composed, and where they entertained many overseas visiting musicians invited to take part in the, by now, burgeoning Aldeburgh Festival. The main entrance gate was festooned with welcome signs in many languages, and the house saw such notables of the music world as Russian cellist and conductor Rostropovich and composer Shostakovich – both great friends of Britten.

I have many fond memories of visiting Red House. It's the personal moments I treasure most. One such was when I called, and his housekeeper – Miss Hudson – met me at the door and told me Mr Britten was upset and wasn't seeing visitors today; his pet parrot had died. But she invited me into the kitchen for a cup of tea anyhow. Ben unexpectedly came in looking very upset – the parrot had been his pet for many years. He told me what had happened, then broke down in tears and cried on my shoulder as I gave him a man hug – something that wasn't commonly done in those days.

On another occasion Ben phoned me one evening and invited me to Red House for 'drinks'. "Don't bring your camera, just come and relax," he told me. When I arrived, the drawing room was already buzzing with conviviality, and I found myself in the company of some of the world's greatest musicians and singers, who were having a musical jam session. I was given a whisky, and the next thing I knew Ben and Rostropovich were sitting side by side at the piano playing Scott Joplin's *Maple Leaf Rag*. Ben knew I was a great blues, ragtime, and jazz fan, and while playing he turned, looked at me and grinned. He and Rostropovich were jamming ragtime music just for me! That was a real 'WOW' moment.

Red House is now home to The Britten-Pears Foundation, formed to safeguard the legacy of Britten and Pears, and to support arts through grants to a wide range of charitable organisations. An archive centre has been established here, which is open to the public.

Ben in his studio at Red House with his dachshund – Gilda (right).

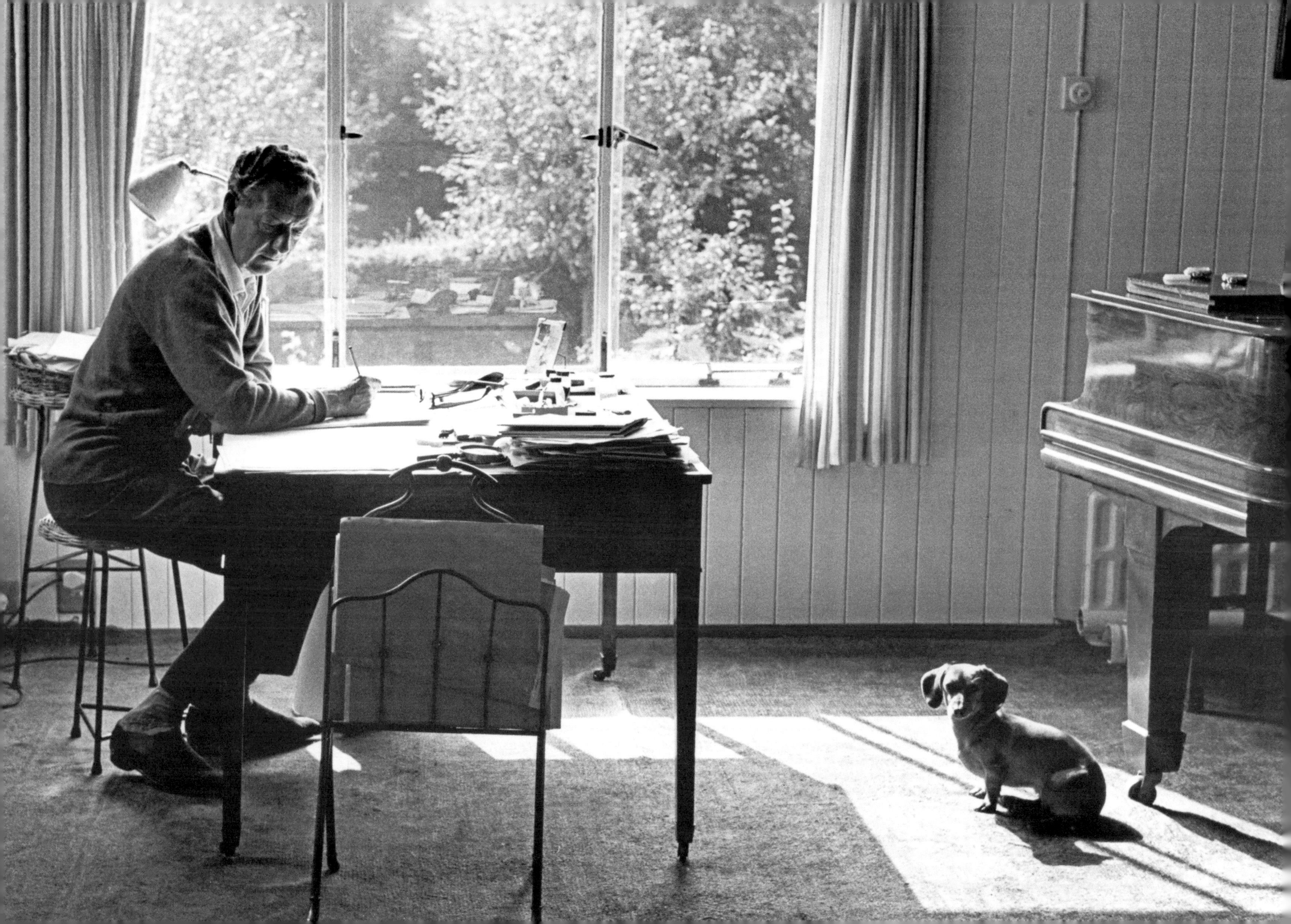

Aldeburgh: its people and other things

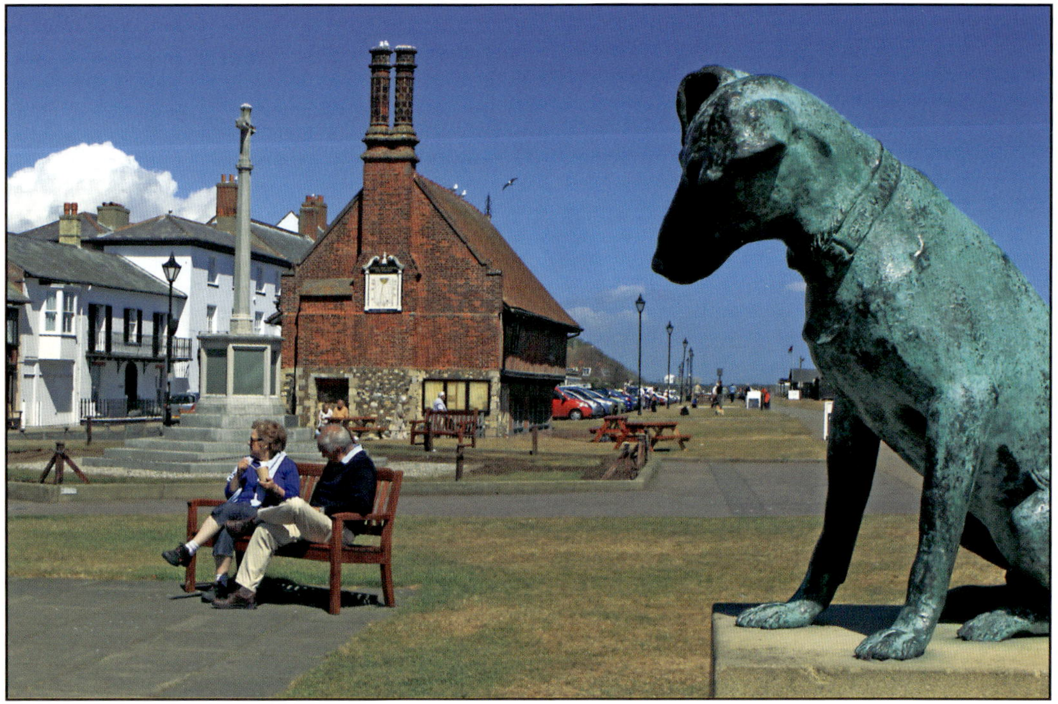

Locals call it the 'lazy wind' – it doesn't bother to go around you, it goes straight through you. When the winter north-easterly winds blow in from the sea, it's time to batten down the hatches, light a roaring fire, and leave the beaches to the tough longshore fishermen.

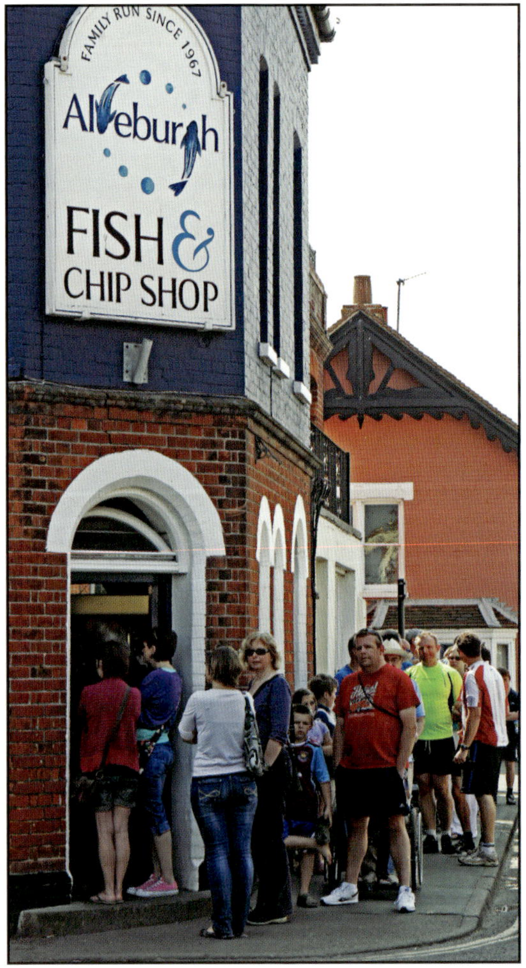

Fortunately the prevailing winds are dry westerlies, having dumped most of the Atlantic wet stuff on the rest of the country before reaching here.

No day trip would be complete without standing in a long queue outside one of the two famous fish and chip shops – run by the same family – waiting to be served with the best fish and chips in the country – so some would claim. Many a well-known person has been seen heading for the beach with this great British fast food takeaway. Aldeburgh is the kind of place you can feel good about doing that.

Hot, lazy, summer days near the beach in Aldeburgh are what most people remember about this user-friendly coastal resort which panders to holiday-makers' needs in the best of classic British understated ways.

Much loved man-and-wife doctor team – Robin and Nora Acheson, who served the town for over a quarter of a century – are remembered by this memorial which overlooks the Moot Hall. It's of their dog Snooks, who would follow his master around the town as Dr Robin made his house calls.

Another even more celebrated medical resident, Elizabeth Garrett Anderson, was the first woman in England to qualify as a physician and surgeon – in 1865. Another first for her was when she moved to Aldeburgh and became Mayor in 1908, becoming the first female mayor, and magistrate, in Britain. These are just three of this amazing woman's achievements – a pioneer in the women's suffrage movement.

Aldeburgh owes much to the Garrett family dynasty. Her father, Newson Garrett, grandson of the Leiston industrialist Richard Garrett, became a wealthy maltster and brewer in his own right and built up his business in Snape, where he constructed one of the largest maltings in East Anglia. He was also responsible for building the town's Jubilee Hall in commemoration of Queen Victoria's Golden Jubilee, where the very first Aldeburgh Festival events took place. He couldn't have imagined, in his wildest dreams, that his maltings would end up being converted into one of the premier music venues in the country. The rest, as they say, is now history.

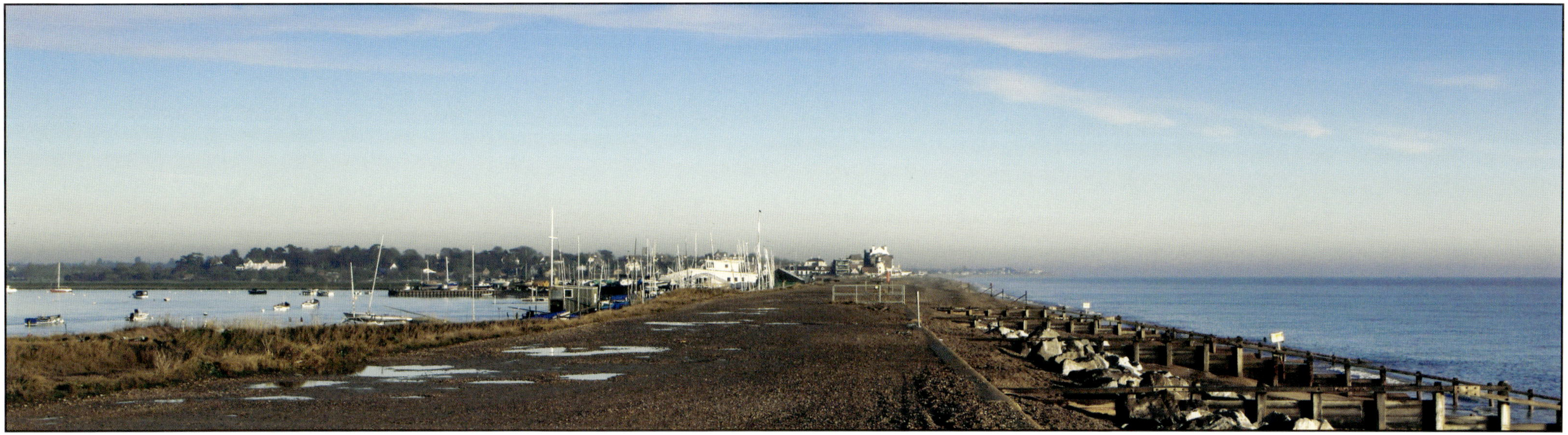

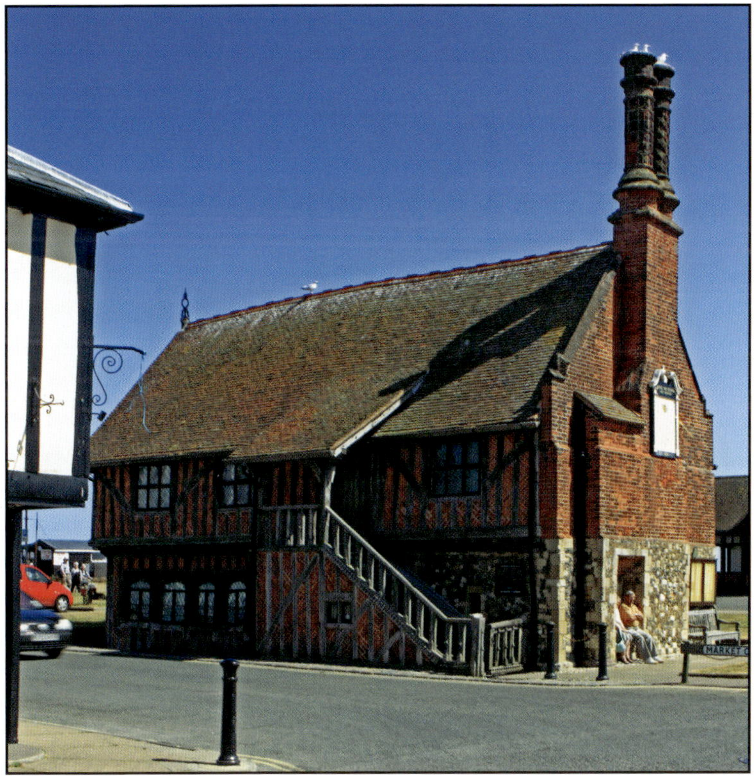

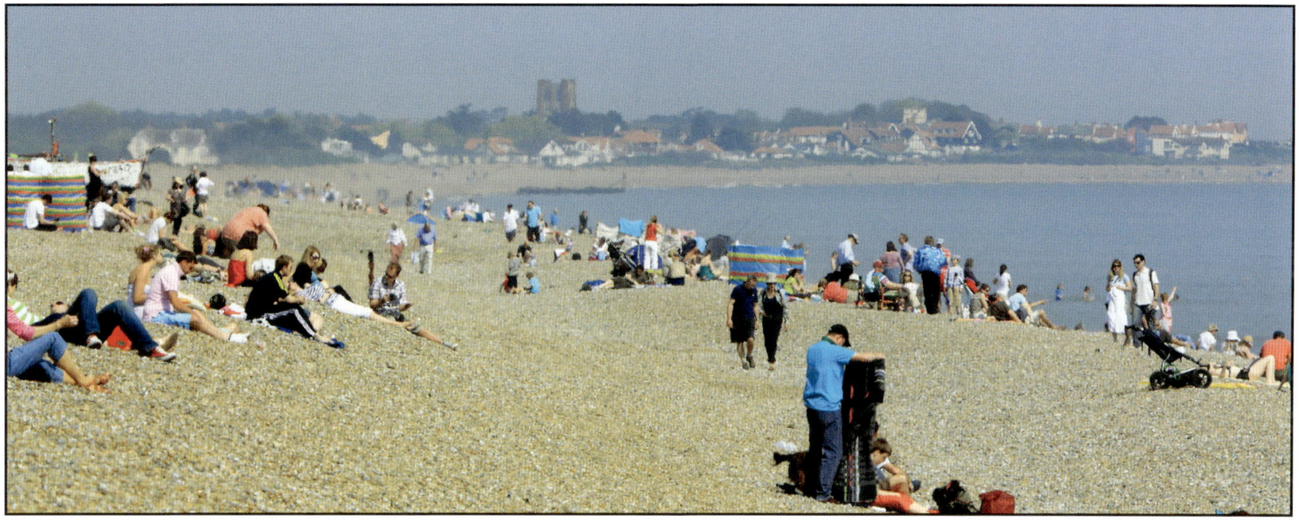

The hundred-metre shingle bank that stands behind the sea wall at Slaughden is all that holds back the North Sea from the River Alde, and the Aldeburgh yacht clubs.

The sixteenth-century Moot Hall, still used for council meetings, was once in the centre of Aldeburgh, then a major Tudor town and leading port and boat building centre – Sir Francis Drake's ship *Golden Hind* was built here. The silting up of the River Alde was the downfall of boat building, and the town slid into gradual decline until it became a popular seaside resort in the late nineteenth century.

Lifeboat spectacle and carnival day fun

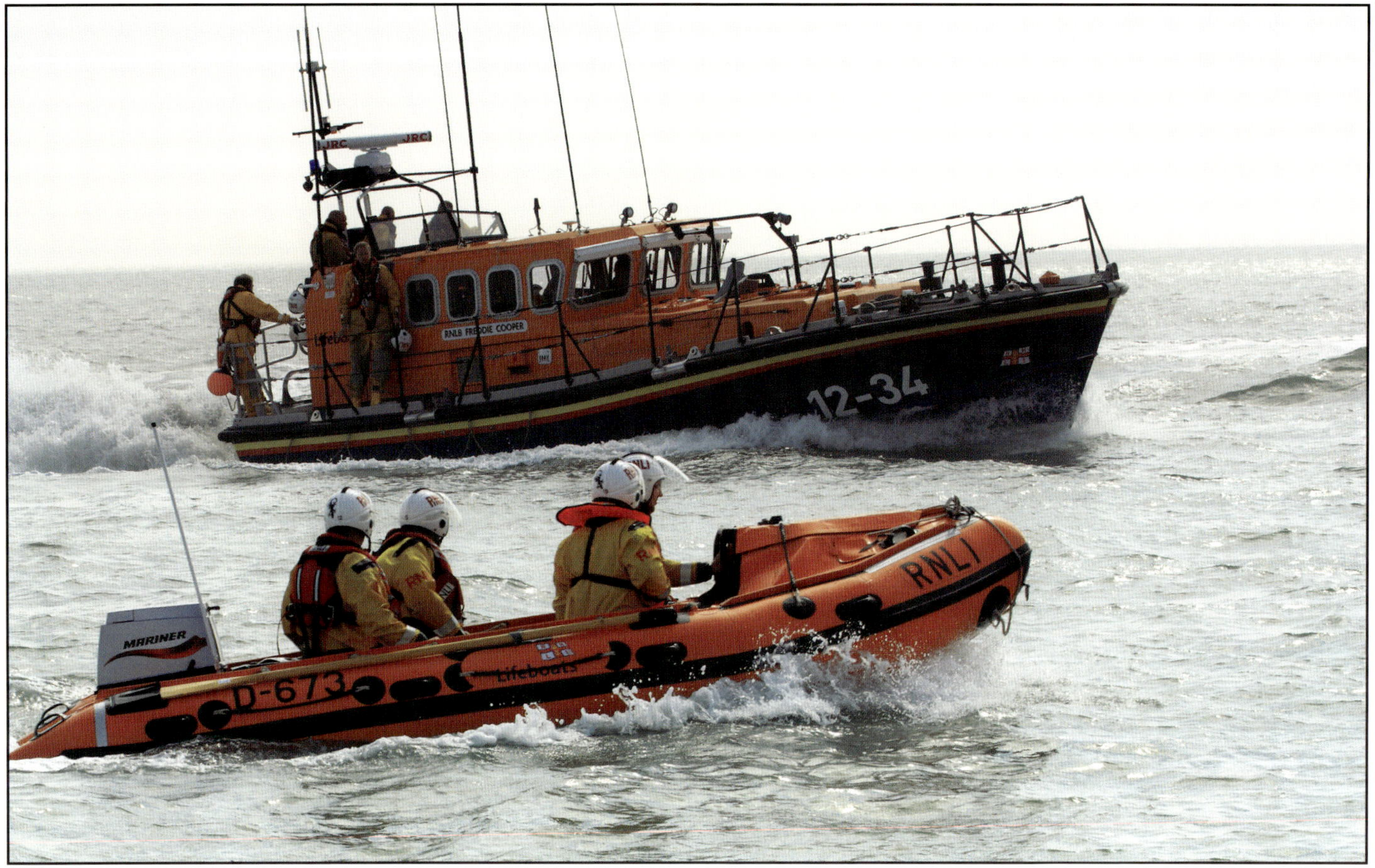

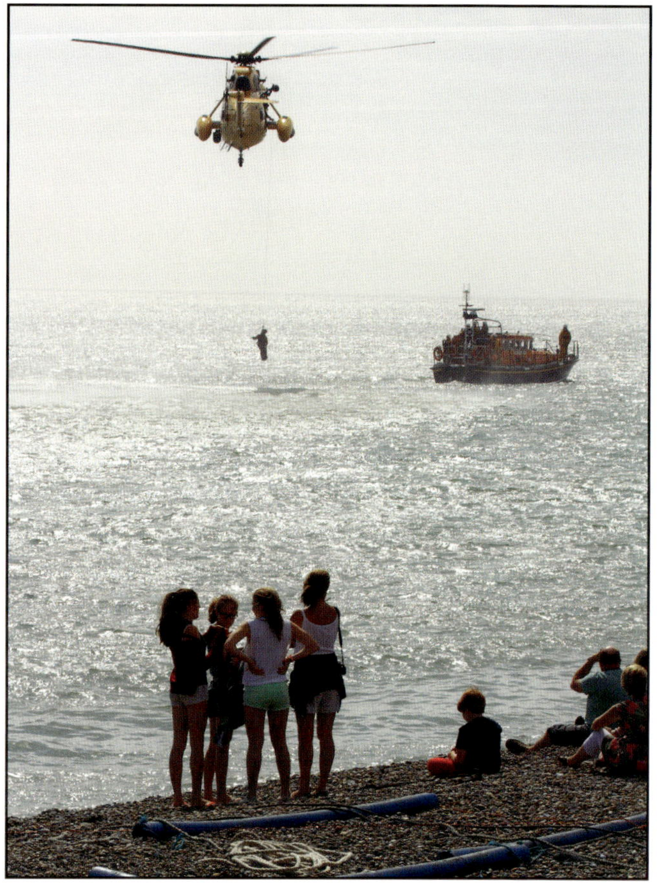

‘Aldeburgh lifeboat is on its way.’ To hear those words on the stricken vessel’s radio must sound like a message from heaven for desperate seamen. Many seafarers have been grateful for the bravery of the crews of Aldeburgh’s Royal National Lifeboat Institution lifeboats, who in all weather conditions launch their boats from the shore – no easy task even in calm conditions – and head out into the sometimes perilous North Sea to rescue fellow seafarers. Britten personally knew most of the Aldeburgh fishermen and crew who manned the lifeboat. They formed a guard of honour at his funeral. There are now two lifeboats on station at Aldeburgh. The all-weather Mersey Class *Freddie Cooper* – a powerful twin-engine, self-righting craft with a range of 140 miles – has a capacity to rescue up to forty-three survivors. The smaller inflatable *Christine* is used for inshore rescues, being a much easier craft to launch and recover from the beach. The current boathouse was built in 1994, enabling the boats to be stored under cover. Both boats and the boathouse were purchased from generous bequests.

On Carnival Day the crew give a demonstration of launching, and how they work with the search-and-rescue Sea King helicopters. In town, houses are decorated, the fun fairs are set up, and Aldeburgh comes alive for its annual August Carnival and Parade of decorated floats and fancy dress.

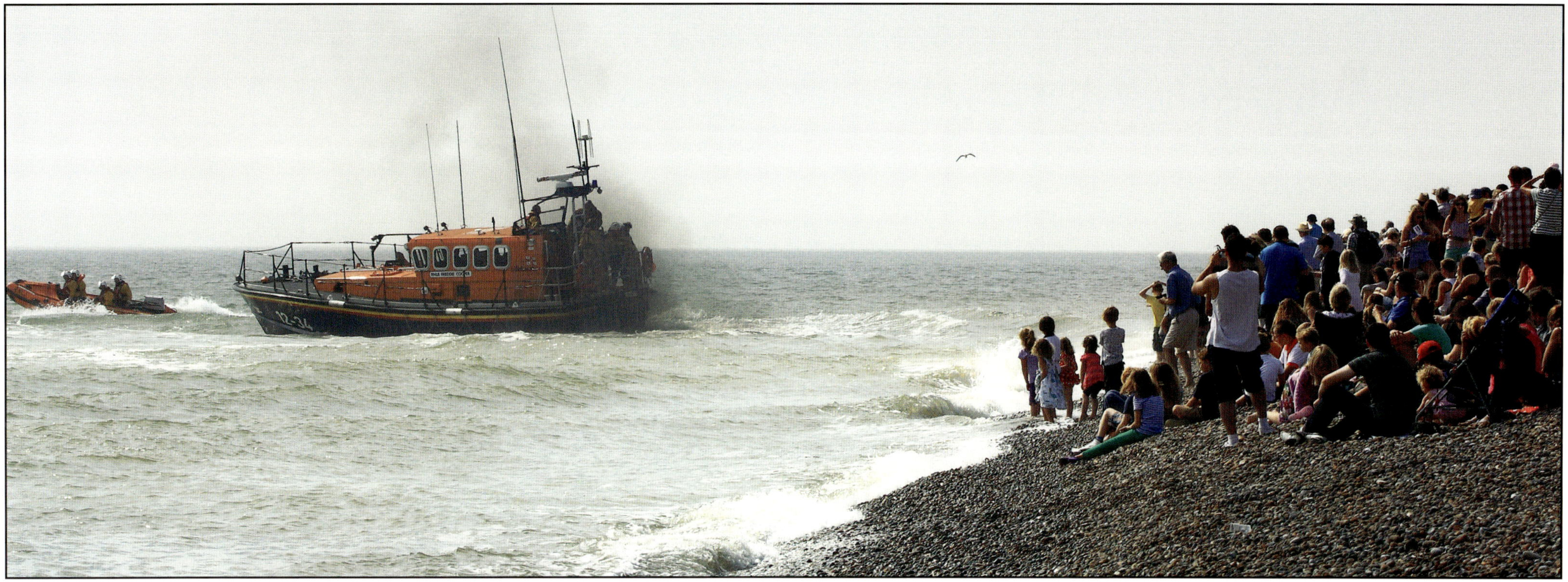

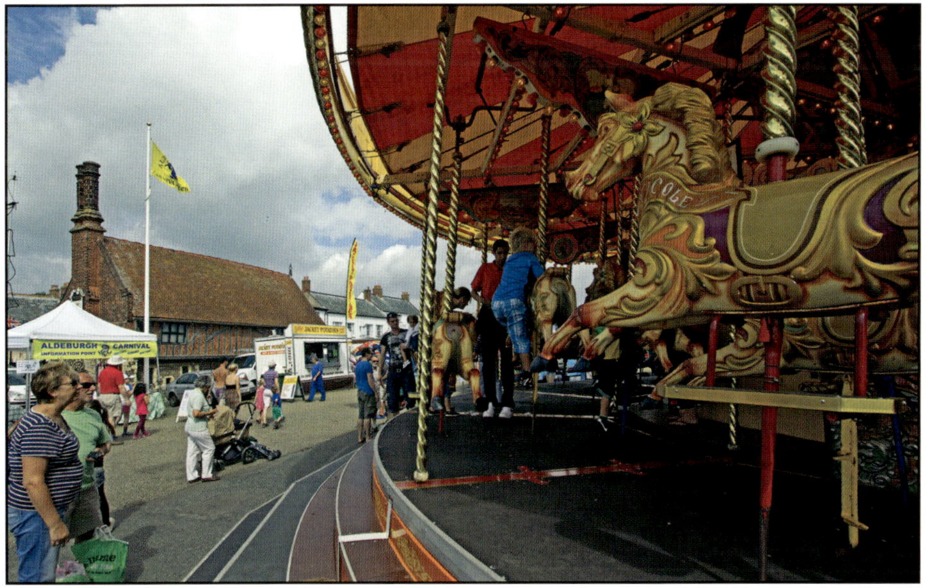
ALDEBURGH CARNIVAL

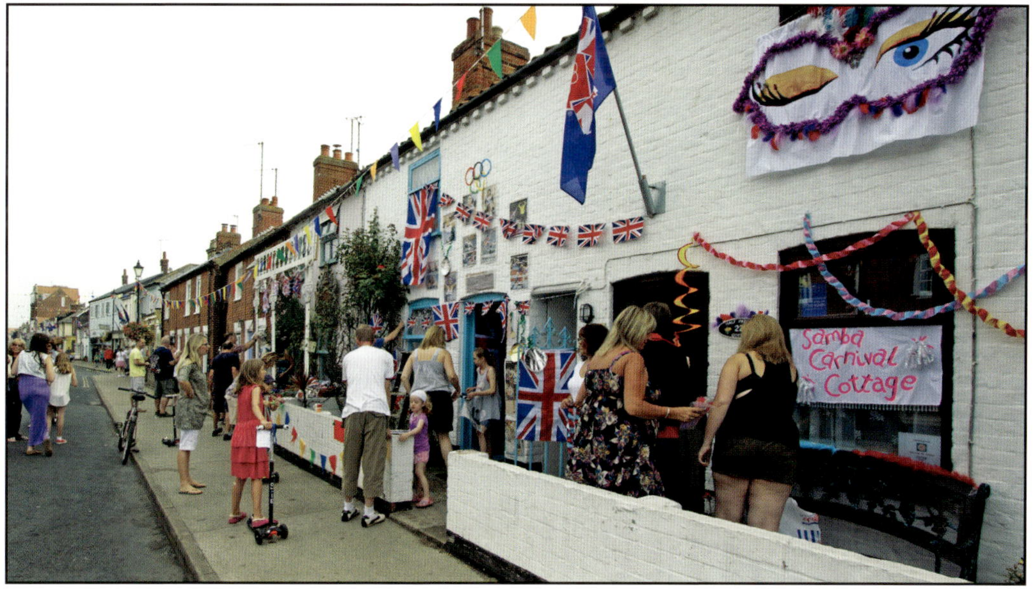
Samba Carnival Cottage

The 'golden hour' on Aldeburgh's beach

Photographers call it the 'golden hour'. That's the hour after sunrise, and the hour before sunset. I'm sure Britten, like me, experienced Aldeburgh as having a special magic all of its own at this time: I know of no other place I'd rather be at sunrise. It feels like Mother Nature is painting her glorious peaceful spectacle just for me. The smell of the ozone, the gentle light, the sound of waves gently lapping the shingle, – even the raucous gulls seem respectful of this hour. Add a touch of early morning mist to the palette, and a fishing boat or two, and the magic is complete.

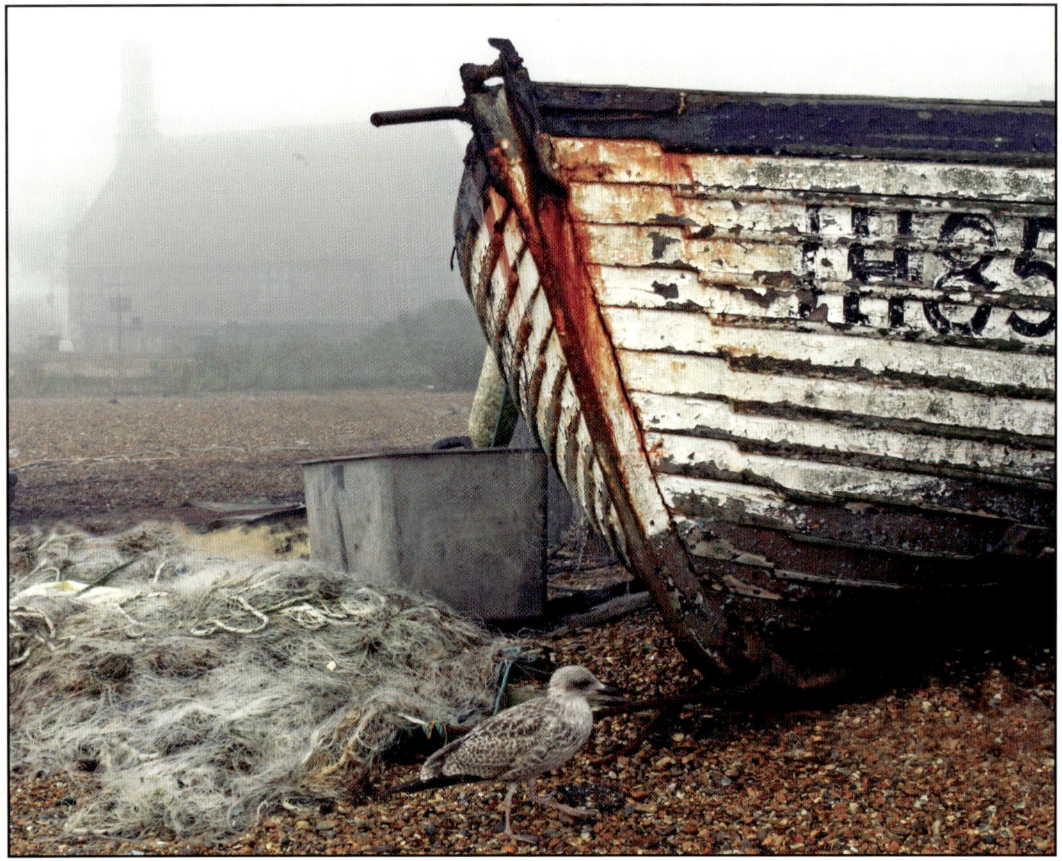

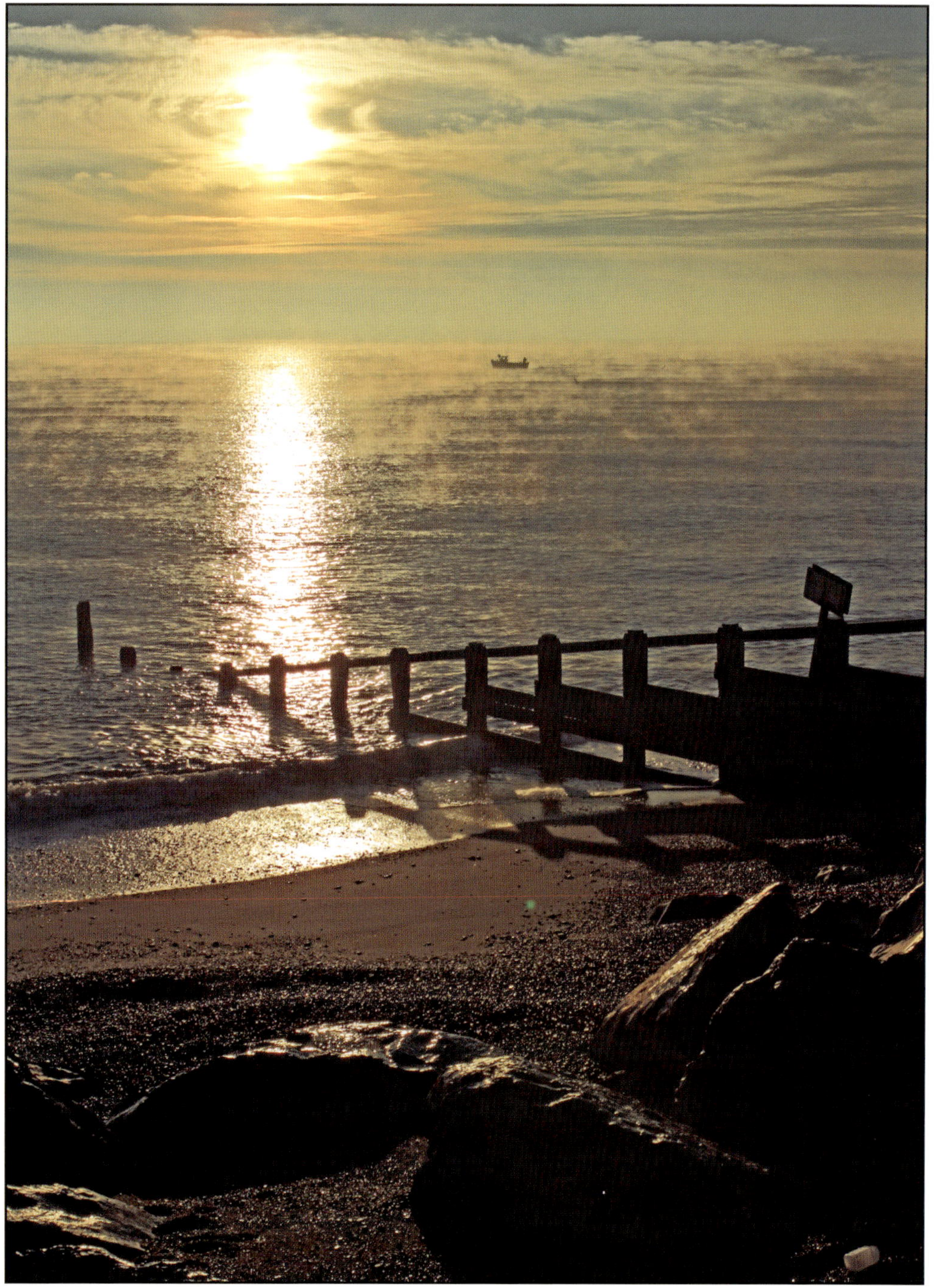

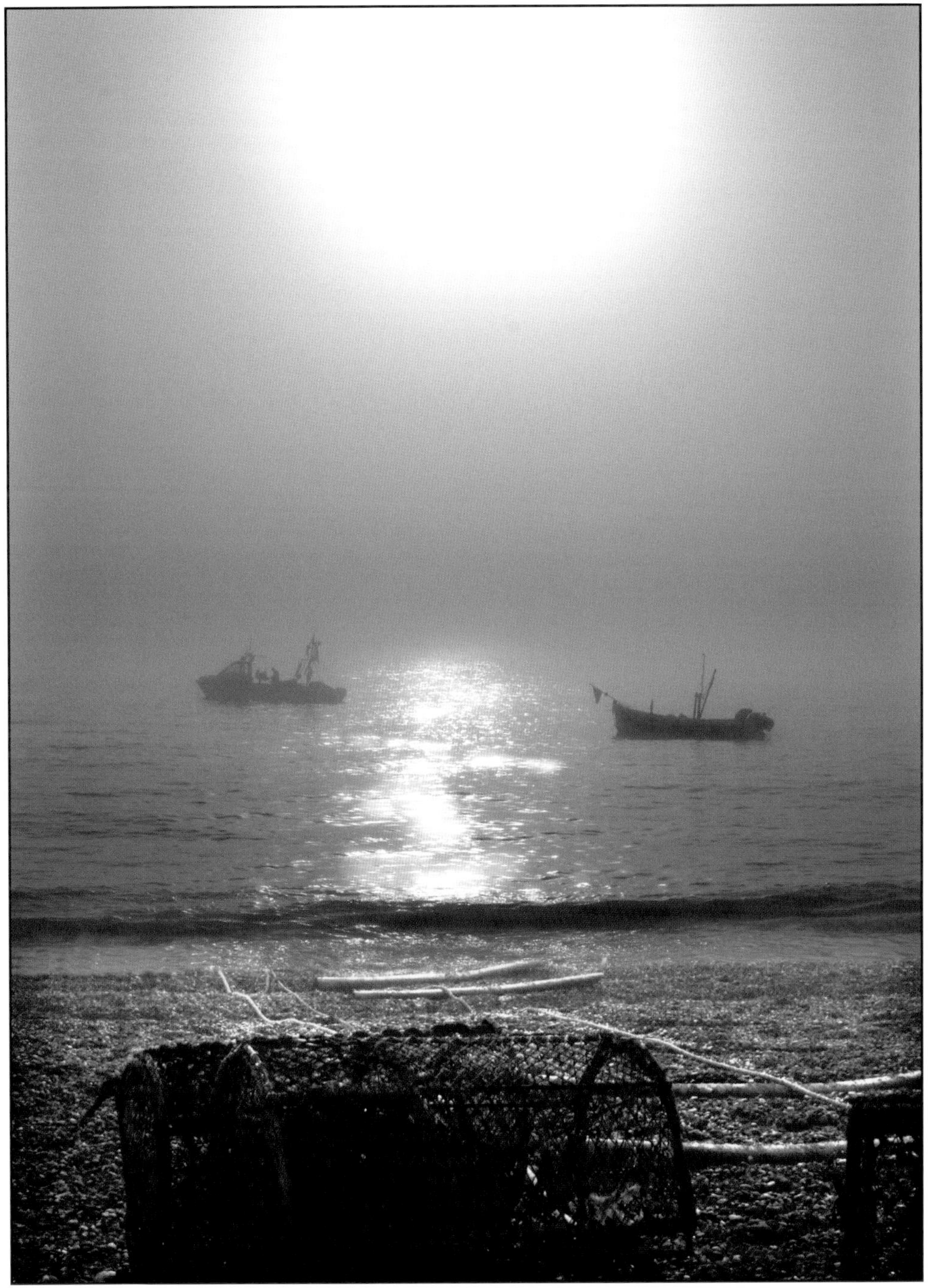

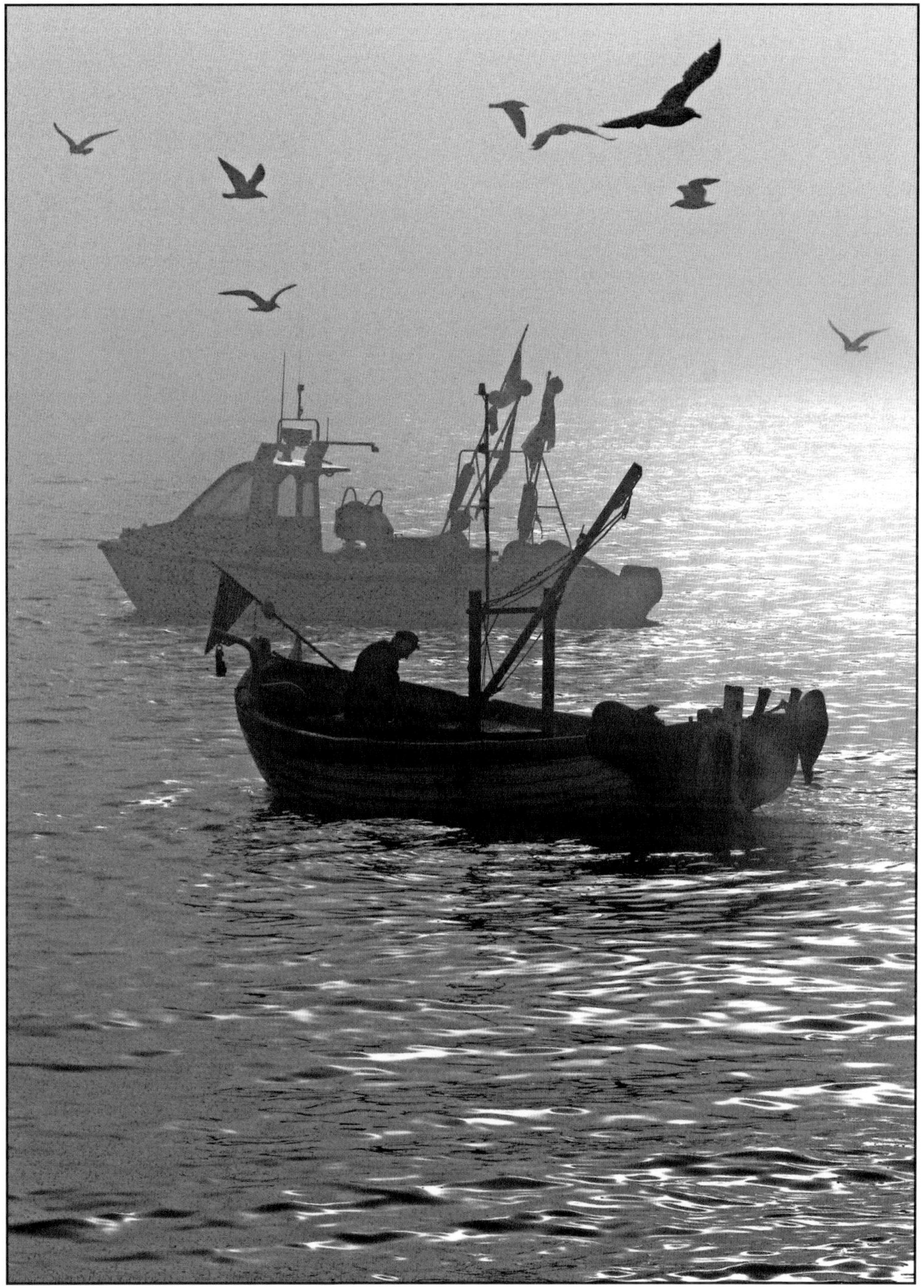

The River Alde from Slaughden to Snape

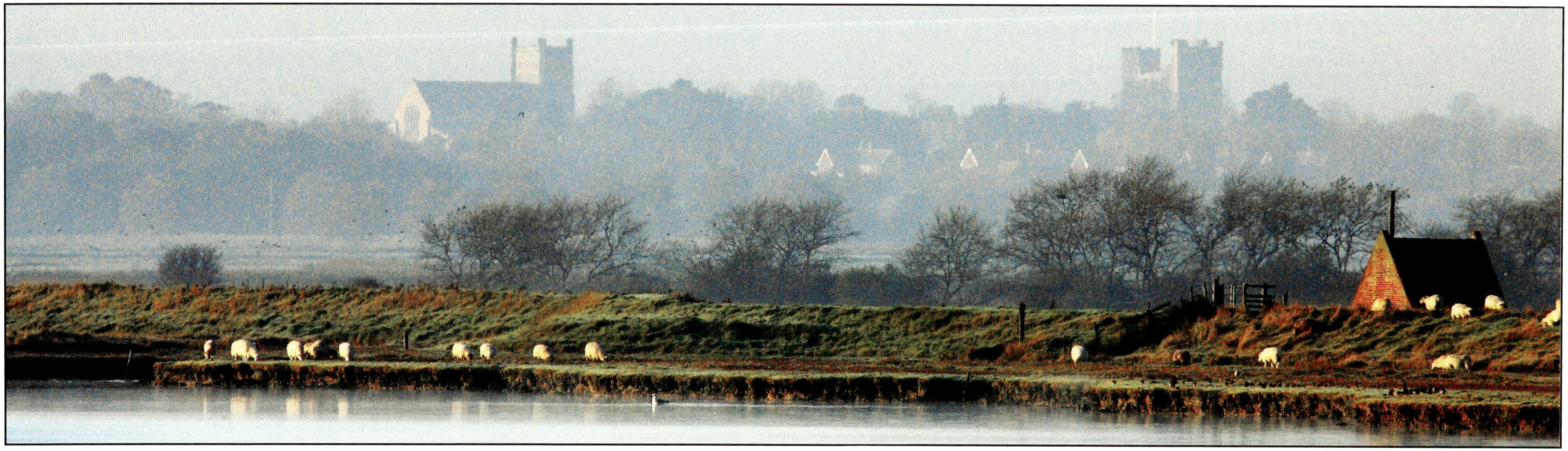

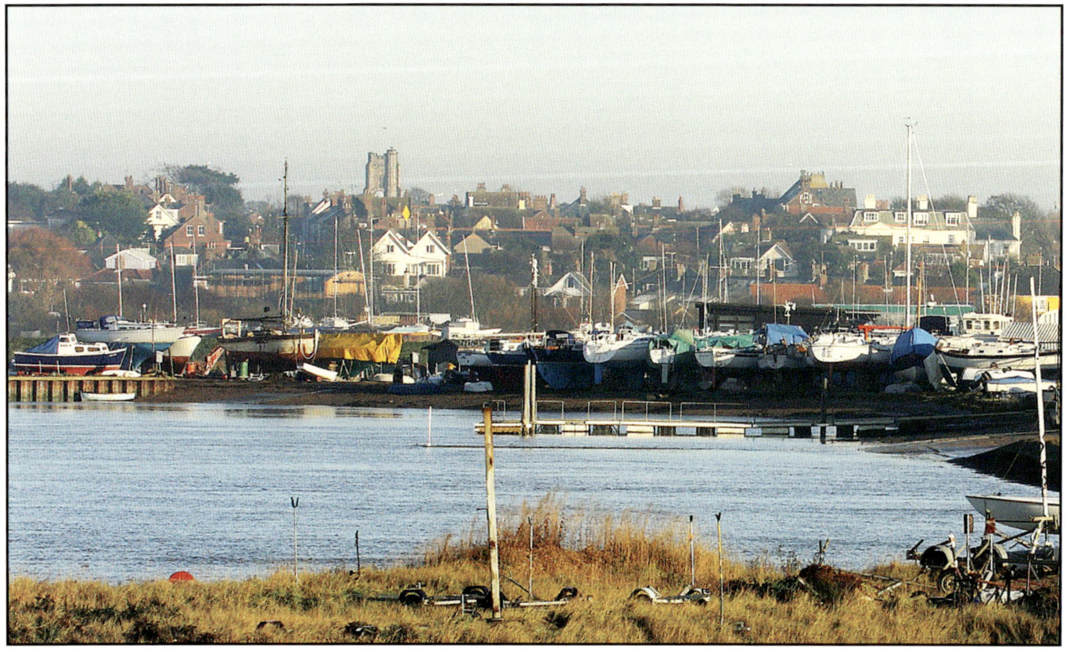

In the misty distance, Orford castle and church (above) can just be seen from Slaughden, where yachts hauled out for the winter vie for space at the boatyards on the banks of the River Alde, overlooked by Aldeburgh town.

Nearby, the largest and most northerly Martello tower in England stands robustly sentinel on top of the sea defences – the only surviving building in what was once the thriving town of Slaughden.

A little way downstream from Slaughden the Alde changes its name to the River Ore; precisely where, and why, is a matter for local argument.

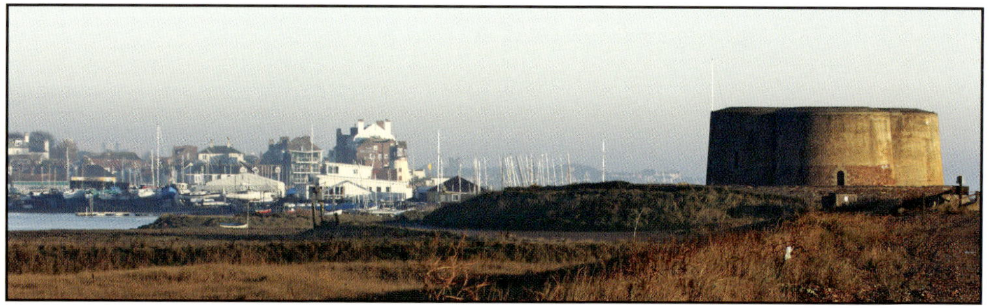

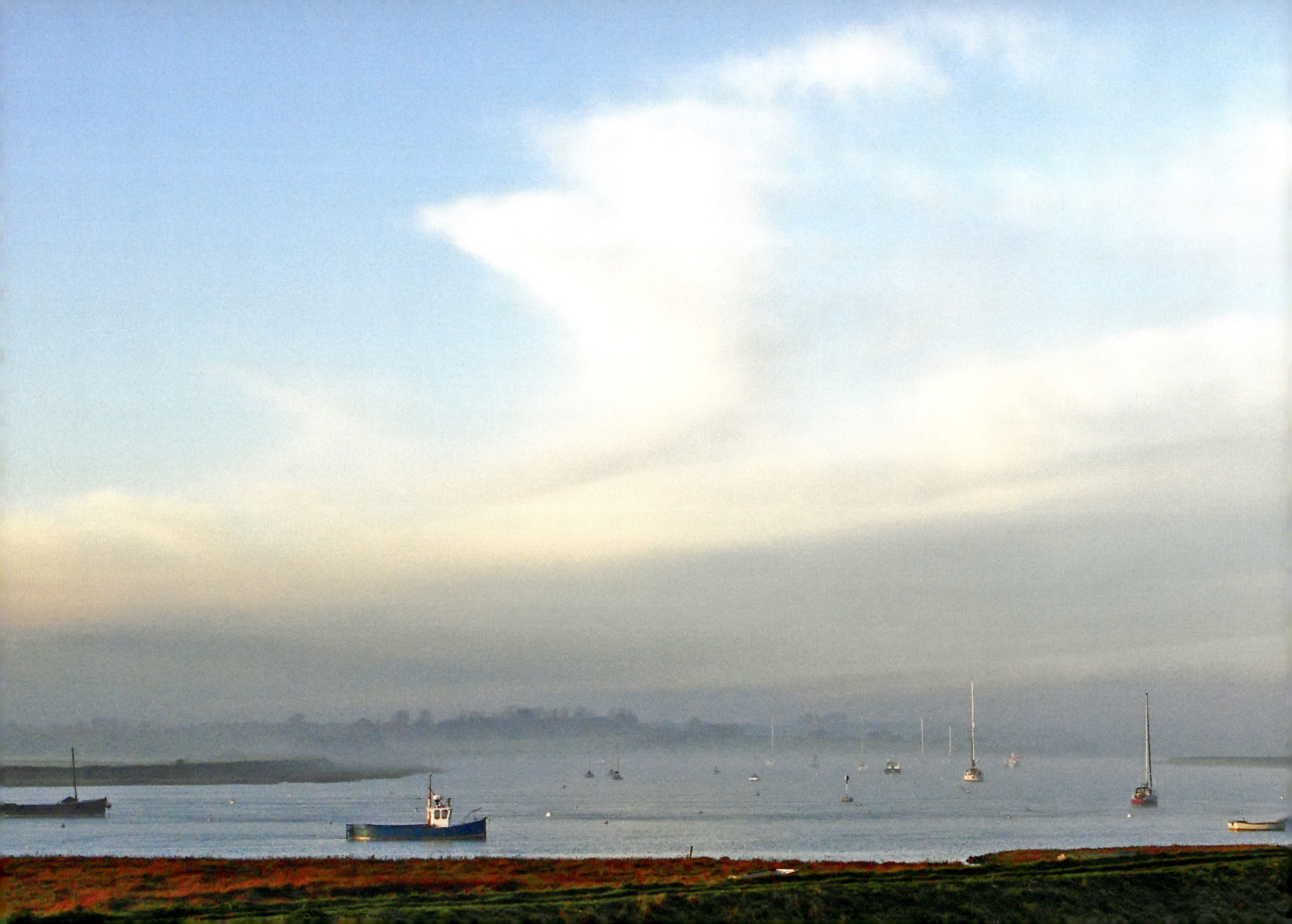

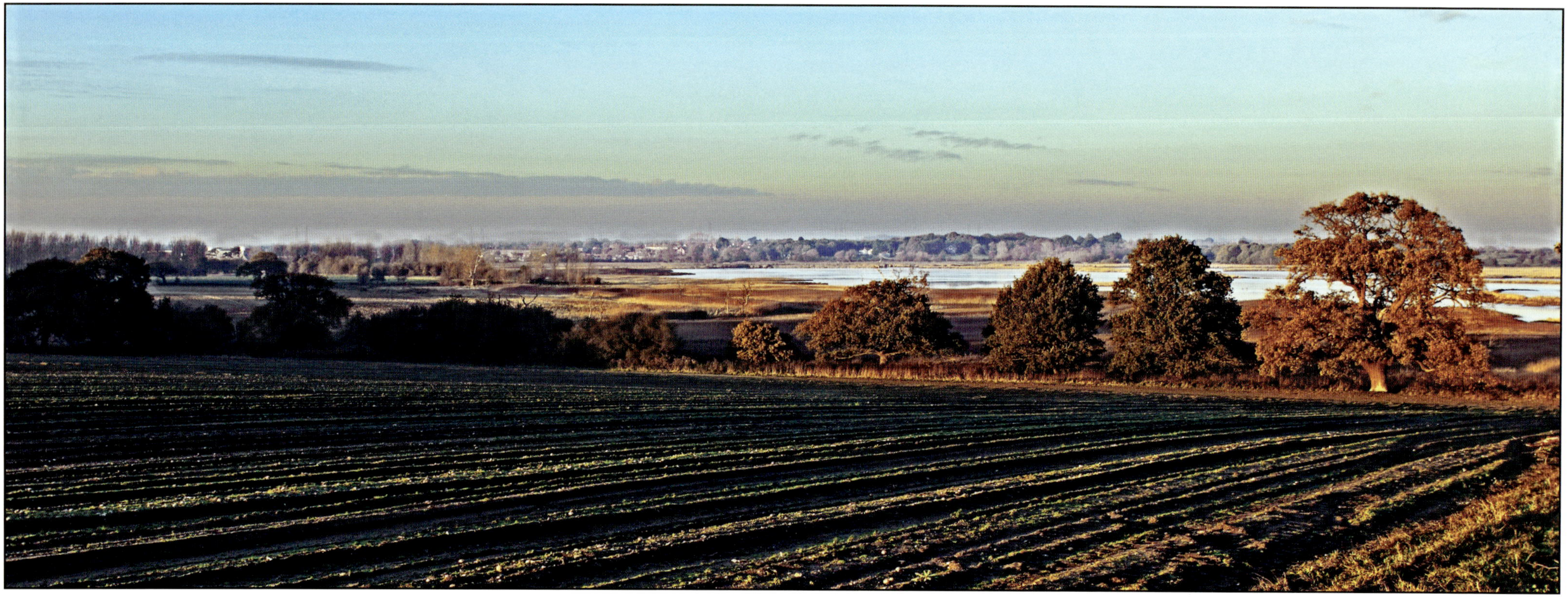

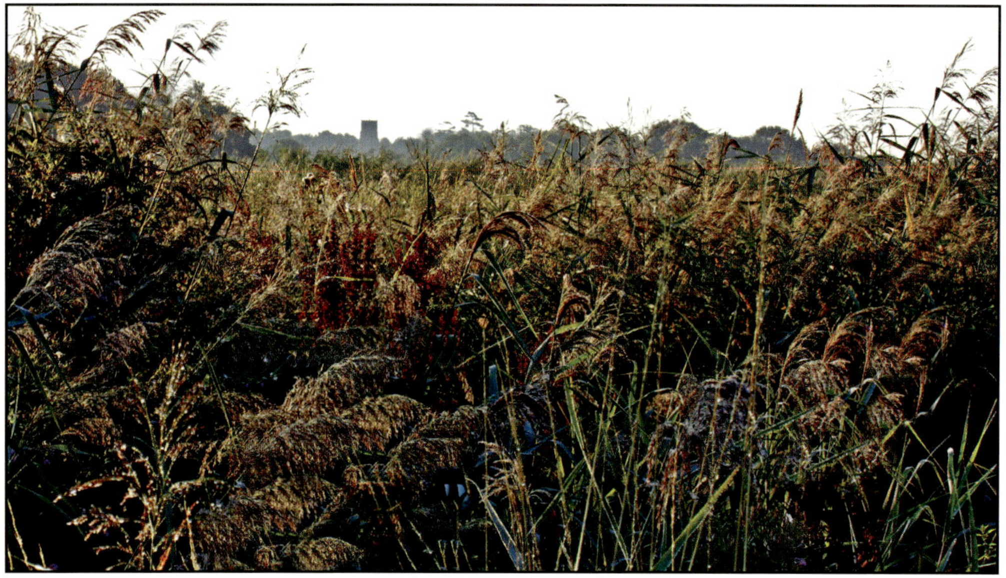

Golden autumn sunlight strafes the newly ploughed field at Iken, as lengthening shadows foretell the approach of winter. The village of Snape and The Maltings can just be seen in the distance (above).

Expert land husbandry by Suffolk farmers ensures good crop yields, even on the light soils of the sandlings. Conservationists give nature a helping hand when farmland gives way to marshes, making them an ideal habitat for wildlife. The lacy ferns, bracken, grasses and reeds make a colourful jumble of delicate foreground foliage to Iken church in the distance (left).

The Alde meanders through the rustling reed beds, coming to a tidal halt at Snape Maltings quay and bridge, the final navigable point for boats.

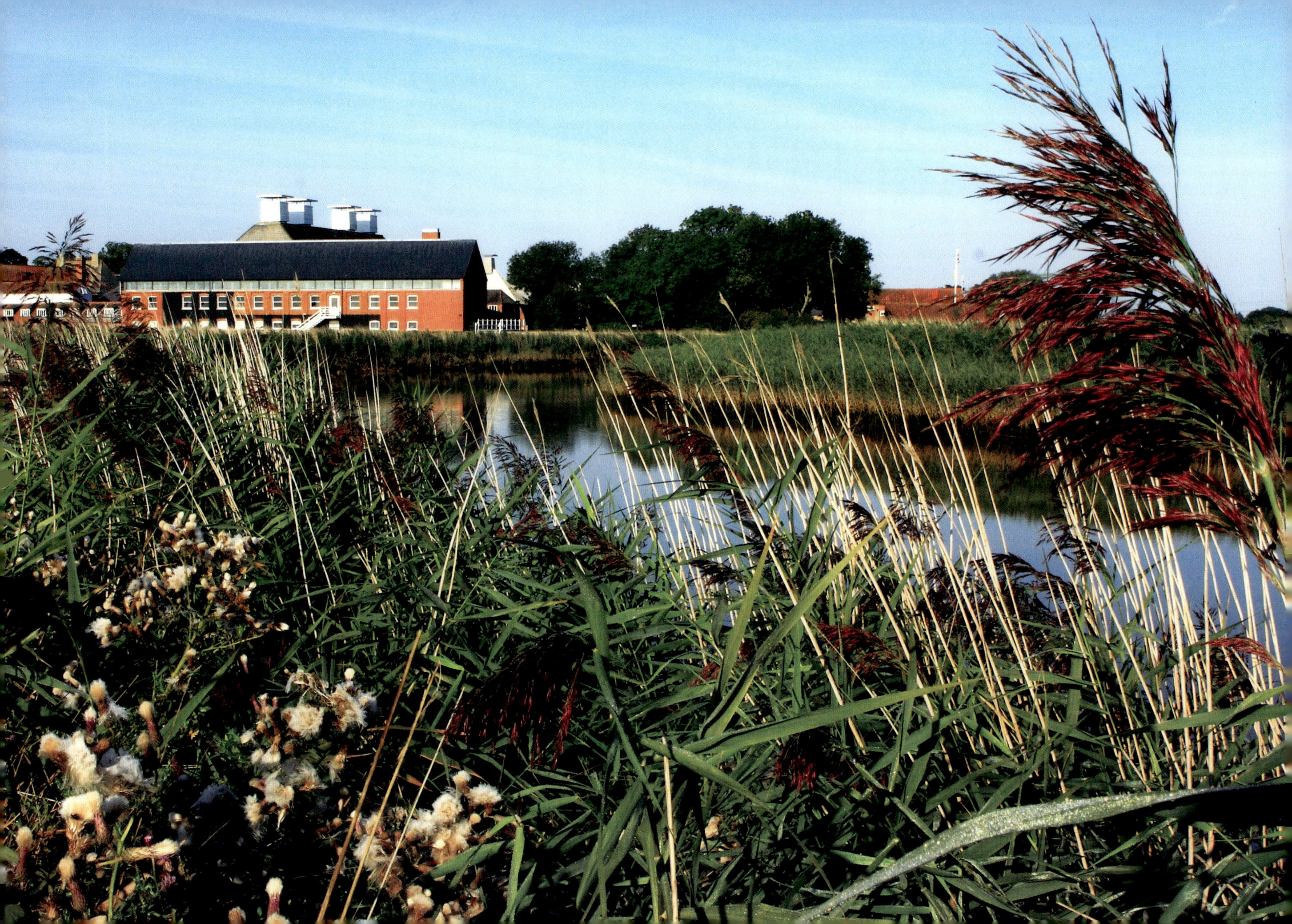

The Maltings Concert Hall – the triumphant beginning

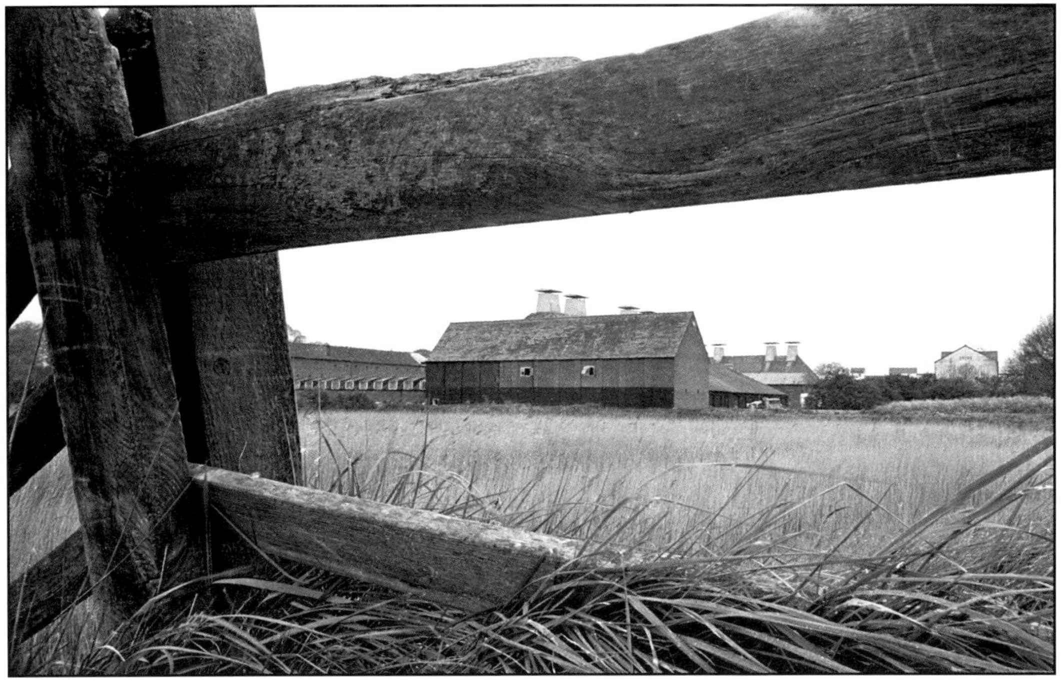

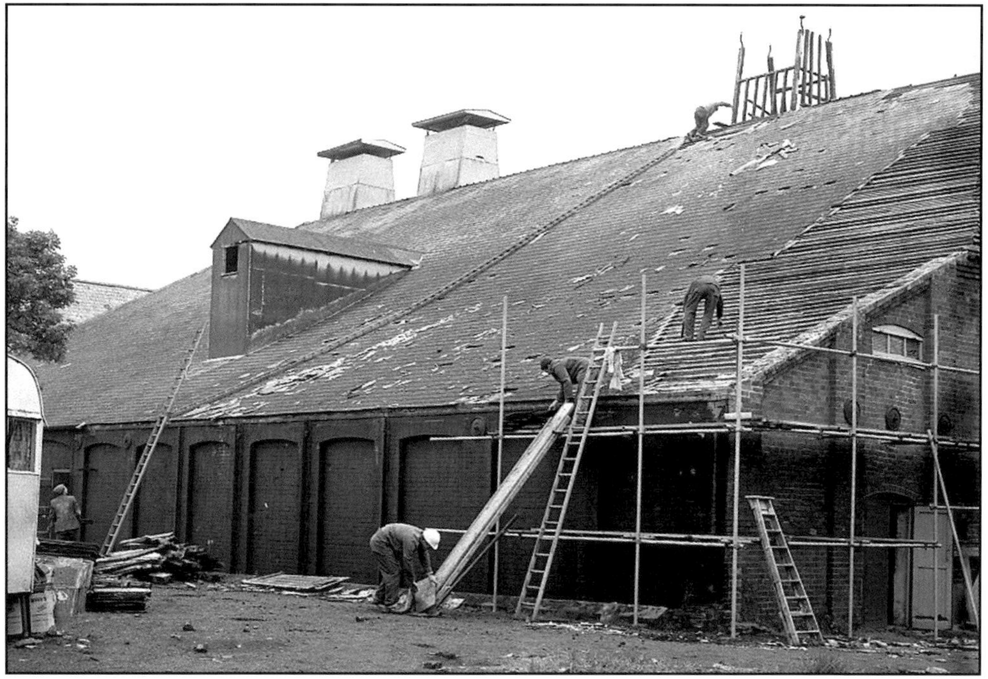

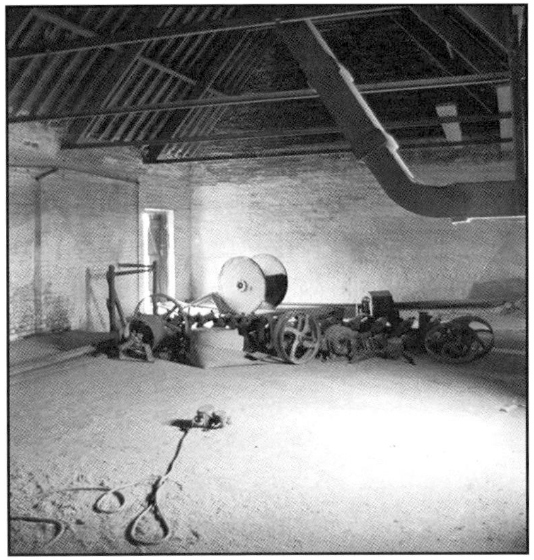

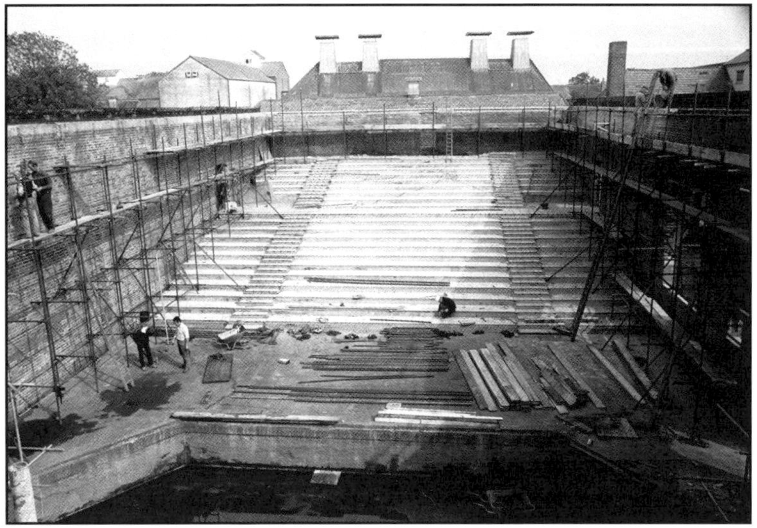

Benjamin Britten first moved to live in Snape in 1937 – he converted the Old Mill, in the village, into a home. From there he had views across the marshes to the maltings. When the maltings closed in the 1960s, Britten looked initially at the redundant building (top and bottom left) as a place to store scenery, then he, and others, had their eureka moment – 'Wouldn't it make a wonderful concert hall?'

A lease was negotiated with the owner, George Gooderham. Arup Associates were appointed as the architects. Fund-raising commenced, and local builders got to work gutting the original building, which was a warren of dark corridors, malting floors and scurrying rats.

The conversion was finished in just over a year.

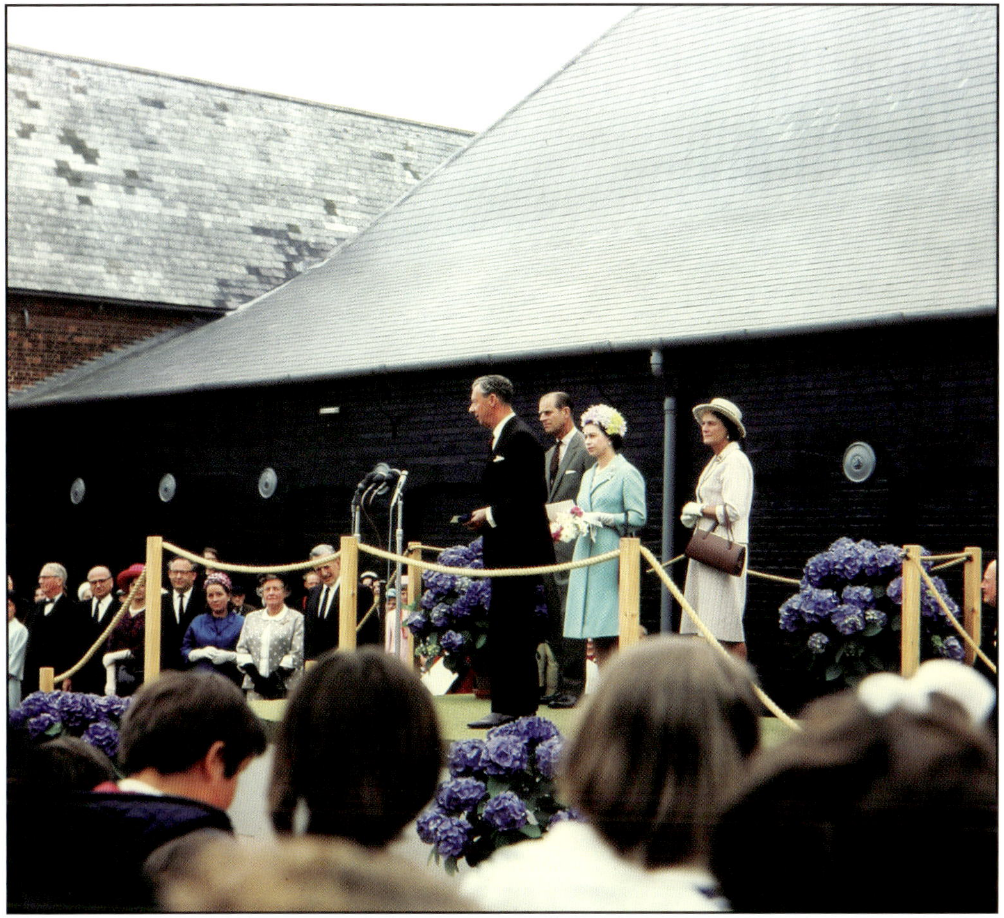

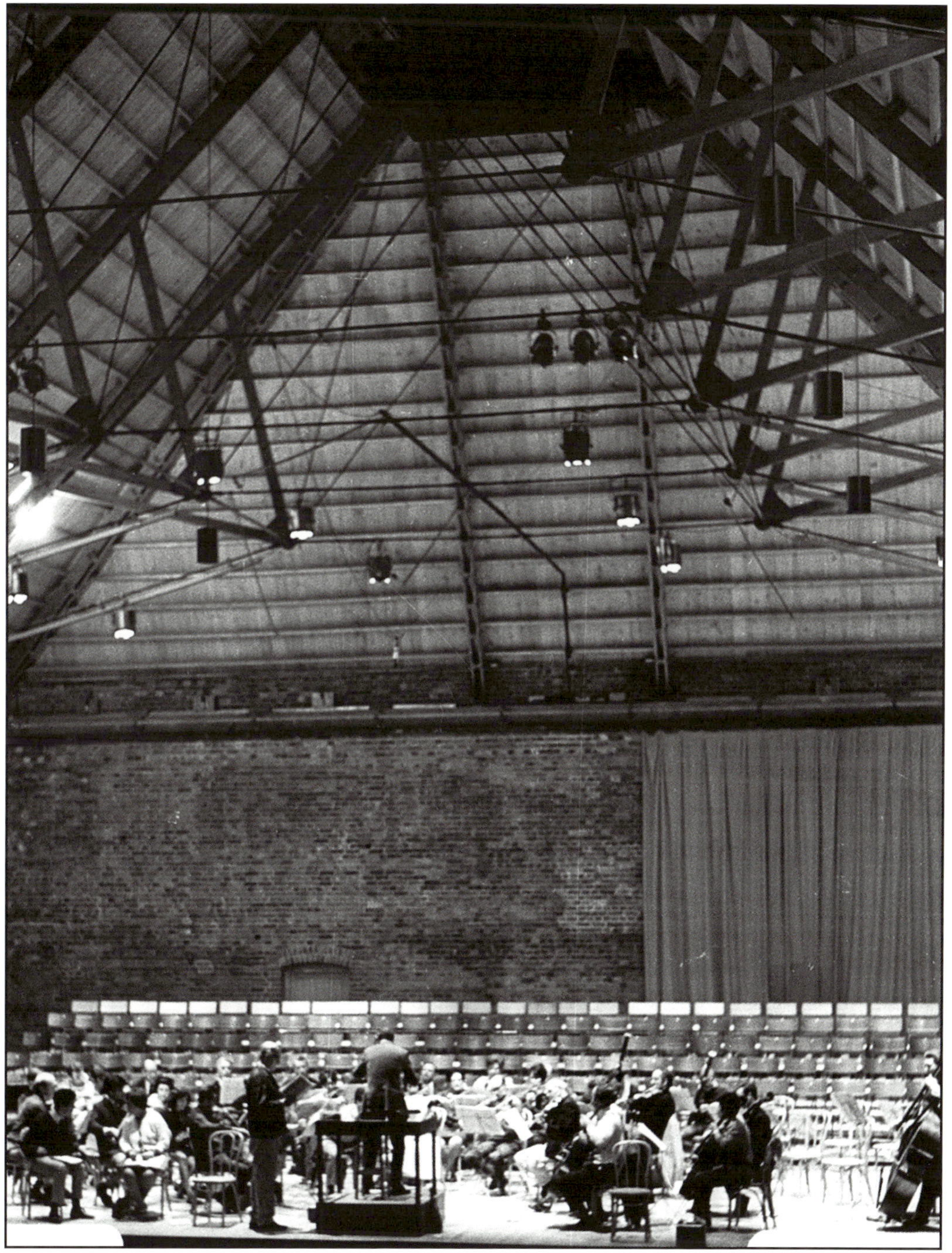

The Snape Maltings Concert Hall was opened in 1967 by the Queen; it was acclaimed a triumph, both acoustically, and in the way it had been sensitively designed.

Britten wrote and conducted a new work *The Building of the House* specifically for the inaugural concert, which opened that year's Aldeburgh Festival. This photograph (right) was taken during the rehearsals for that occasion.

Very quickly it became a popular venue, not only as a performance hall but also as a recording studio, and televised productions were held here. It was the televising of the opening night of the 1969 Festival that probably led to the disastrous fire when the roof caught alight, believed by many at the time to be the result of powerful lighting setting fire to the timbered roof.

The tragic fire

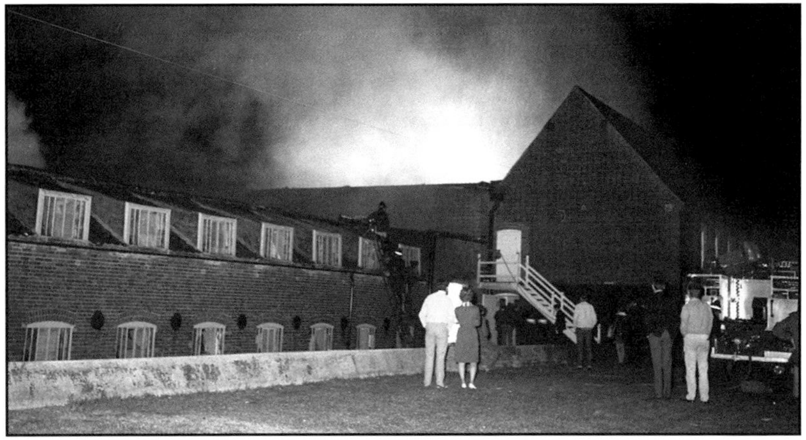

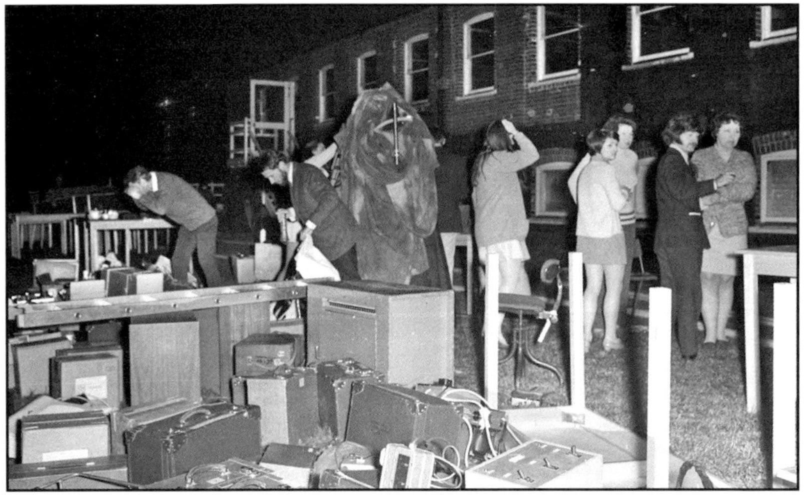

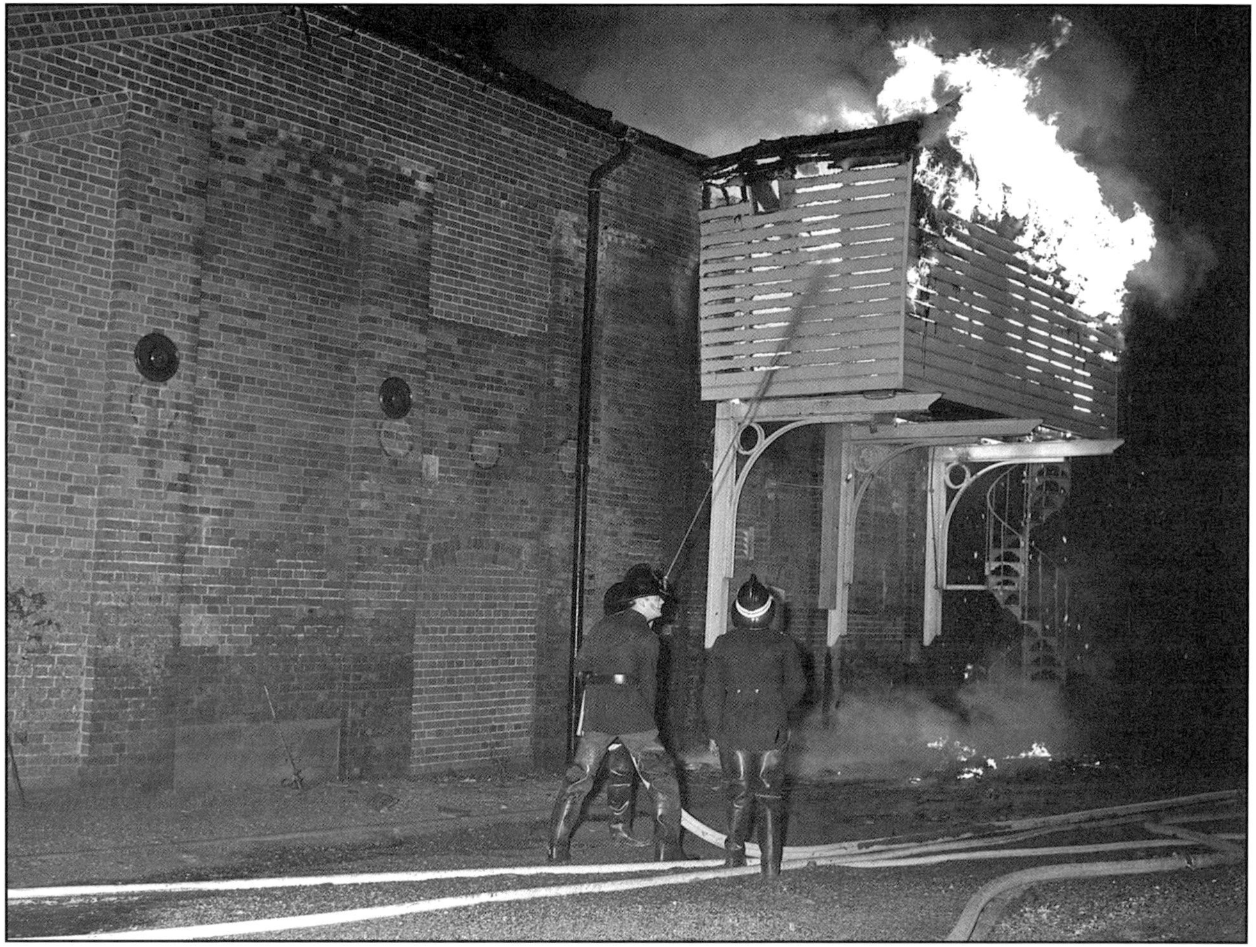

The opening night of the 1969 Aldeburgh Festival had just finished, the audience and most of the cast had left – then someone smelt smoke. Within minutes the whole of the Maltings Concert Hall roof was ablaze. Those left in the building, mostly backstage staff, rallied to the call and removed as many costumes, sound gear, and anything else they could lay their hands on, away from the rear dressing rooms to the grass outside. Everyone was in a state of dazed shock. I received a phone call from the landlord of the adjacent Plough and Sail public house to say the Maltings was alight. By the time I arrived, fire appliances from all over Suffolk were in attendance, but there was little they could do to save the main hall and roof from total destruction.

In the spirit of those early Aldeburgh Festival days, alternative venues were found, and most of that year's Festival programme went ahead away from the blackened debris of the concert hall.

'It will rise again like the Phoenix from the Ashes'

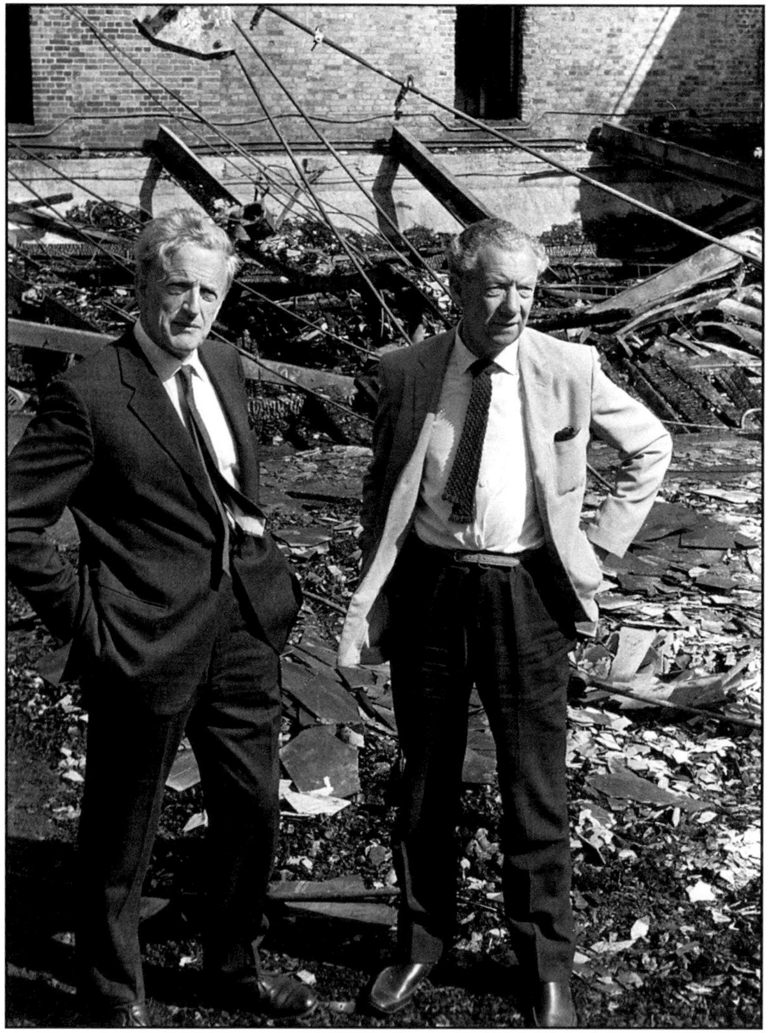

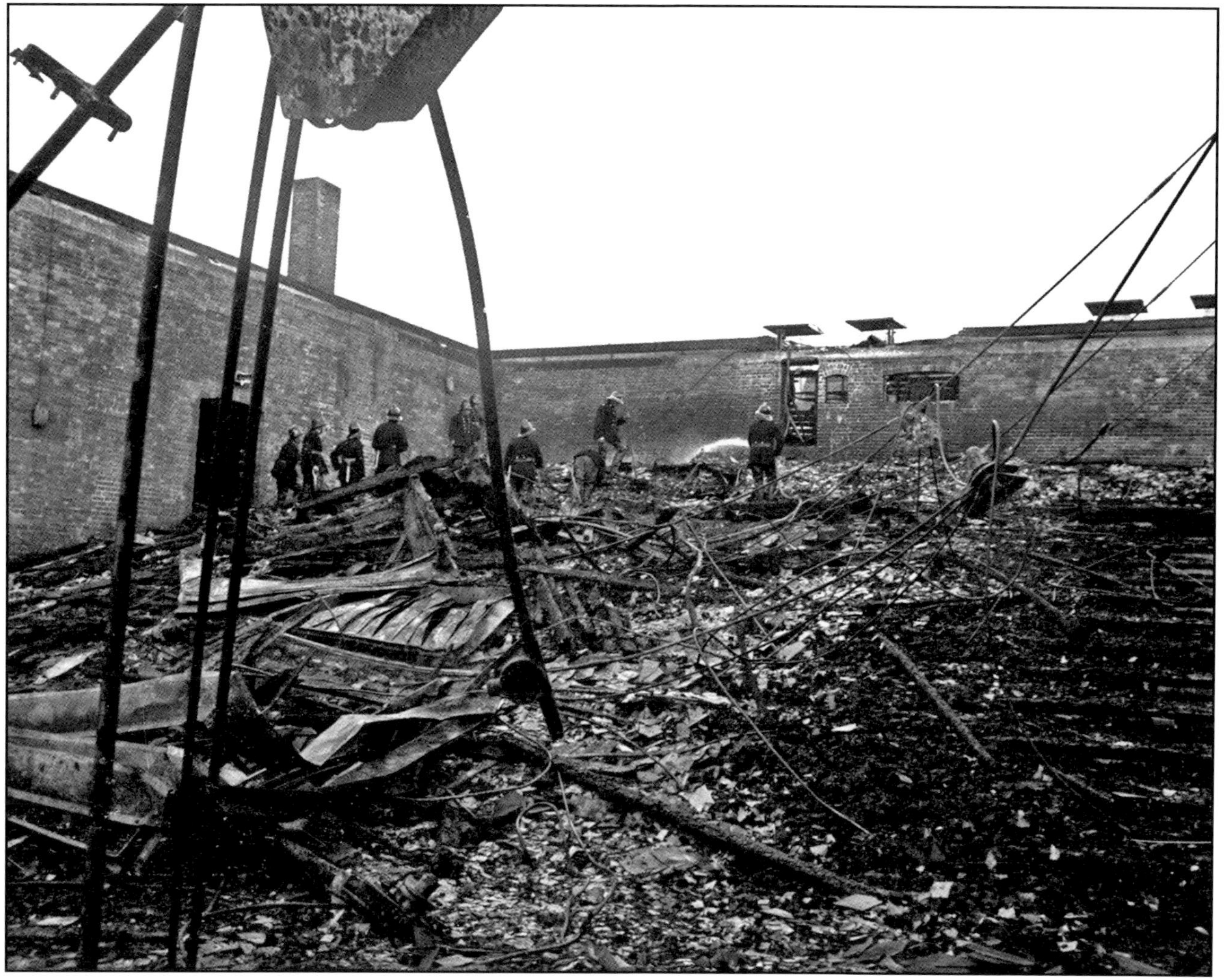

The next day Britten and Pears stood in the still-smouldering wreckage when Britten declared 'It will rise again like the Phoenix from the Ashes'. Amazingly, in only twelve months, and after intensive fund-raising activities, the re-build was completed, incorporating many modifications based upon two years' experience of using the original concert hall. Ben later commented 'In some respects we were lucky to have had two bites at the same cherry – the second time around we've got something much better.' A happy spin-off from the intense heat of the fire was even better acoustics resonating off the soft red brick walls, making it, as one BBC audio technician declared – 'a sound man's dream'.

The Queen reopened the new Concert Hall in time for the start of 1970 Festival.

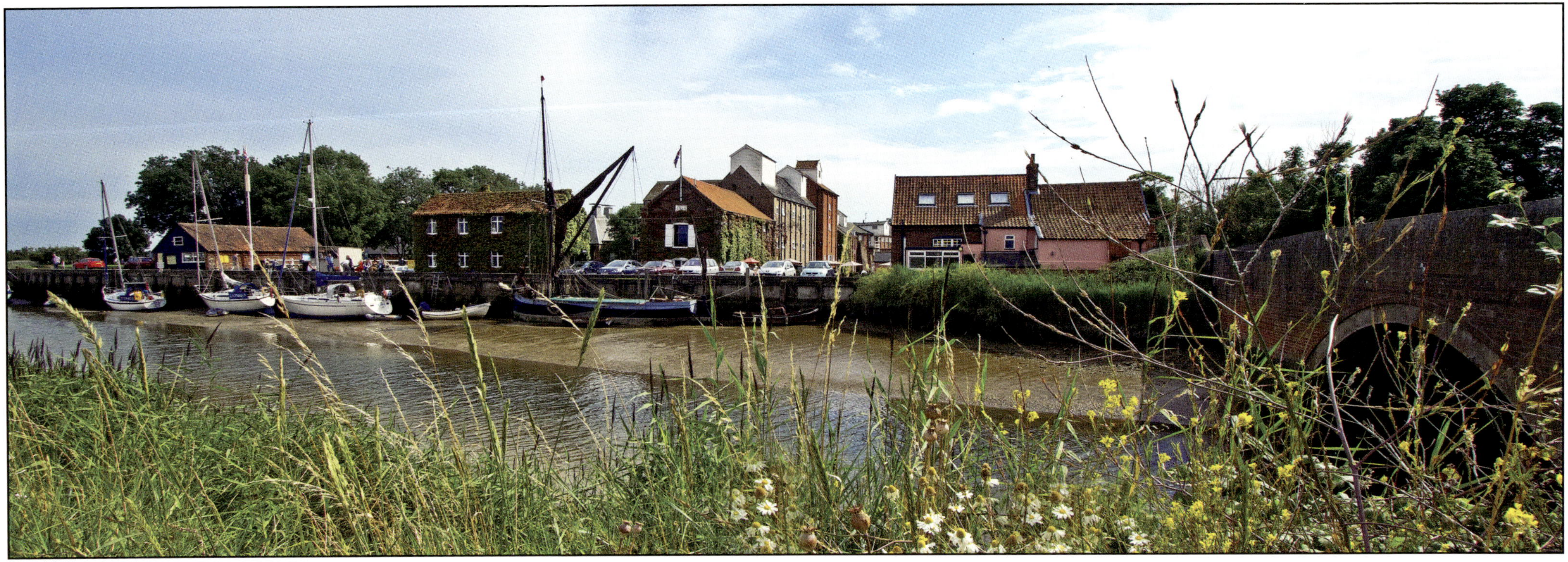

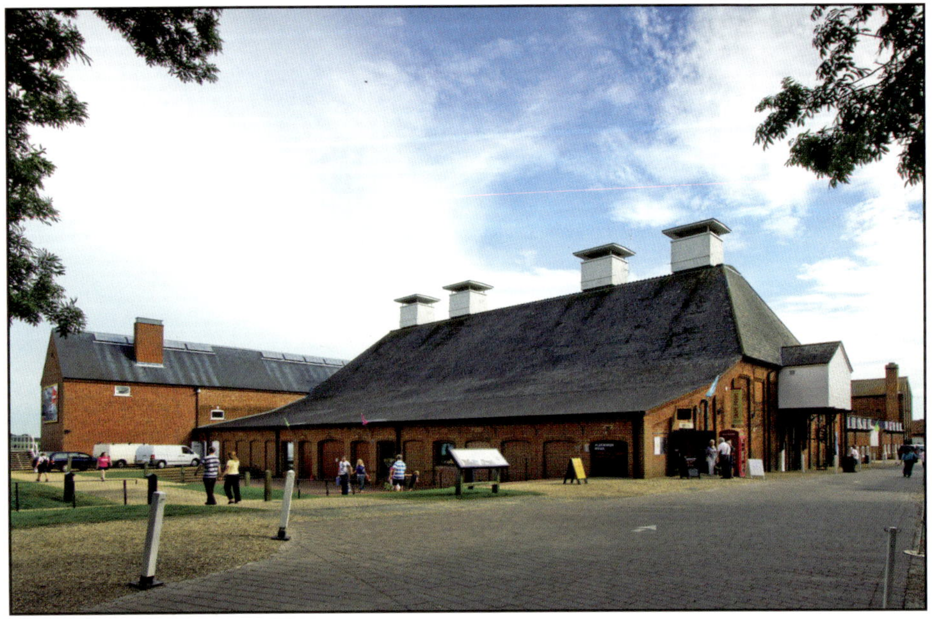

Much has changed since the last commercial barge laden with barley offloaded its cargo at the Maltings quayside. Today's boats tied alongside the harbour wall, awaiting high water, are all leisure craft.

The most recent significant changes have occurred since 2006 when Aldeburgh Music purchased Snape Maltings Concert Hall and its rehearsal facilities, together with additional redundant buildings. Since then an extensive programme of developing the music facilities has been undertaken. Britten and Pears' original vision of creating a centre of musical excellence, where the world's most talented musicians could be nurtured, has been achieved. The concert hall and its facilities are now the premier music venue in the country outside of London, attracting top class musical talent.

The remainder of the buildings are in the ownership of the Gooderham family, who bought the entire complex in the mid-sixties. They have developed residential units, and established a thriving retail centre. Throw in some excellent riverside walks, and it becomes one of Suffolk's major tourist attractions.

Barbara Hepworth's 1970 *Family of Man* bronze sculpture (right) is, at the request of the Hepworth estate, on permanent loan to the Maltings from the Fitzwilliam Museum, Cambridge, as a memorial to her friends Benjamin Britten and Peter Pears.

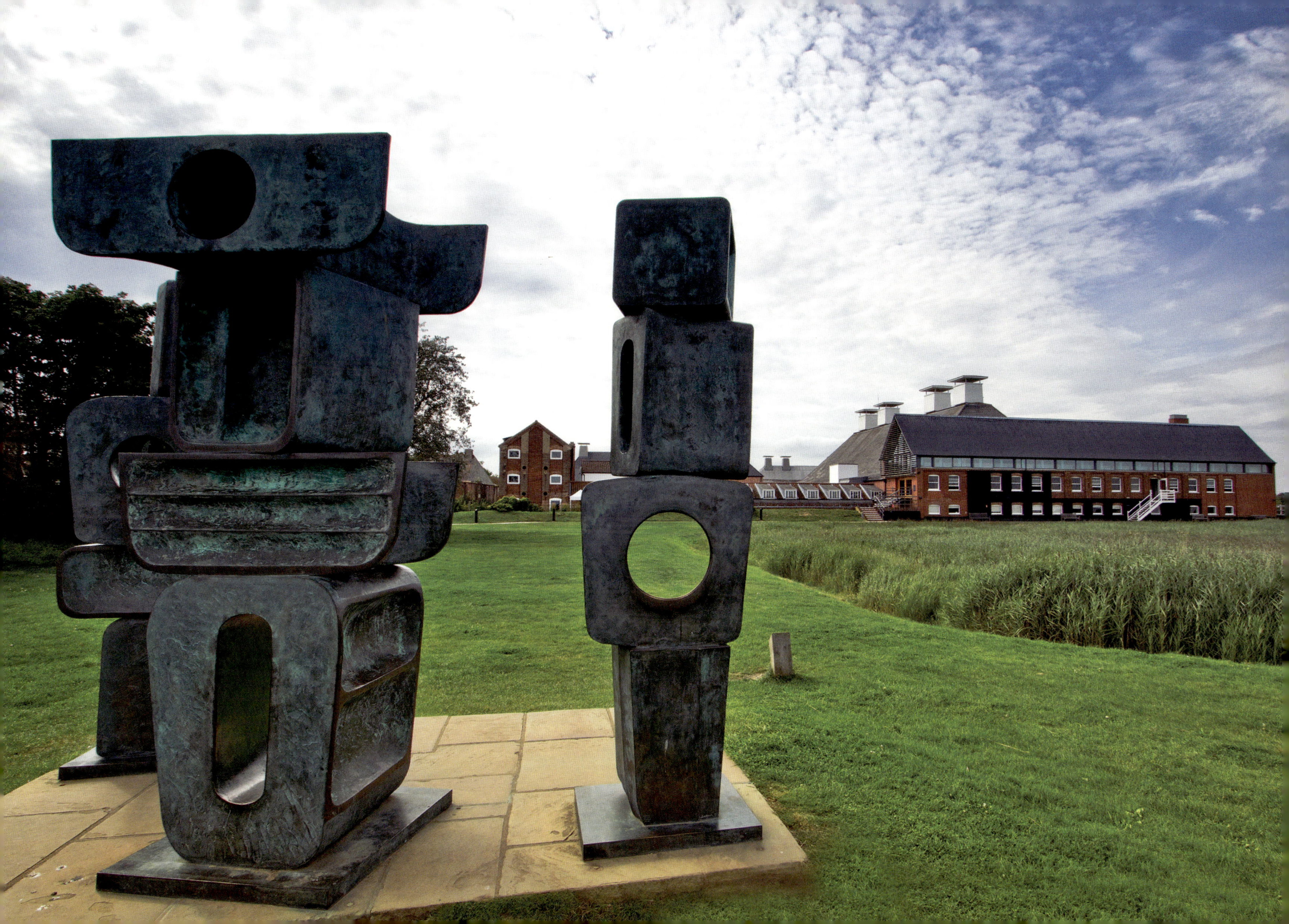

Suffolk pubs – music venues for centuries

Music venues of another kind have long been popular along this Suffolk coast, especially with those who worked the land and fished the sea. Folk singers, jazz musicians, morris dancers and others gather in Suffolk pubs to play music, or dance, and sing their traditional songs. Some get paid to entertain, but most do it simply to make music for the sheer enjoyment of doing so – like they do in the popular Eel's Foot pub at Eastbridge (right).

Morris dancing cannot claim to be traditionally Suffolk – its origins are in the Midlands – but it has been adopted by the county and is now a popular Suffolk pub entertainment. Local groups travel around the countryside performing their colourful traditional dances to the accompaniment of accordions, bells and whistles.

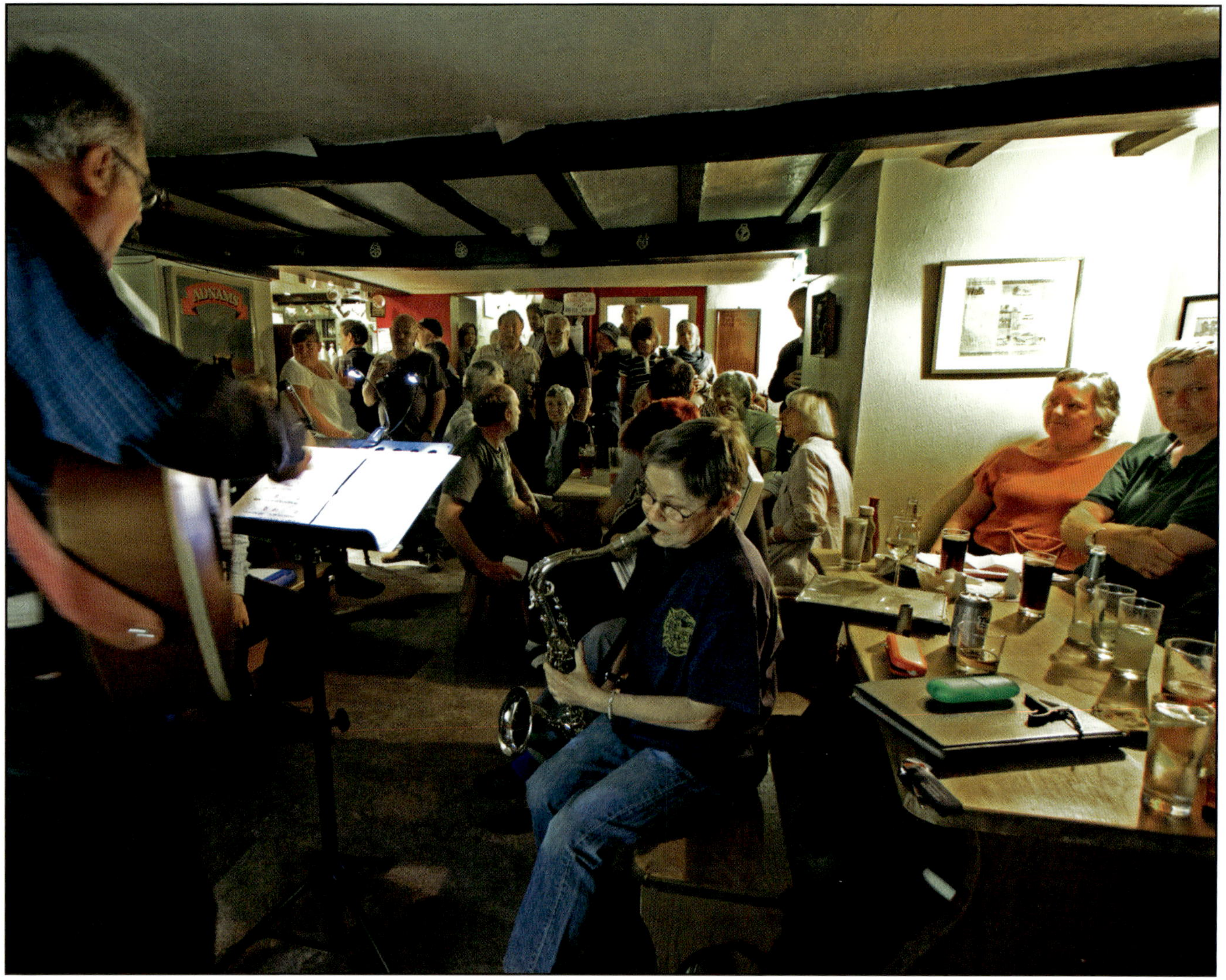

The Eel's Foot at Eastbridge, not far from Leiston, is an alehouse dating back to 1533, and is probably Suffolk's leading pub venue for folk music. Their Old Squit night takes place most Thursday evenings and everyone is welcome to come along to sing, bring an instrument and play, or just listen while enjoying a drink with good food in the age-old friendly atmosphere of this popular village pub, where even the oak beams seem imbued with music of generations long past.

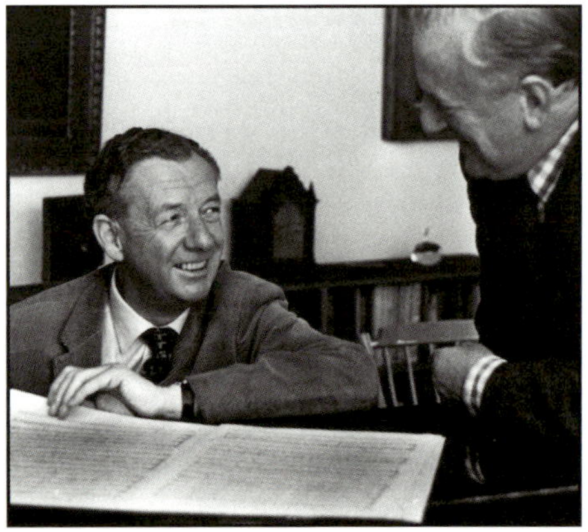

Benjamin Britten and Peter Pears enjoyed getting around a piano at Red House and singing folk songs as light entertainment for their guests. Some of the lyrics could be playfully saucy at times, and always brought a relaxed 'thoroughly enjoying the occasion' smile to Ben's face. He arranged several folk songs.

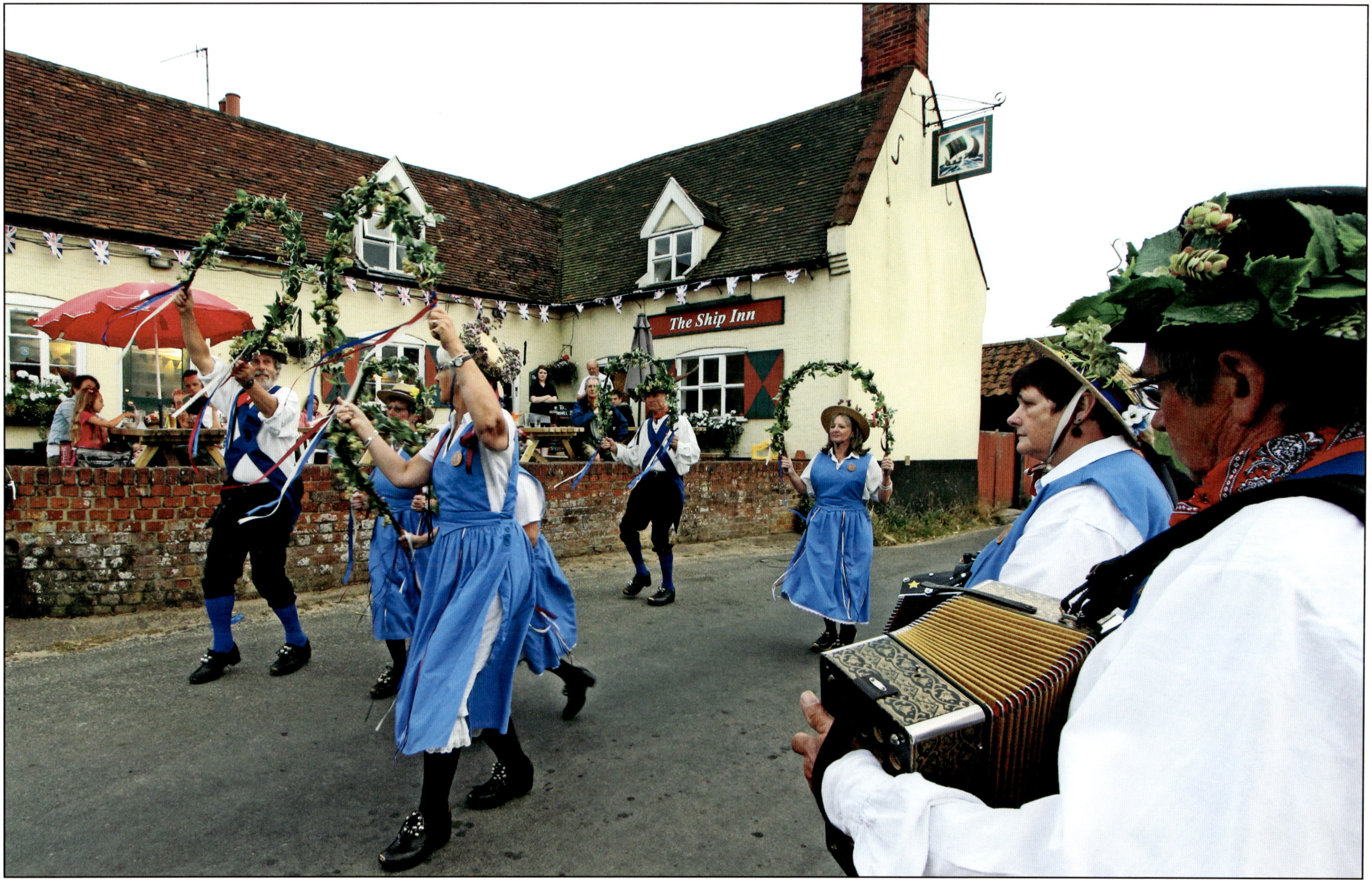

The Point Devis Morris Group from Blythburgh dance outside the Ship public house at Blaxhall, a village close to Snape Maltings.

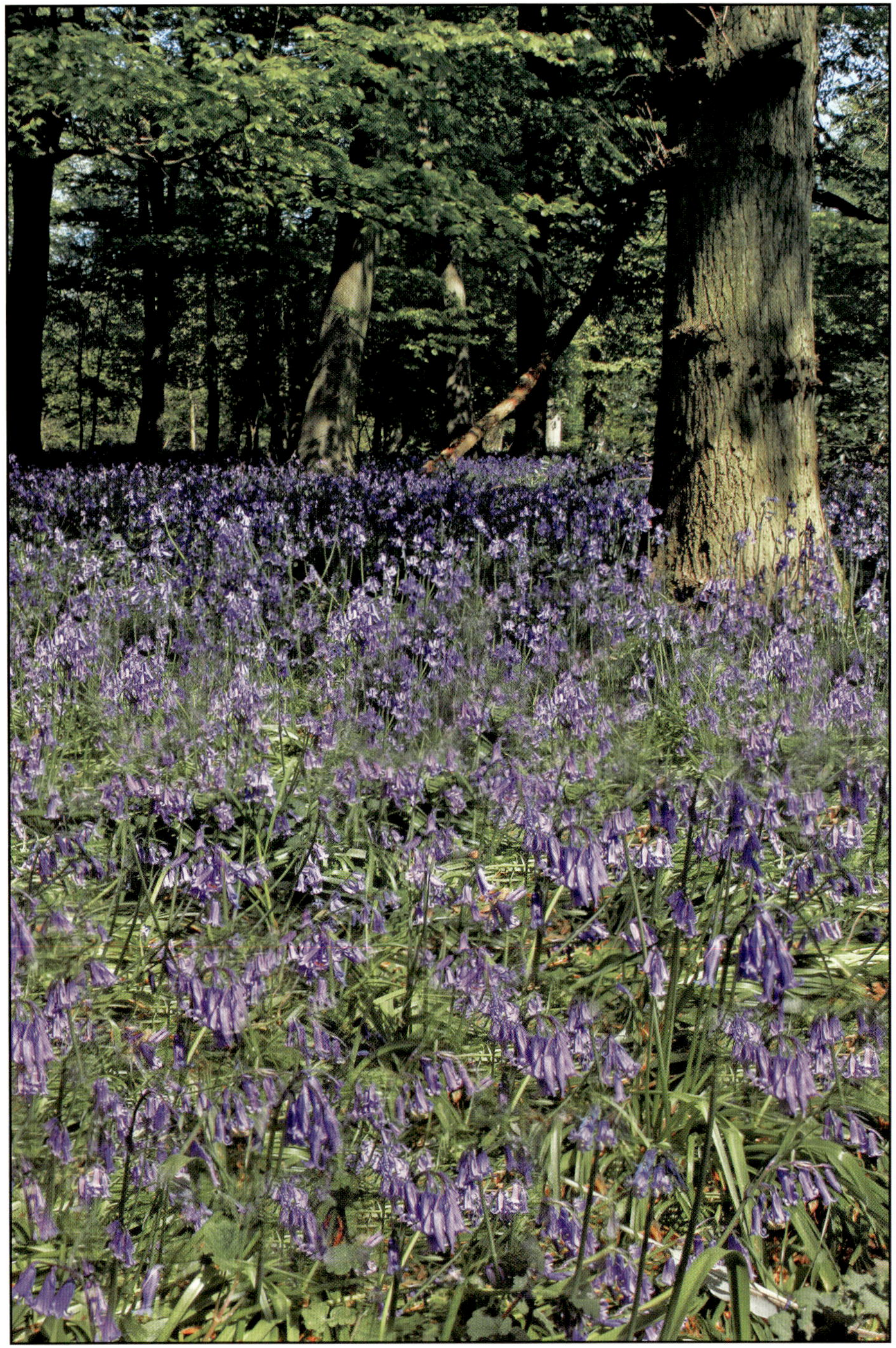

Staverton Thicks

It's easy for one's imagination to run riot, standing quietly in this most atmospheric of all Suffolk's woods at Staverton Thicks (right) near Butley, on the road from Woodbridge to Orford. This former thirteenth-century hunting park has some of the oldest oak and holly trees in the country – four hundred or more years old. Wizened oaks, twisted and tormented by age, stand in memorial to those that have succumbed to mossy decay and fallen to the forest's graveyard below, there to trip the carelessly planted foot as one stoops to dodge the low overhead foliage that has been grazed to deer-browsing height.

A number of protected woodlands abound in this part of Suffolk – Benjamin Britten knew most of them. In the springtime some are carpeted with bluebells, others with daffodils, and in the autumn with golden leaves. All are the habitat of deer – once the prize of the nobility who hunted these woods.

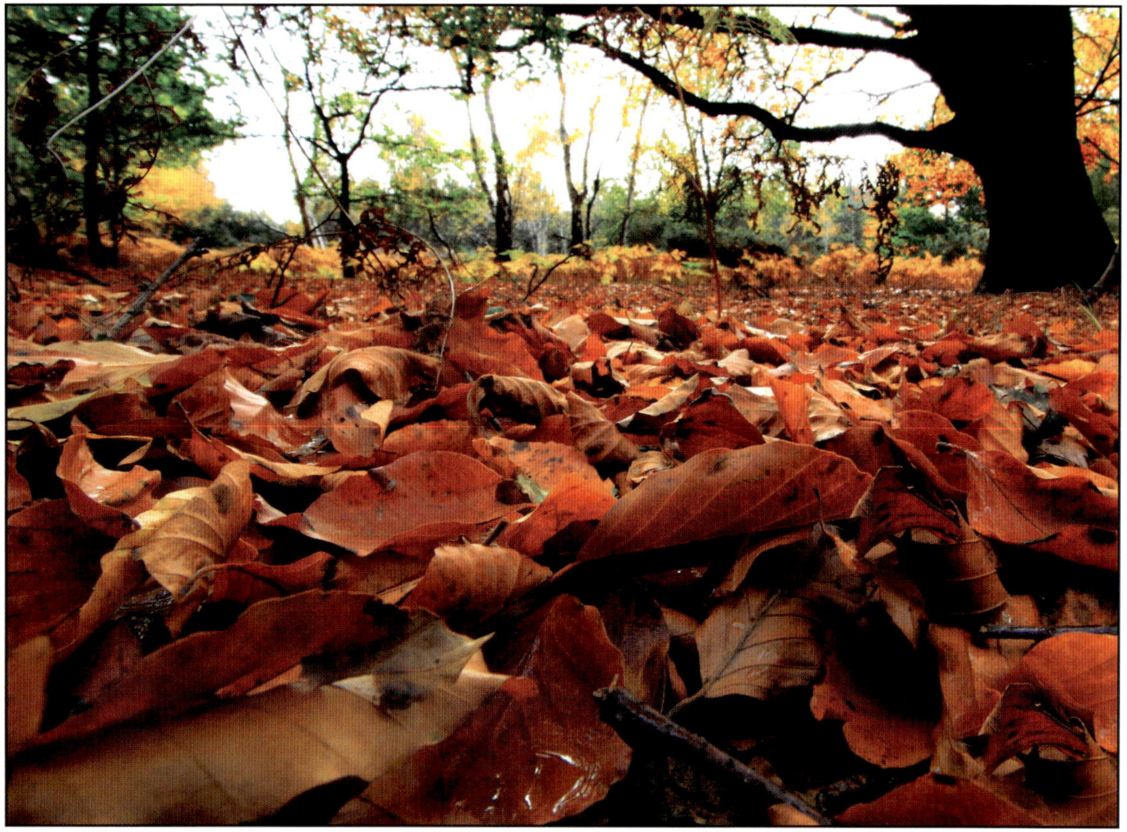

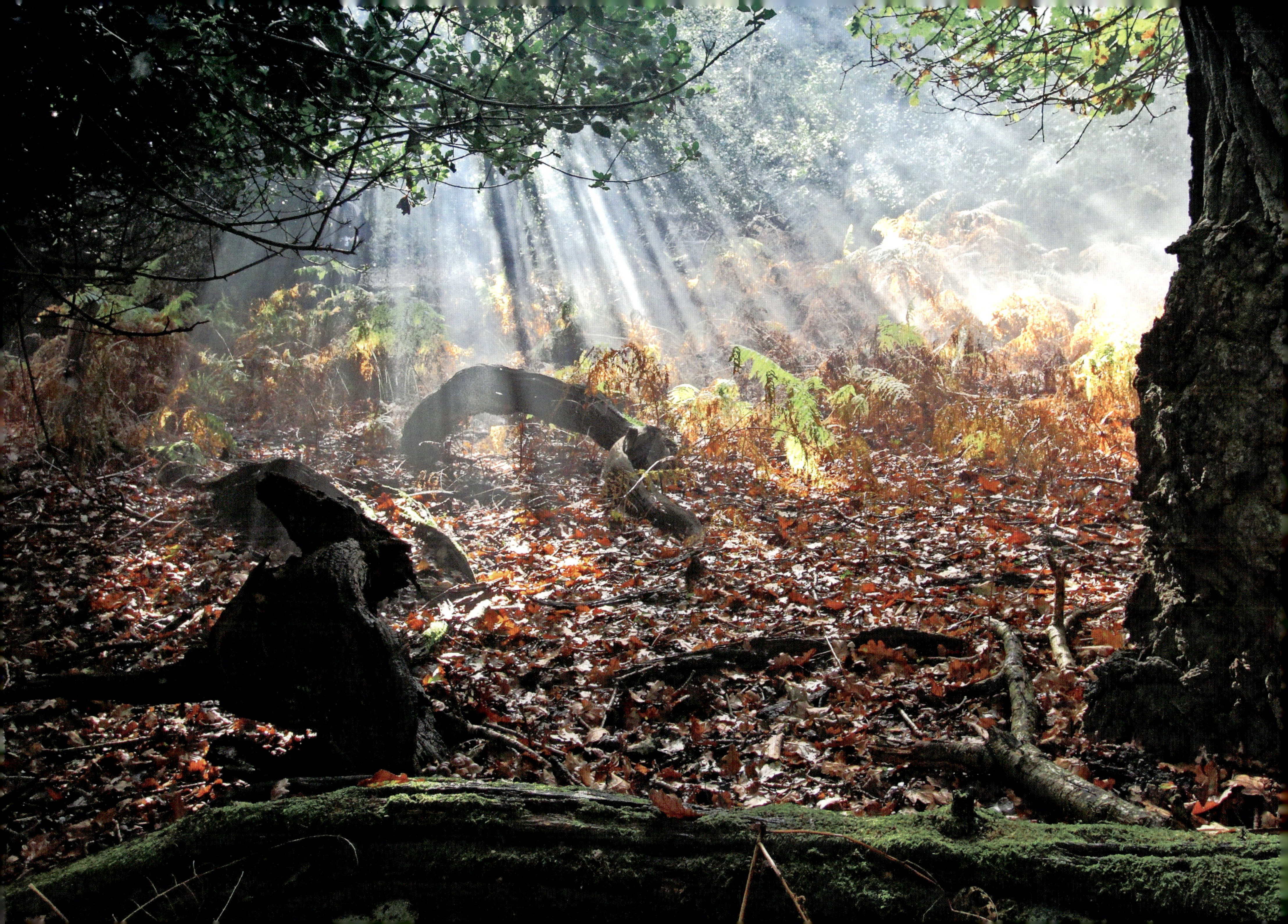

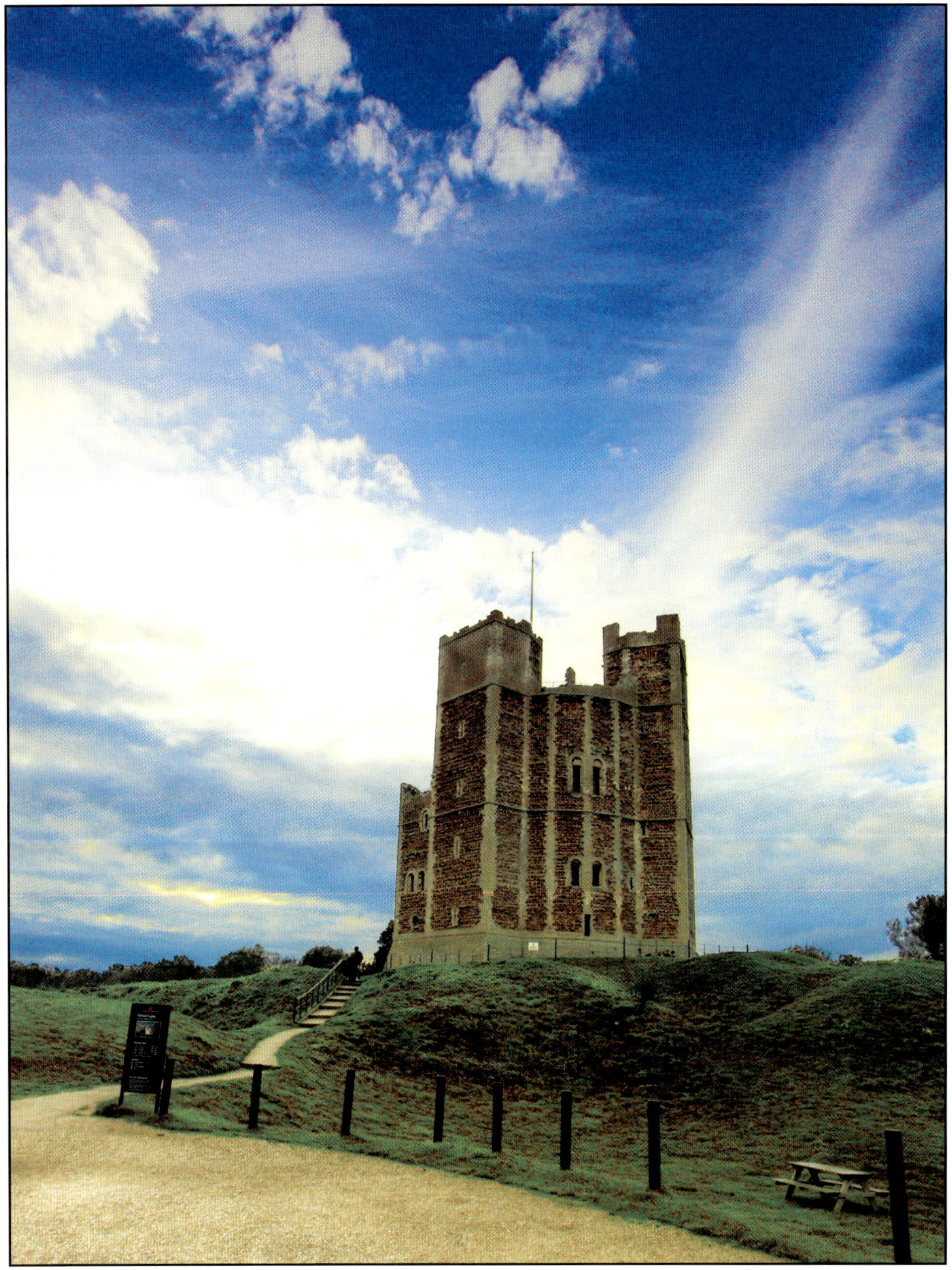

Orford – defiant in defence

The Suffolk coast has played its part in the defence of the realm. The quaint village of Orford has long been associated with buildings of a military nature. Henry II built a castle here in 1173 to maintain a watchful eye on the rebellious Bigod family – the hereditary Earls of Norfolk. In 1216 the castle, which hitherto had a rather unexciting history, was 'captured' by Prince Louis of France at the invitation of the English barons who were disillusioned with King John.

Only the keep remains, but it is one of the most complete in the country. English Heritage maintains the property which is open to the public most days.

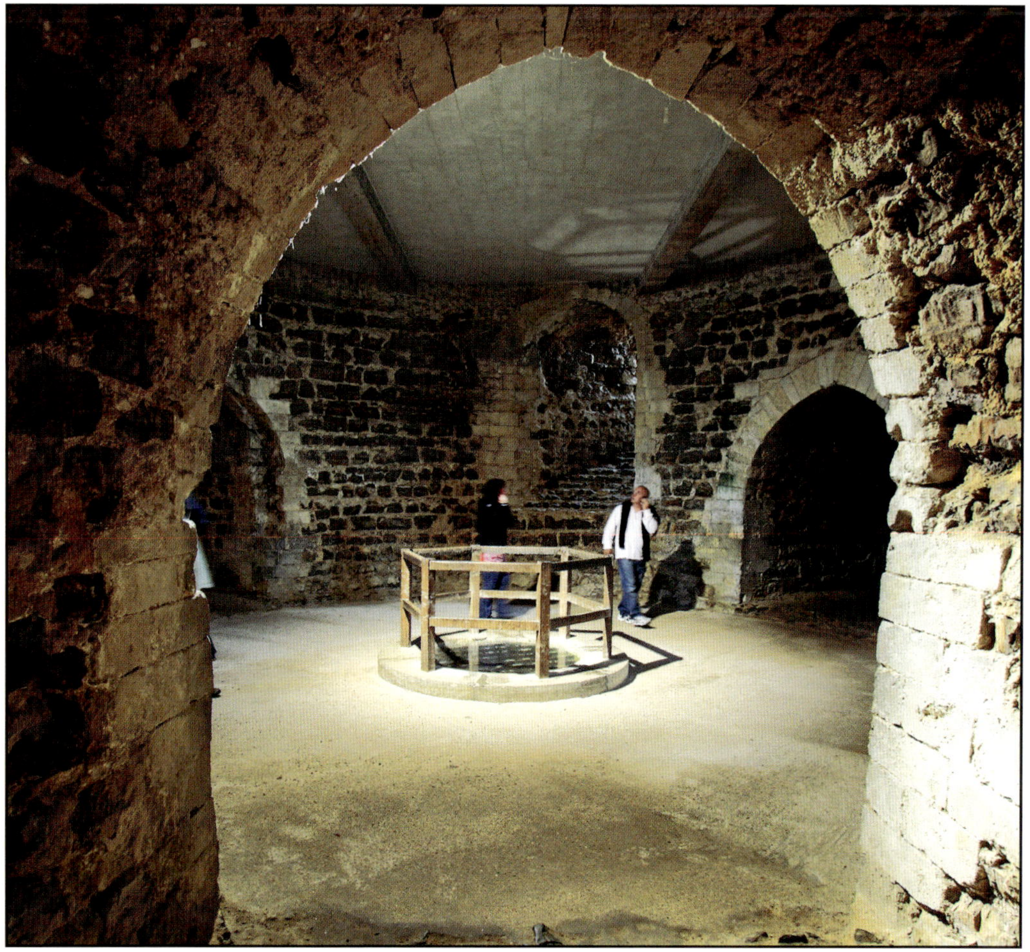

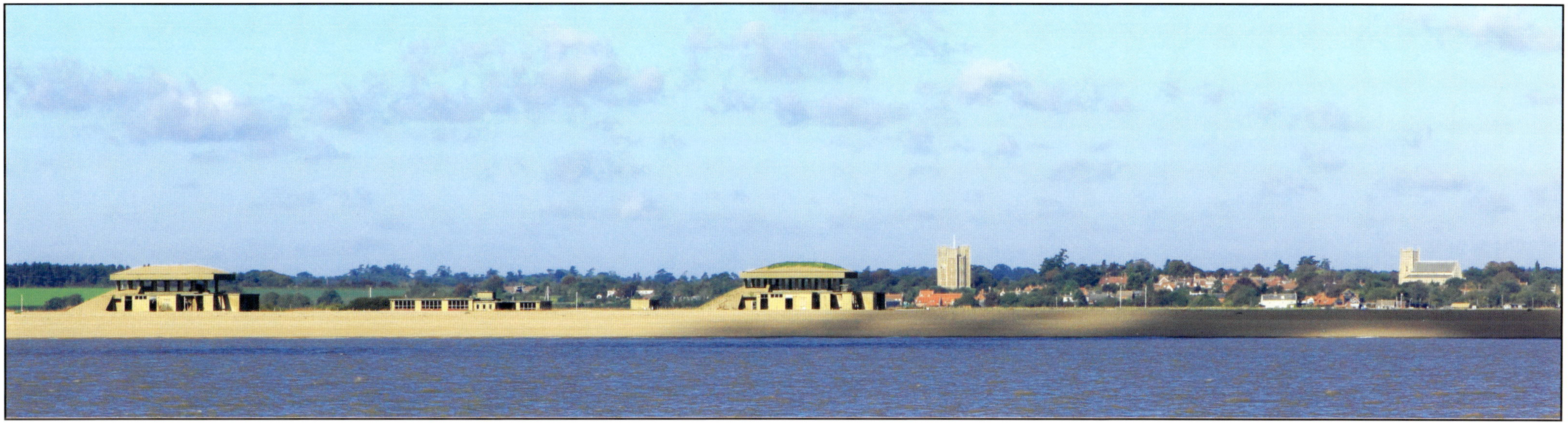

From 1913 until the 1990s the spit of land separating Orford village from the sea – Orfordness – was a top secret no-go area in the forefront of military and scientific ingenuity. Used originally to test night flying and parachuting during the First World War, it took on a more sinister role after the Second World War under the guise of the British Atomic Weapons Research Establishment, carrying out highly secret weapons testing. Latterly it hosted the equally secretive UK-US Cobra Mist project – a cold war early-warning system that turned out to be an expensive disappointment. Orfordness is now a much more friendly place and is owned by the National Trust as a nature reserve.

(Below) Orford village looking north from the top of the castle. The church has hosted many Aldeburgh Festival productions.

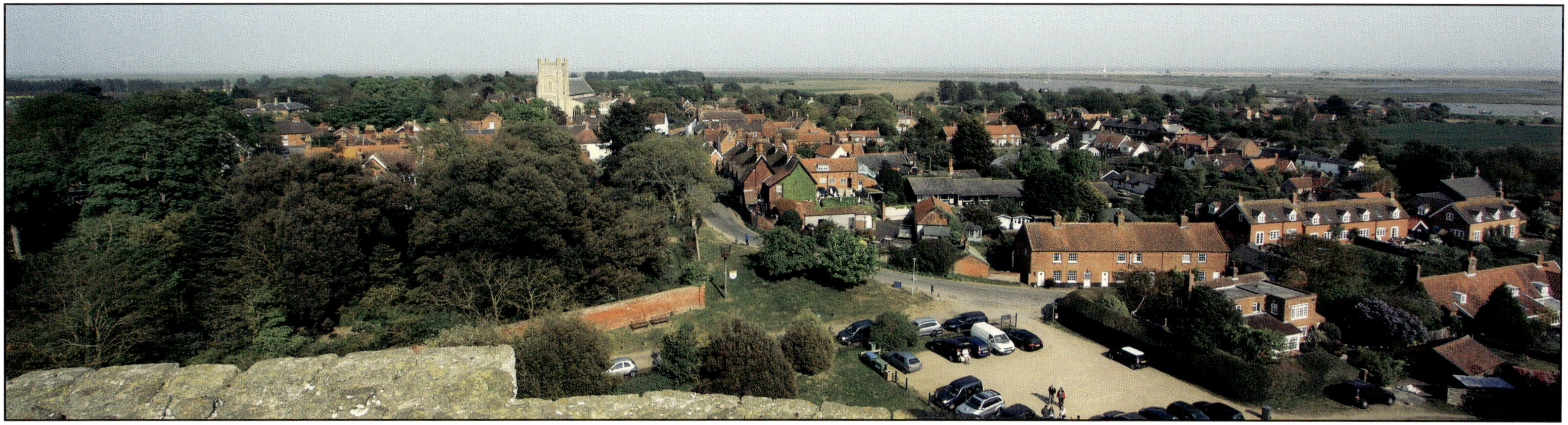

Orford's St Bartholomew's Church cum Opera House

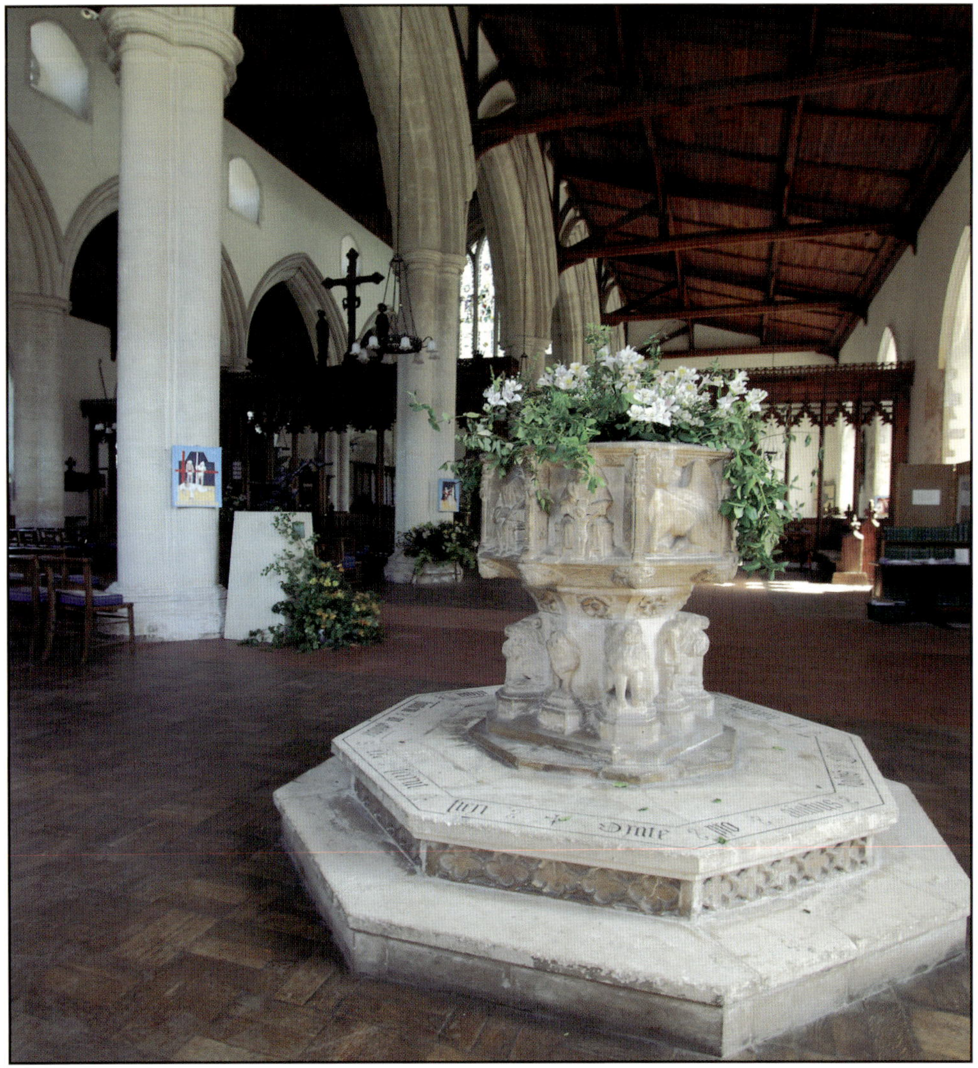

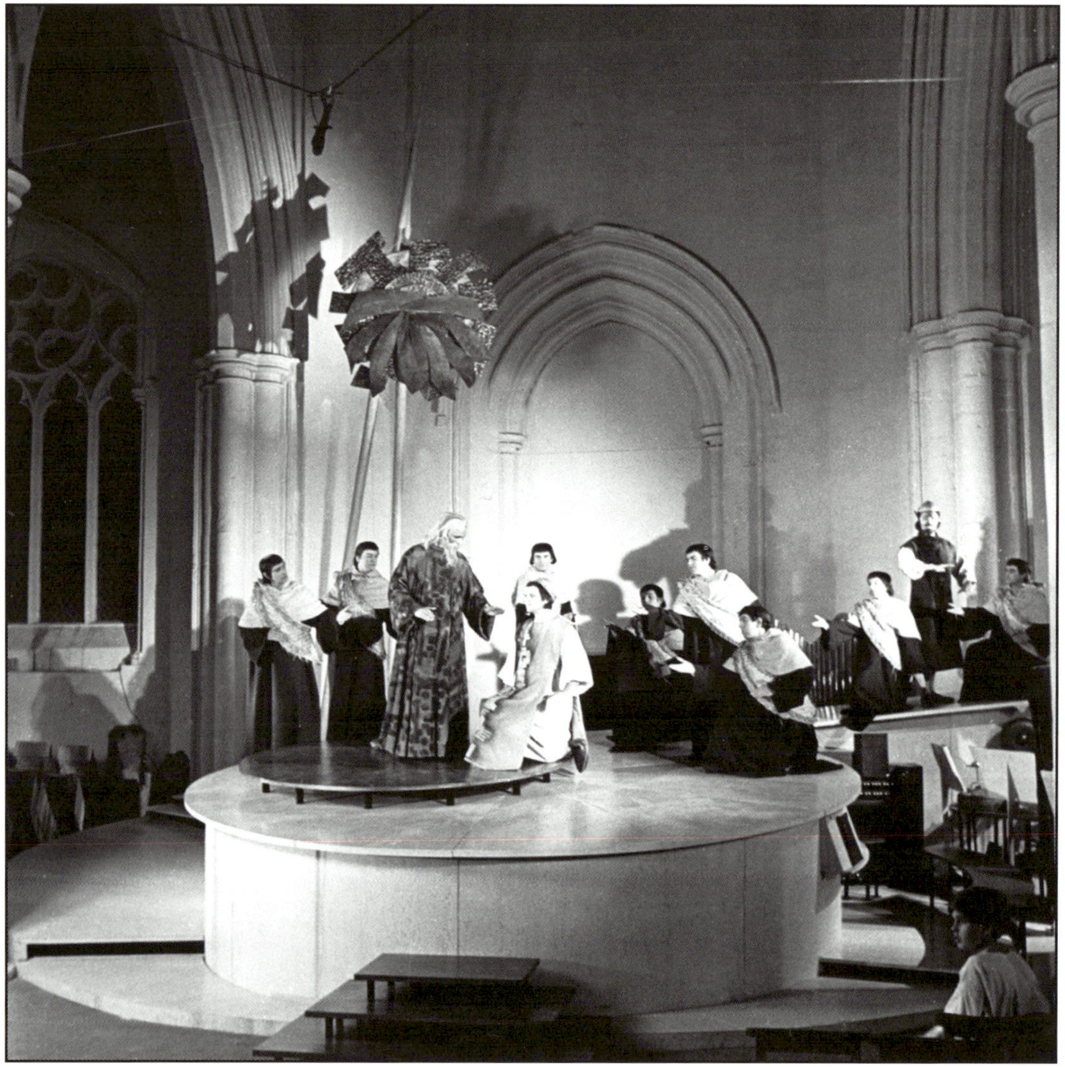

St Bartholomew's Church is still used as an Aldeburgh Festival venue. The good acoustics and the fact that there is a lot of open space and no fixed pews make the church an ideal setting for Britten's church parables – *Curlew River, The Burning Fiery Furnace* and *The Prodigal Son* (above). *Noye's Fludde,* Britten's version of the Chester mystery play about the Noah legend, was the first Britten opera to be staged here when dozens of schoolchildren from all over Suffolk had their first taste of performing in an opera, including the young treble singer Michael Crawford, who went on to international fame as a TV star and a singer in a number of smash hit musicals.

The beautiful font is a feature of the interior. Remains of the first Norman church stand outside in the churchyard.

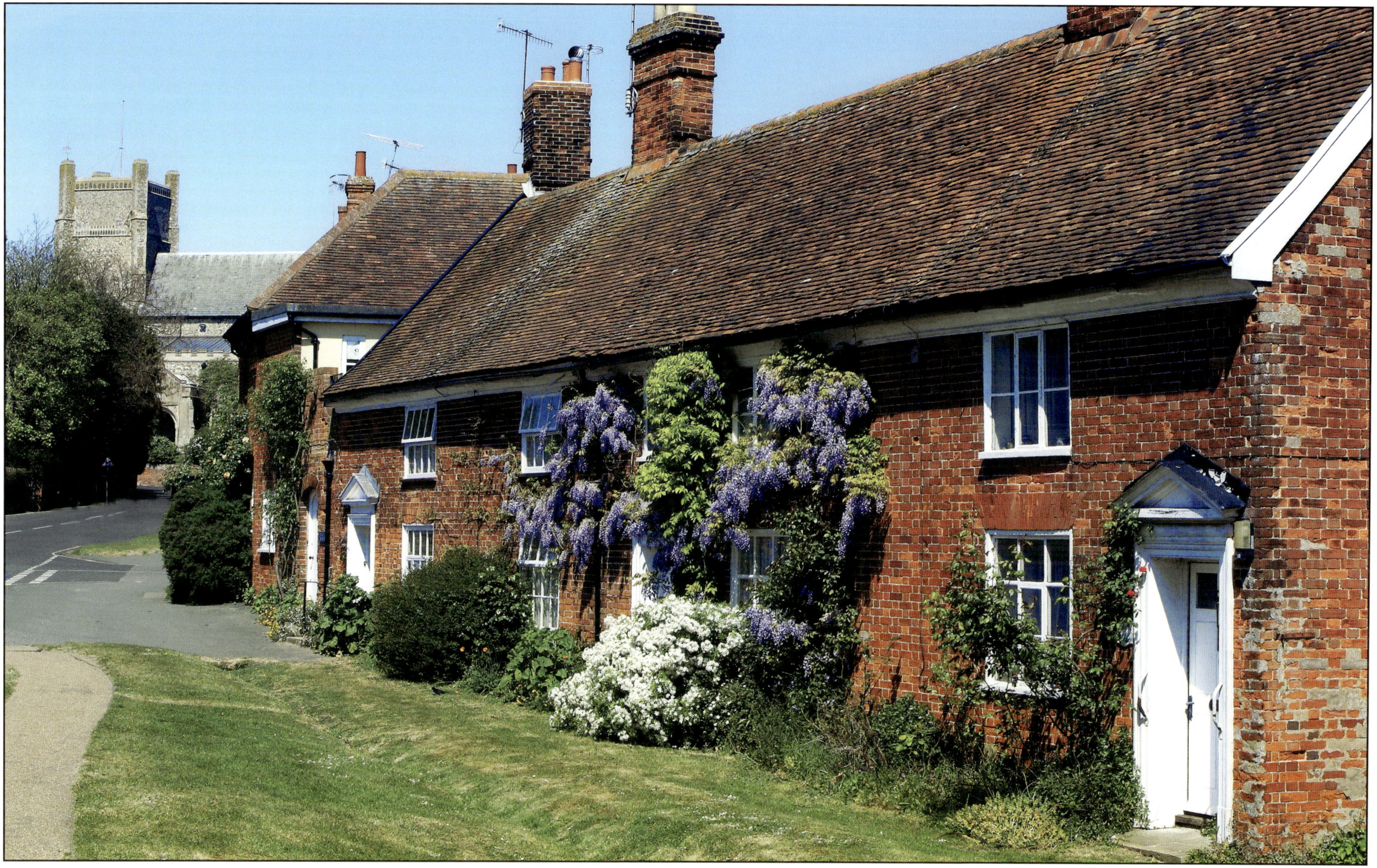

The wide street from St Bartholomew's Church to the quay is lined with houses made of red brick – Suffolk Reds. Most of the houses along this street are now second homes. No visit to Orford is complete without sampling produce from the oysterage and smokehouses – some of the best seafood to be had anywhere.

The Suffolk Punch Trust Colony Stud, Hollesley

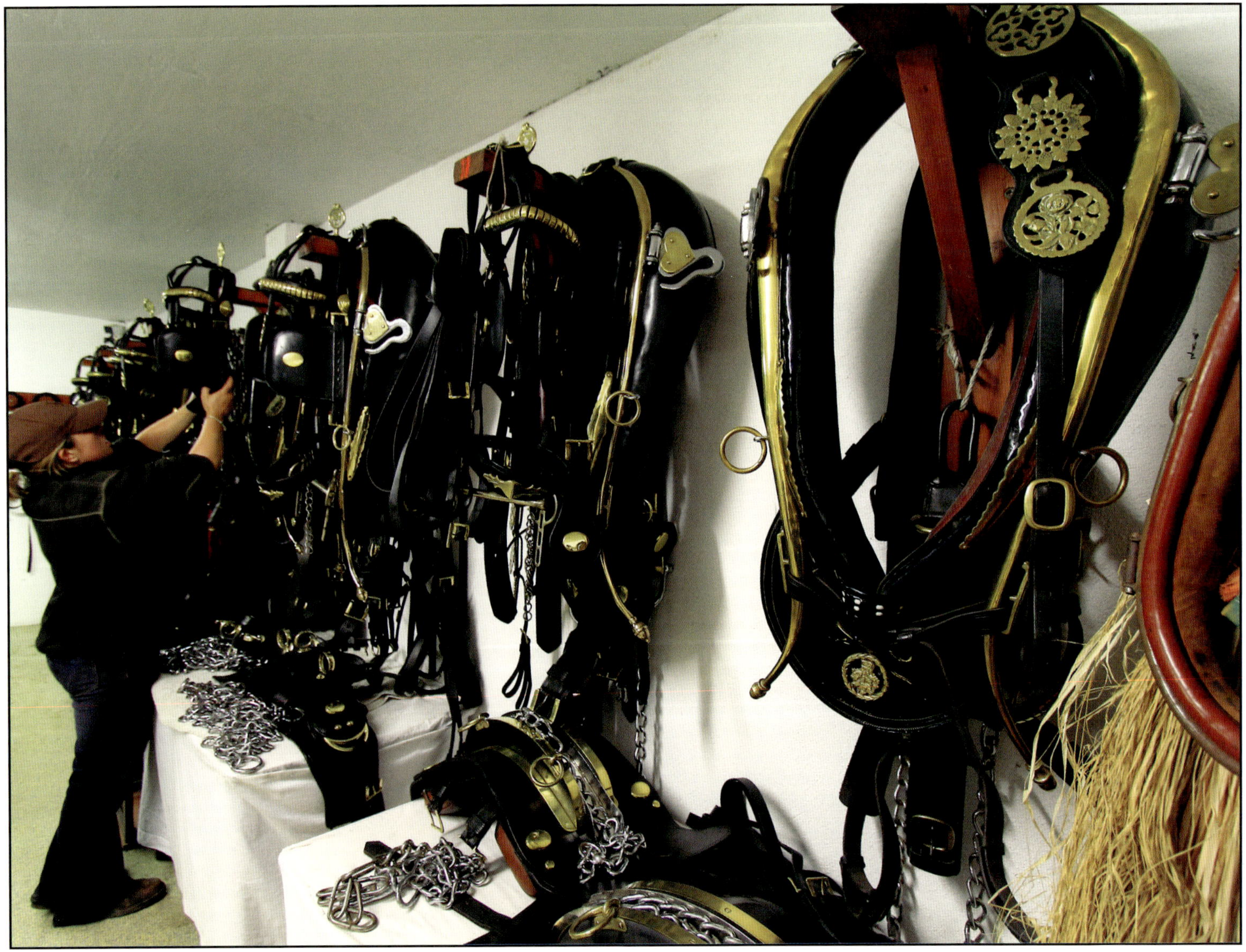

It's a labour of love in the harness room to keep all the brass work and leather of the harnesses in pristine condition – worthy regalia for the mighty Suffolk Punch. The foundation sire of all Suffolk Punch horses was *Crisp's Horse* foaled near here in 1768 – then known as the Suffolk Sorrel. All Suffolks owe their existence to this one horse.

The Suffolk Punch Horse is rarer than the Giant Panda, and would certainly qualify for inclusion in Britten's *Noye's Fludde* ark. Fortunately, these iconic working horses were saved from virtual extinction thanks, in no small measure, to a prison. The farm at Hollesley Bay Colony Stud, between Orford and Bawdsey, has bred Suffolk Punch horses for 250 years, making it the oldest stud of its kind in the world. Latterly it was part of the prison service at the Hollesley Bay Colony. Originally a borstal, it had the largest prison farm in the country, and the Suffolk Punch was used to work their land. Britten took an interest in the stud, having been introduced to its work by Fidelity the Countess of Cranbrook – the first chairman of the Aldeburgh Festival, who was also chairman of the Hollesley Bay Borstal governors.

In 2002 the Trust was set up as an educational charity to raise funds to buy the stud and horses after the prison service announced plans to sell off all their farms.

Since then, the Trust has developed the site into a popular tourist attraction, with a special remit to provide educational opportunities for all age groups. An exhibition hall illustrating Suffolk life, a café, a magnificent harness room (left), a collection of horse-drawn vehicles, and working demonstrations, are just some of the other attractions for visitors to The Suffolk Punch Trust.

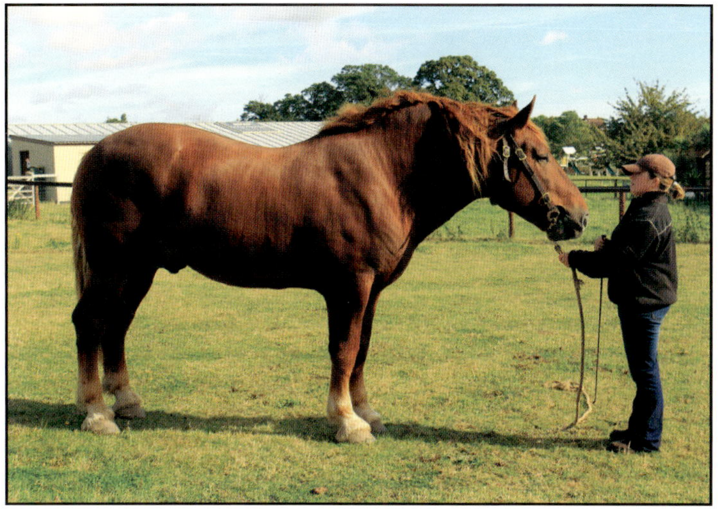

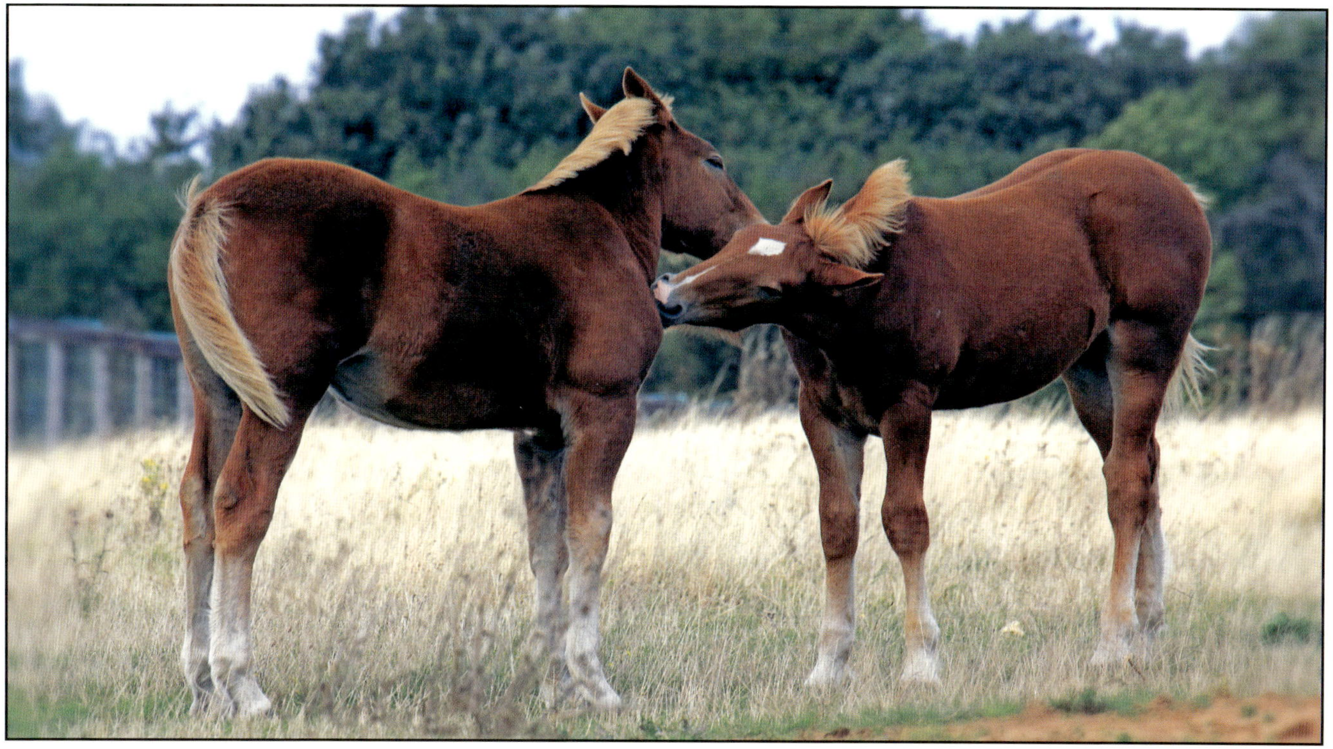

It is said the ideal Suffolk Punch has a 'face like an angel, a body like a barrel and a rear like a farmer's daughter'. *Besthorpe Achilles* (above) was supreme champion when first shown at the Suffolk Show. Two of his sired foals (right) affectionately groom each other, and another is being trained to harness (below).

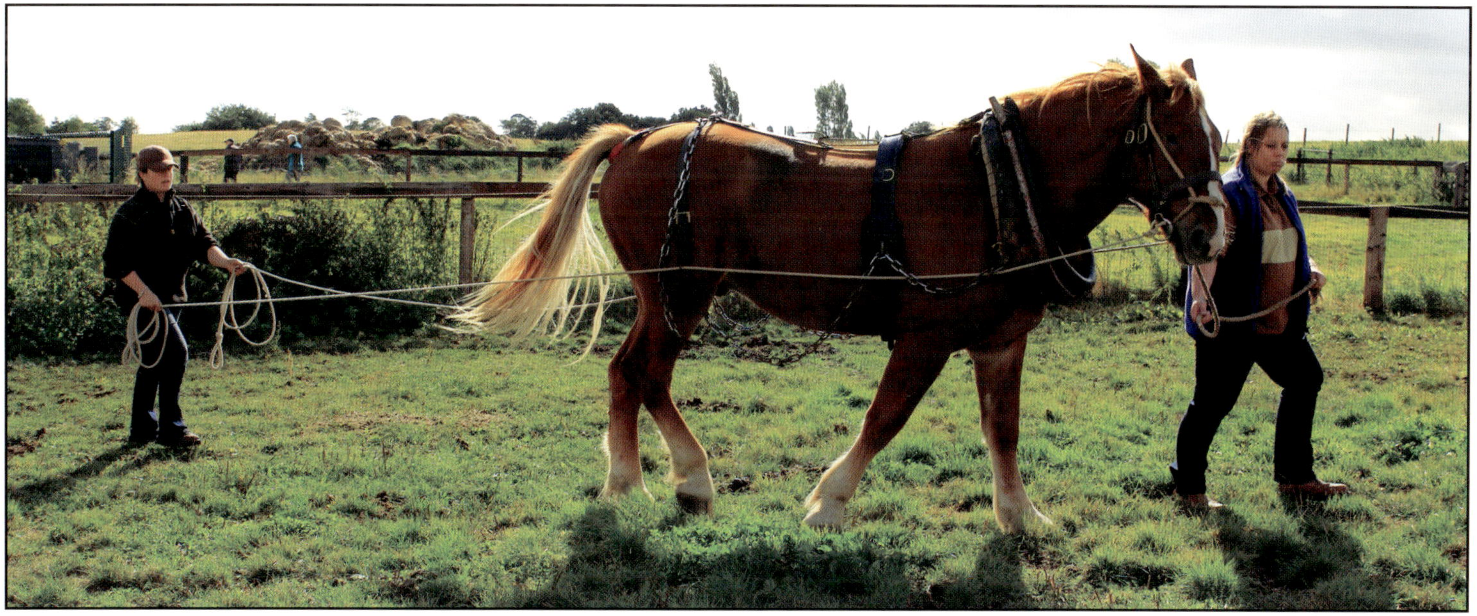

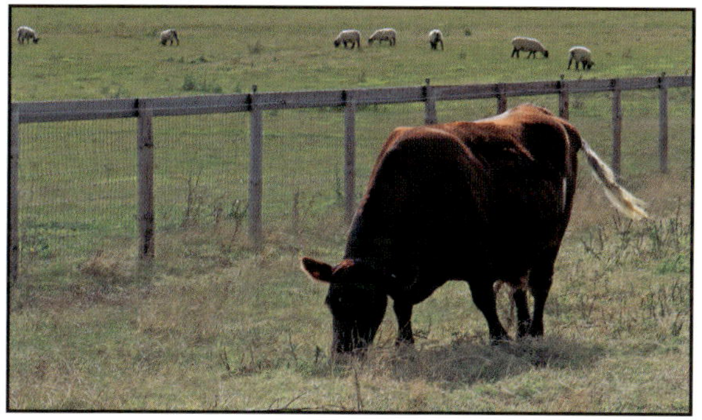

The Trust also has the oldest registered flock of Suffolk Sheep in the world, and Red Poll cattle (seen above). The Suffolk Punch, Red Poll cattle and Suffolk Sheep are known as 'The Suffolk Trinity', famous farm animals, originating from within the county, that have been exported and bred across the globe.

Woodbridge
'I'm back in Suffolk'

'Now I really feel I'm back in Suffolk – look at that big sky and the brilliant clear light,' Ben remarked as we approached Woodbridge station having travelled from Ipswich together on the train. He'd been in London for a few days and was feeling tired, and homesick for his birth county.

Approaching Woodbridge by train gives unrivalled views across the River Deben, a sight that can lift the heart of the most weary of travellers.

With 1400 years of recorded history to draw upon, the 'town fathers' have looked after their heritage well. No longer the boat-building centre it once was, it now relaxes into the more leisurely pursuits of caring for the needs of yachtsmen, and the thousands of tourists who visit every year.

Thomas Seckford – Master of the Court of Requests to Queen Elizabeth I, and one of Suffolk's greatest fourteenth-century benefactors – bequeathed substantial assets to the town that still benefit today's residents. He built the Shire Hall (opposite right) and Seckford Almshouses, and owned the Tide Mill, and many other properties. The Seckford Foundation continues to do good works to this very day, especially in the field of education.

The recently restored Tide Mill (opposite top left) is one of only two operating in the country – working now for demonstration purposes only. It's probably the earliest of all surviving tide mills, one having been recorded here in 1170. The ebb and flow of the tides entering the mill pond turns the water wheel, which in turn powers the grinding stones. It was still operating commercially until 1957, then fell into dereliction, but was saved by the hard work and money raised by enthusiasts. It is a Grade 1 listed building and now a major tourist attraction.

The Shire Hall stands in the middle of the Market Square, where weekly markets are held. It's still used as a council chamber, and is a popular venue for civil marriages.

The railway line effectively cuts the river off from the town. Crossing the pedestrian bridge over the line gives a fine panorama of the waterfront, portent of the delightful riverside walks ahead.

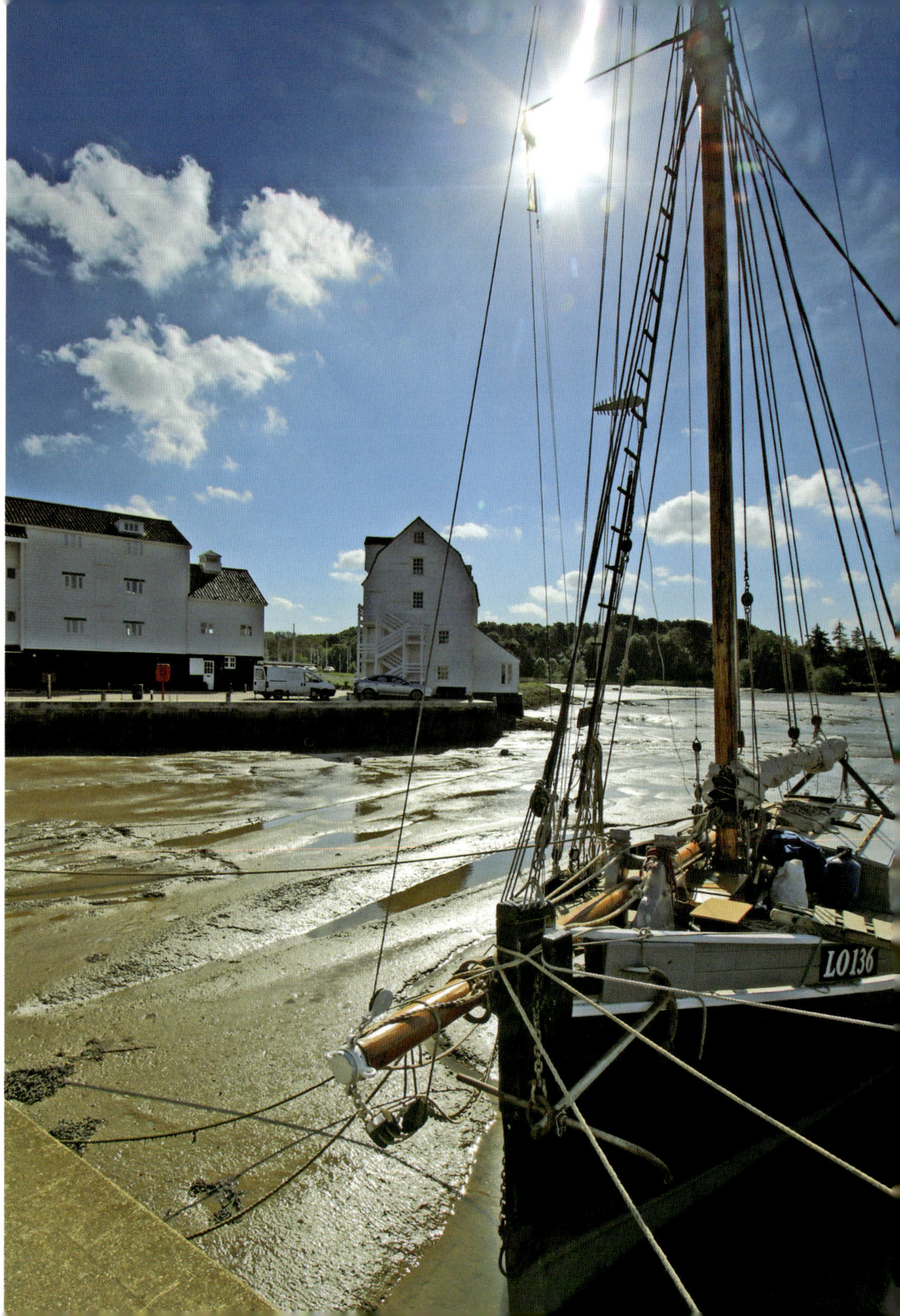

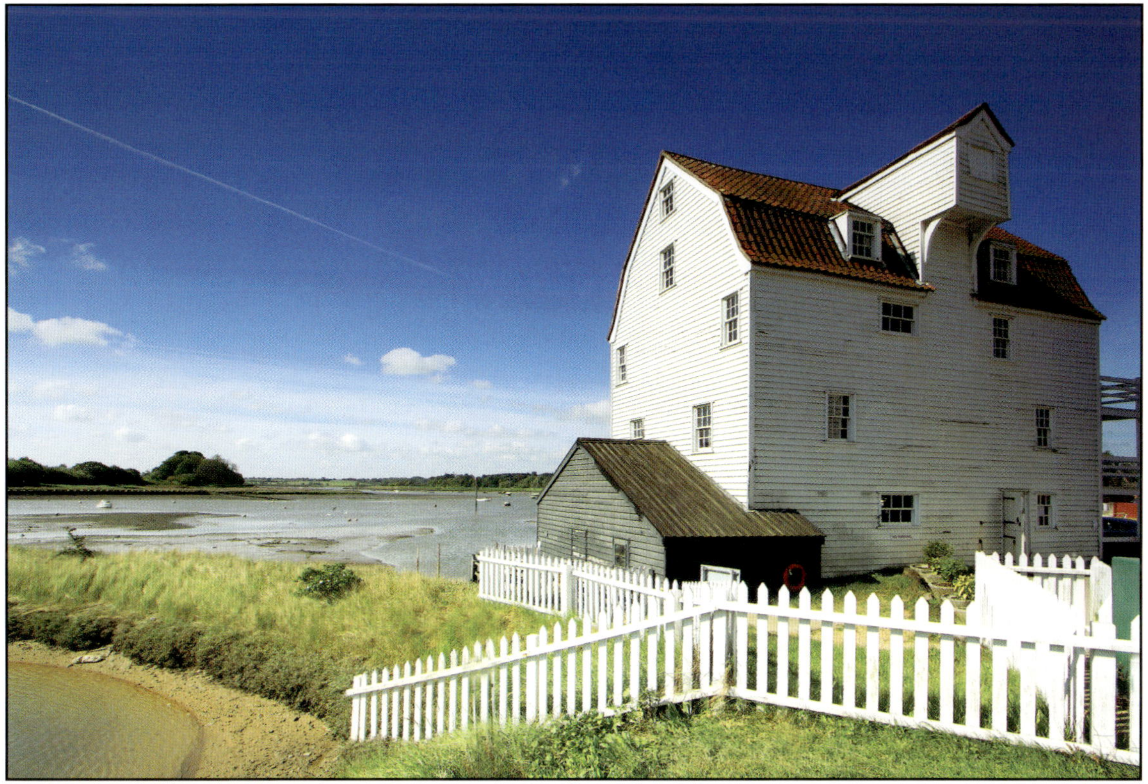

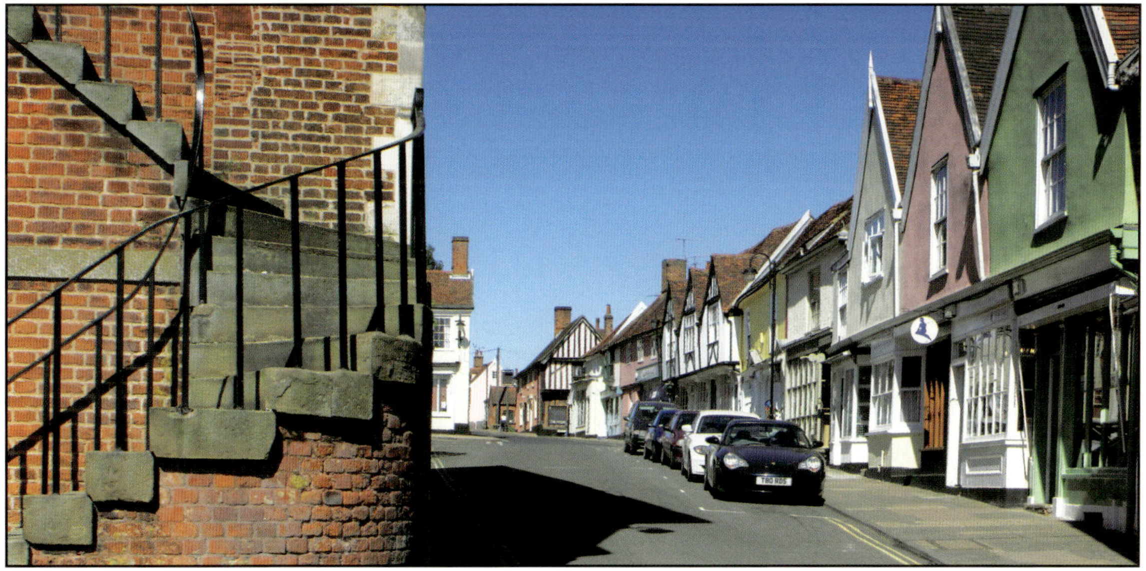

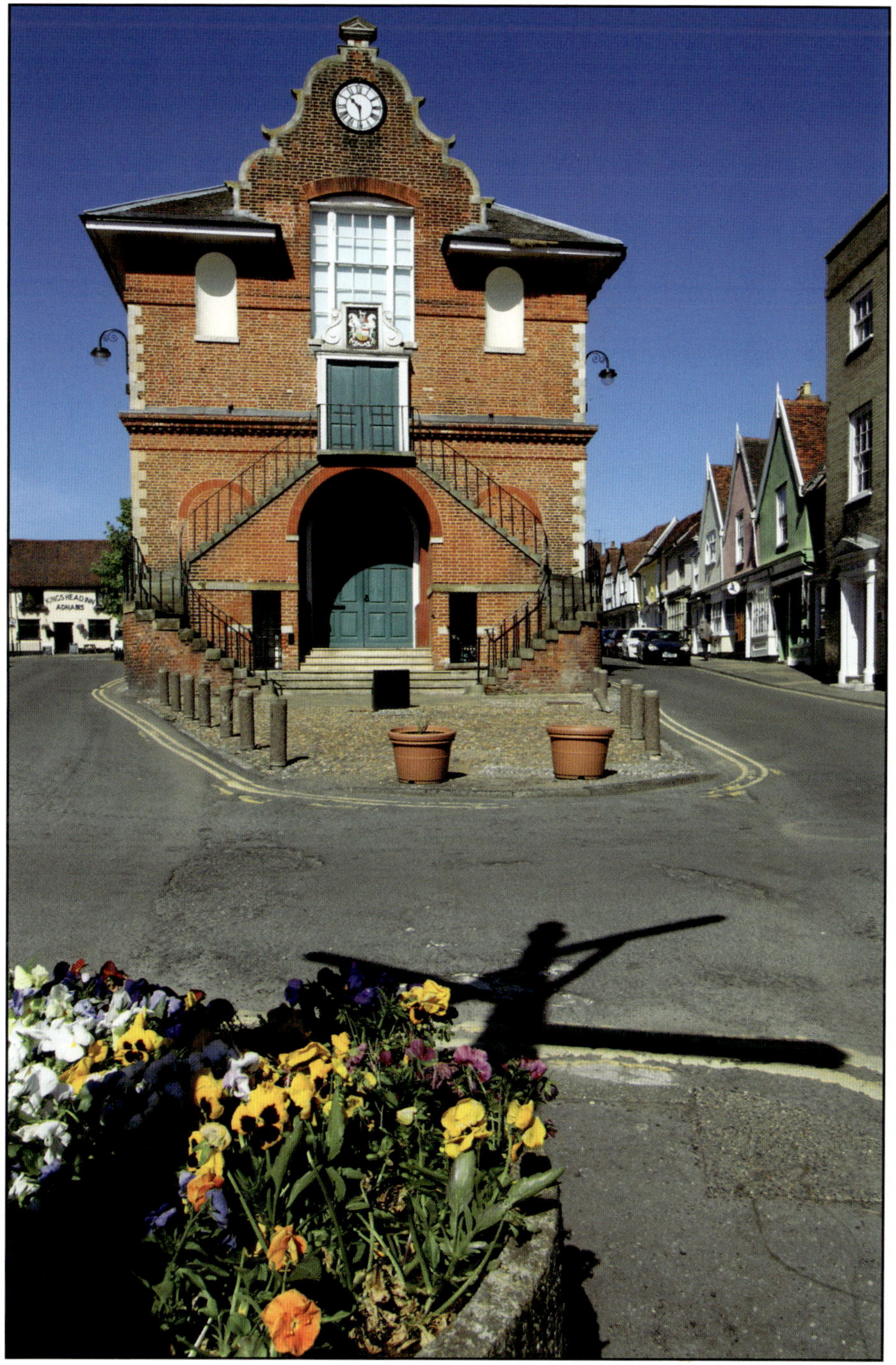

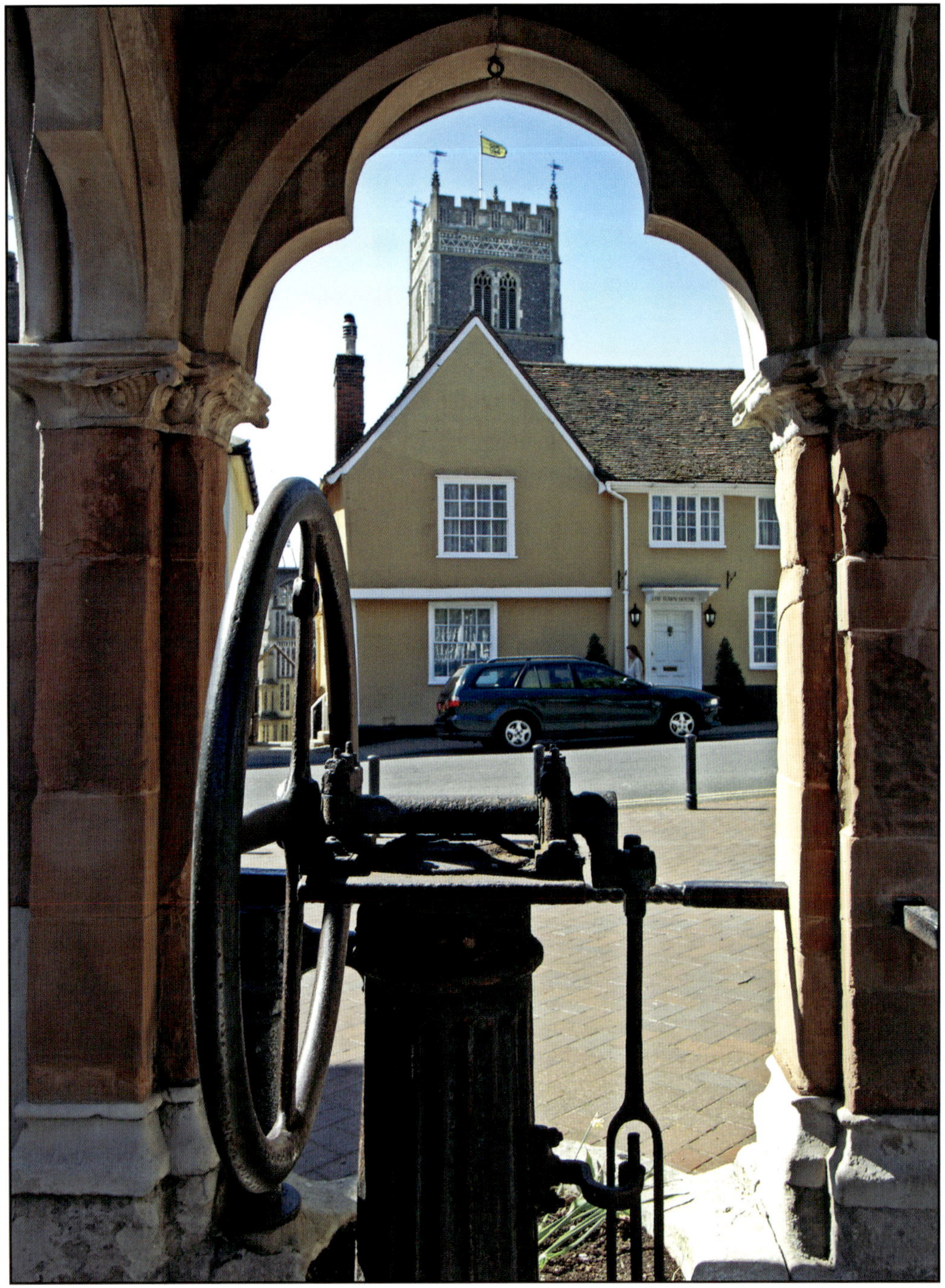

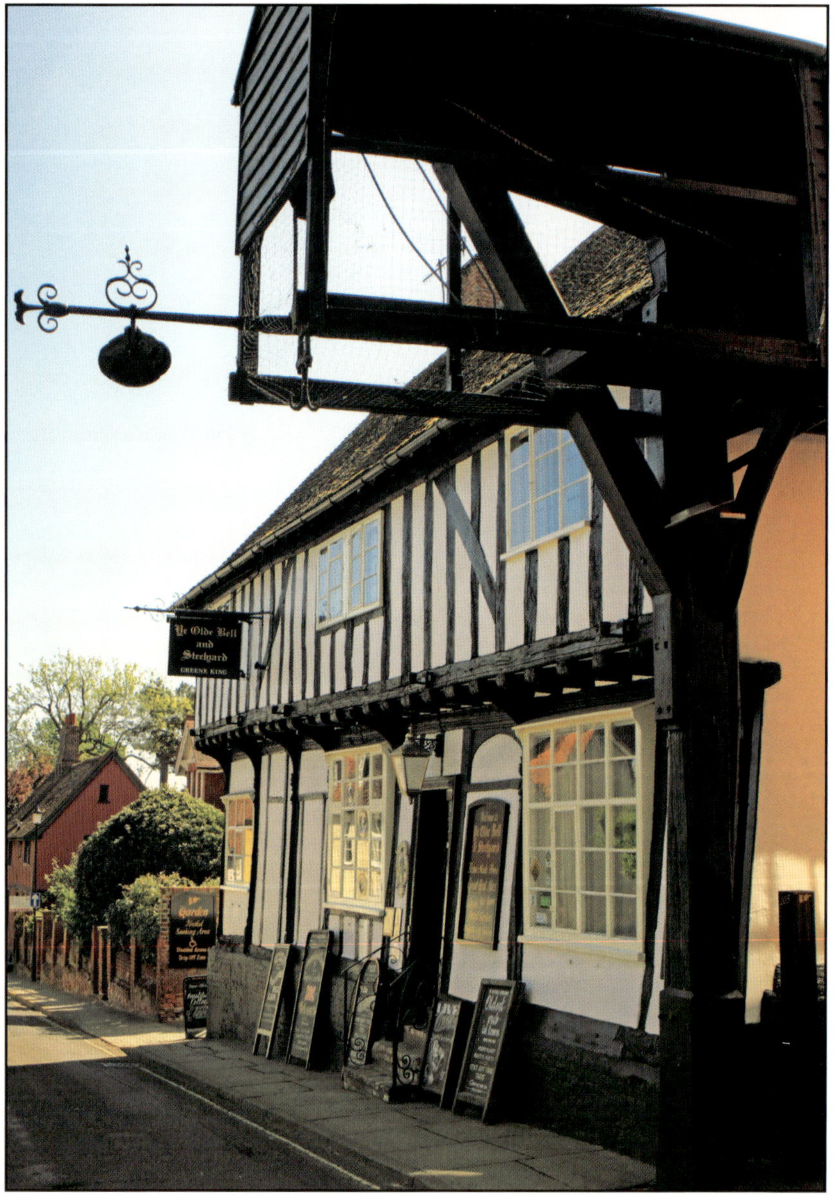

The Shire Hall water pump on the Market Square frames the house and the medieval St Mary's Church. The Old Bell and Steelyard public house (above) in New Street is steeped in history, but only became a pub in the mid eighteen-hundreds. The 'steelyard' is a weighing machine, a forerunner of a public weighbridge.

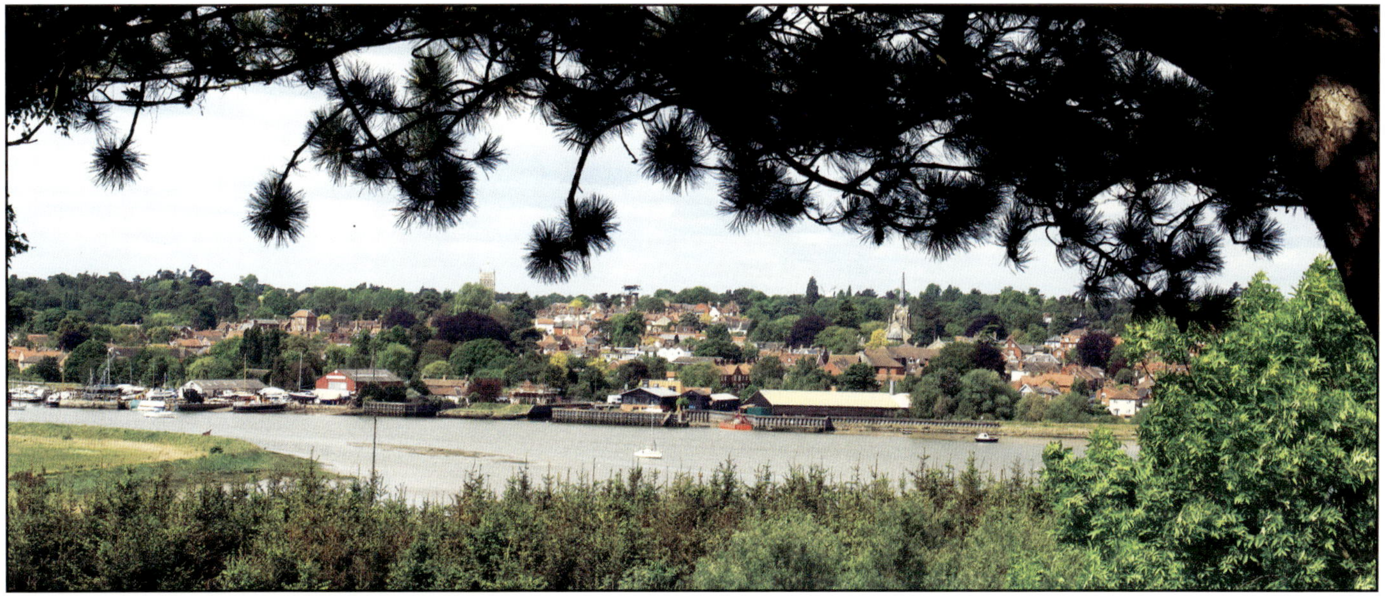

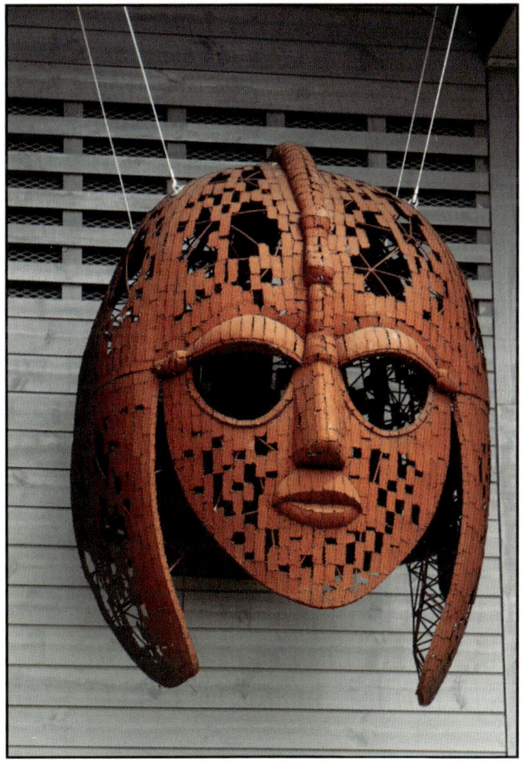

Sutton Hoo burial ship

In 1939 self-taught Suffolk archaeologist, Basil Brown, discovered one of the richest and most important seventh-century Anglo-Saxon burial ships just across the River Deben at Sutton Hoo, near to where the above photograph of Woodbridge was taken. It contained the treasure of Raedwald, King of East Anglia.

The site is now run by the National Trust where they have a visitor centre based on the burial ship. The model of the masked helmet (left), one of the most iconic finds at the site, welcomes visitors to the centre. The original artifacts are in the British Museum.

The picture (right) of the excavation was not taken by me – I wasn't born then! It is such a significant archeological photograph I had to include it. The photographer's name is not credited, but I believe it could be by Henry Clarke, my boss when I worked for the East Anglian Daily Times after leaving school. He photographed the site during the excavation. It has all the hallmarks of his photographic style.

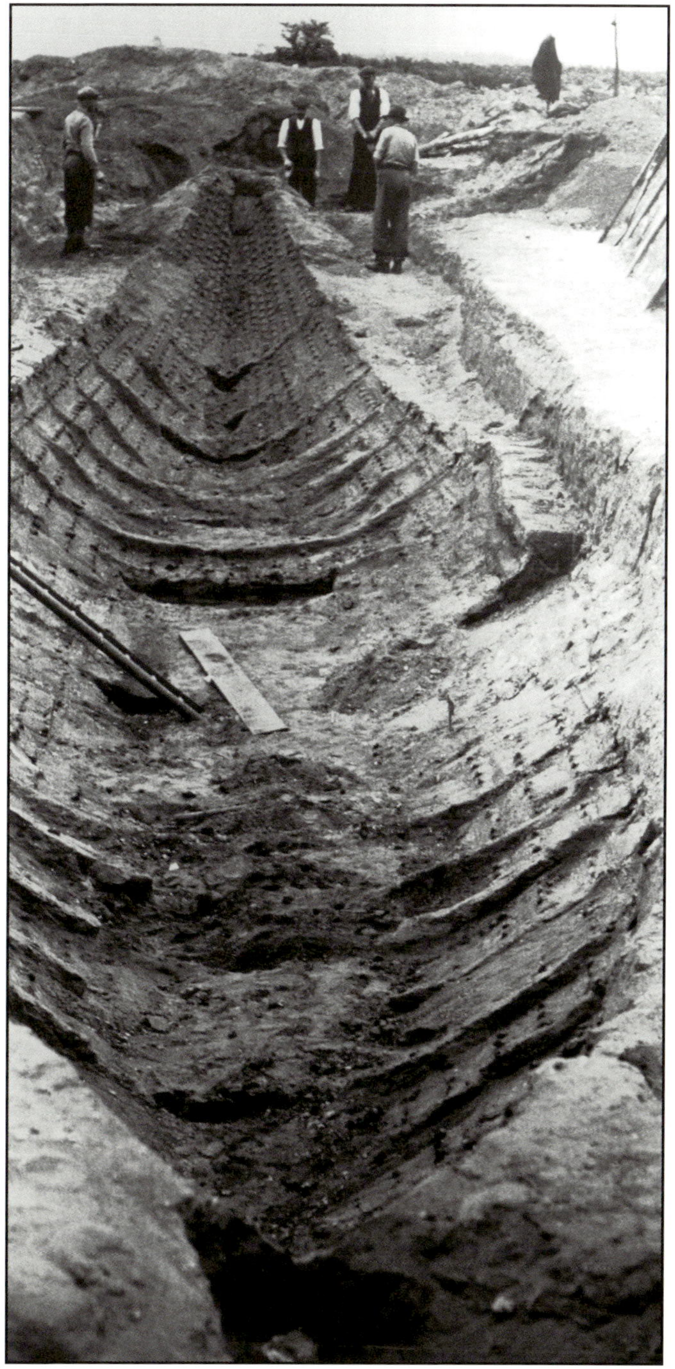

The delightful River Deben

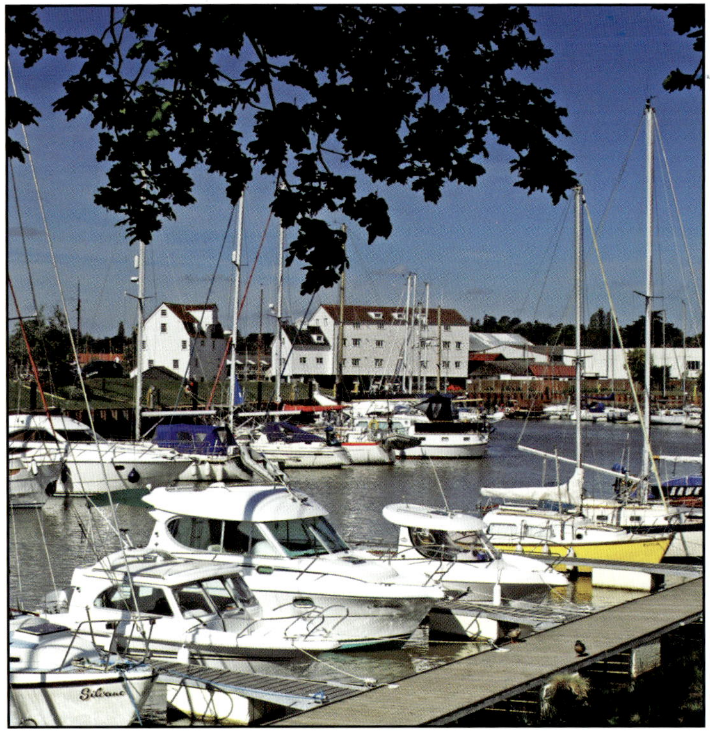

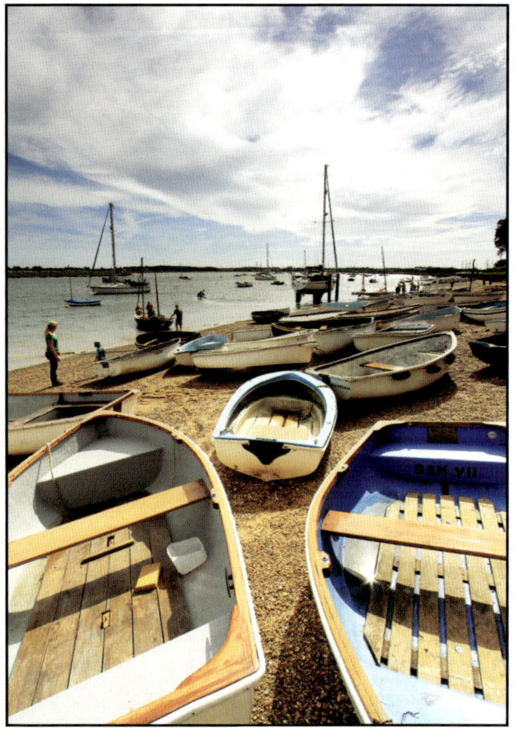

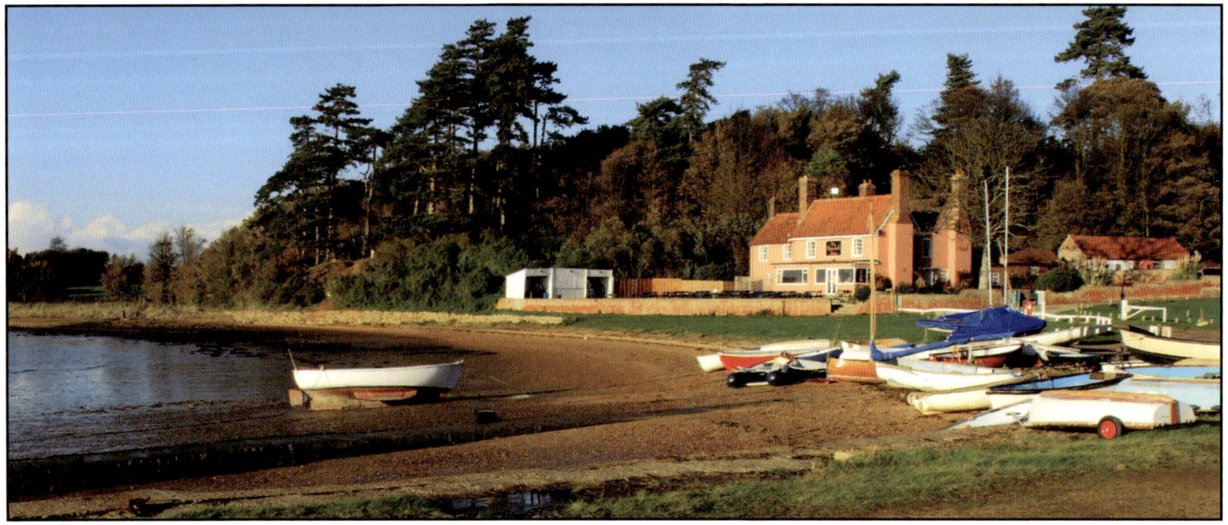

The River Deben has for generations been a vital commercial waterway for boats laden with agricultural cargo, cement and ballast, plying between Woodbridge and Felixstowe Ferry and then out into the North Sea and beyond. However, to spot a commercial craft working on the river these days is almost as scarce as finding hen's teeth.

Despair not: there are more waterborne vessels using the river now than ever before – all leisure craft. From Bromeswell, the upper end of the tidal reach, down to Felixstowe Ferry, hundreds of pleasure boats are moored on this attractive meandering river that is within the Suffolk Coast and Heaths Area of Outstanding Natural Beauty.

Yachtsmen sailing downstream from Woodbridge Tide Mill Marina (top left) need to keep a careful watch while navigating between the closely moored yachts either side of the buoyed channel. Soon the busy nautical playground of Waldringfield hoves into view (top right), home to the Waldringfield Sailing Club. The riverside Maybush Inn is a popular foodie pub for boaters and landlubbers alike.

Further downstream, passing the well-used anchoring spot called 'The Rocks', the isolated Ramsholt Arms (bottom) comes into sight. Apart from the concrete quay – a relic from past commercial interests – the pub is the only sign of habitation hereabouts.

Moored boats come thick and fast as we approach the mouth of the Deben, with Felixstowe Ferry on one side (opposite page), and Bawdsey on the other.

Bawdsey Manor (overleaf) was purchased by the RAF during the Second World War and became RAF Bawsdey, a top secret establishment for the Ministry of Defence, where Sir Robert Watson-Watt carried on the development of RADAR, an invention that played a significant part in winning the Battle of Britain, and the Second World War.

The Manor is now a conference and education centre.

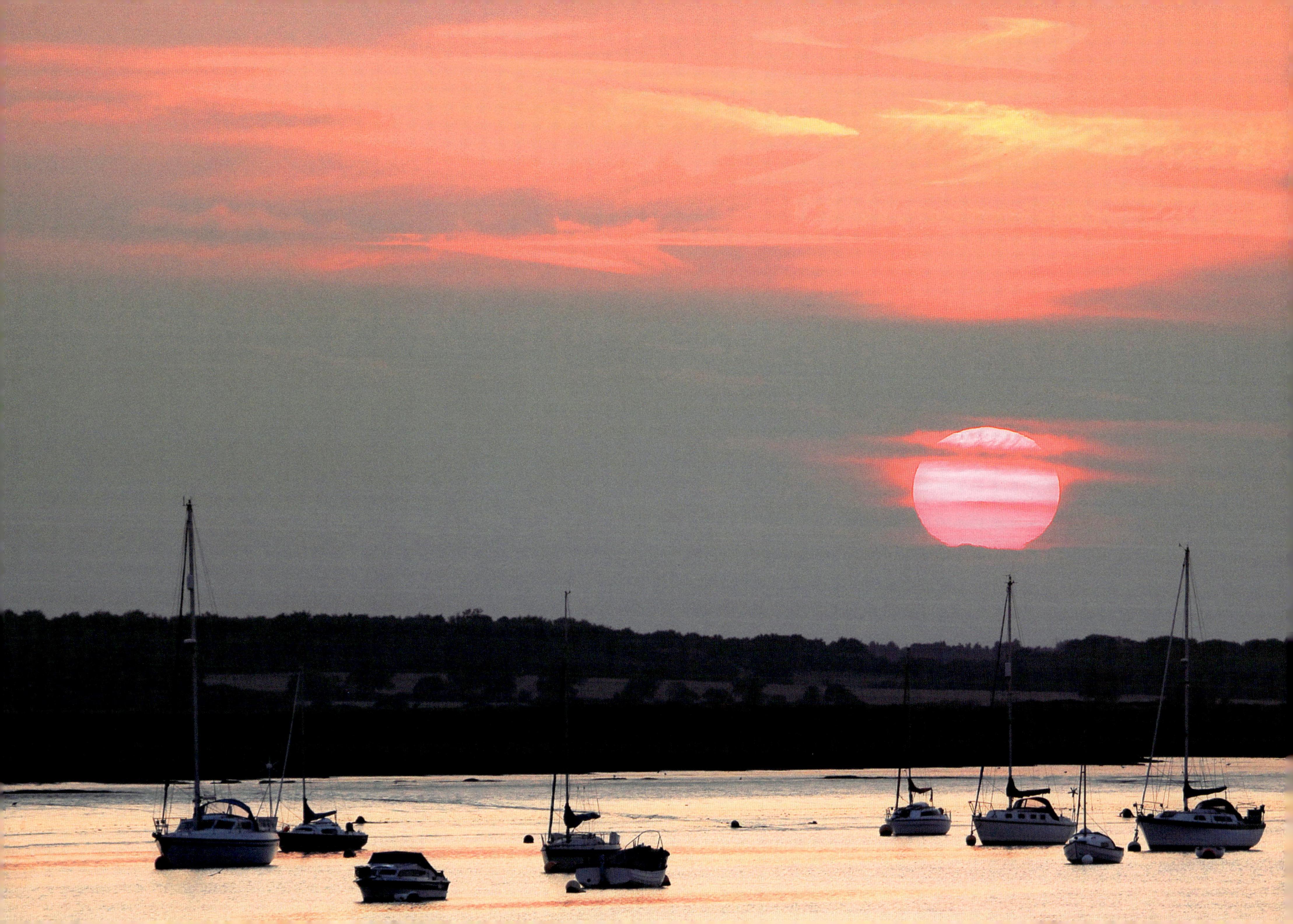

Felixstowe – the old meets the new

Depending on which history books you read, Felixstowe is said to be the site of the last opposed sea-borne invasion of England. What is indisputable is that on 2nd July, 1667, a 2,000-strong Dutch force landed at Felixstowe in an attempt to ransack and destroy the ships in and around Harwich harbour. This invasion fleet was repelled by the men of the Duke of York and Albany's Maritime Regiment stationed at Landguard Fort – Britain's very first commando unit. Ever since then, a fort has stood defiantly at the mouth of the River Orwell, defending the strategically important entrance to Harwich harbour. It ceased to be a military base in 1957 and is now a fascinating visitor centre and museum operated by English Heritage.

Felixstowe really came into its own after the railway line was built in the late Victorian period, when it became a fashionable seaside resort, and Felixstowe Ferry Golf Course is one of the oldest golf courses in the country. Mrs Wallis Simpson resided in the town for six weeks in 1936 before her divorce hearing at Ipswich County Court, which paved the way for her to marry King Edward VIII, an event which precipitated his abdication of the throne.

Today Felixstowe is not only a popular seaside resort but has the UK's busiest container port, where some of the largest container ships in the world dock.

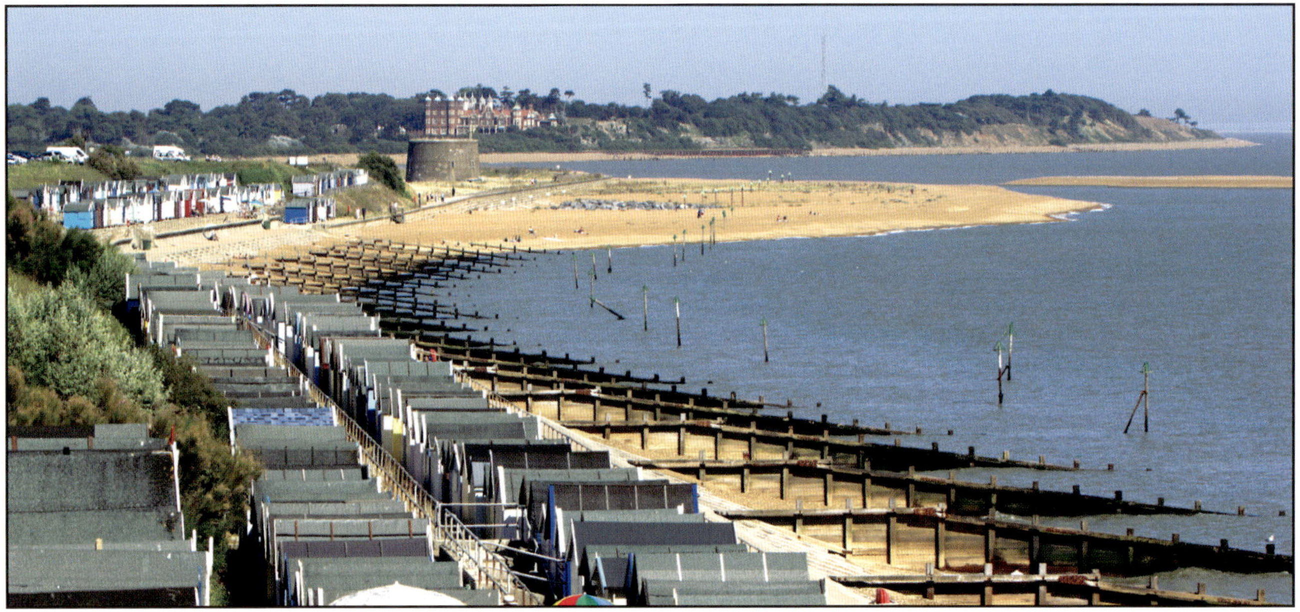

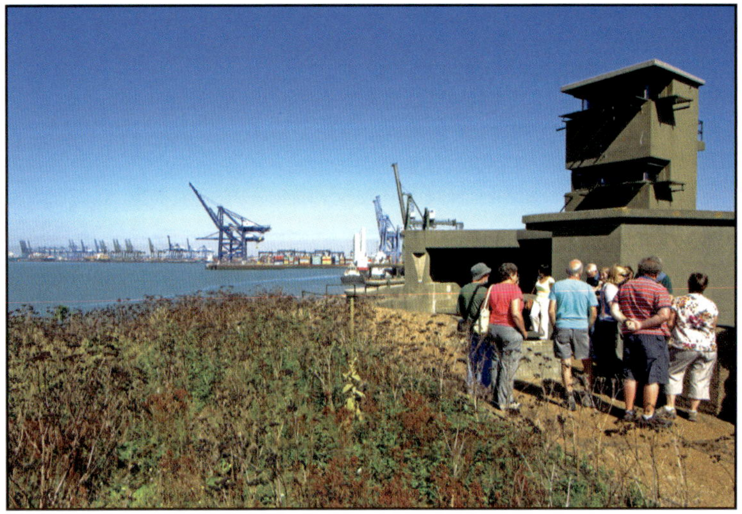

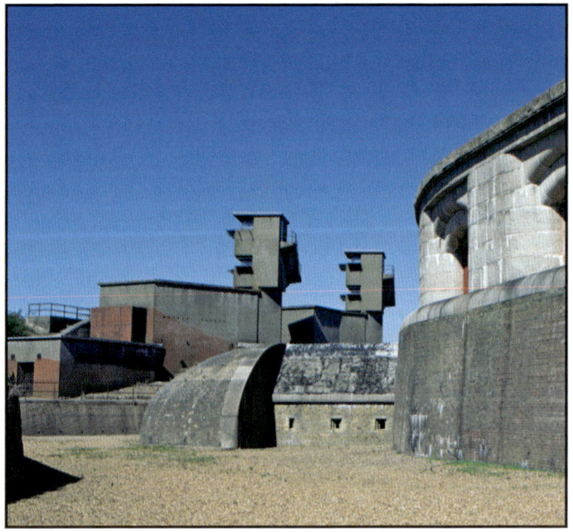

Felixstowe is surrounded on three sides by water. To the north, the mouth of the River Deben (top) is guarded at Old Felixstowe by two Martello towers – Bawdsey Manor can be seen in the background. To the south, Landguard Fort (above), now a museum, stands overlooking the mouth of the River Orwell, and Harwich and Felixstowe Ports. As testament to its formidable gunnery power, it was never challenged, and no shots were ever fired in anger from here during the last two World Wars.

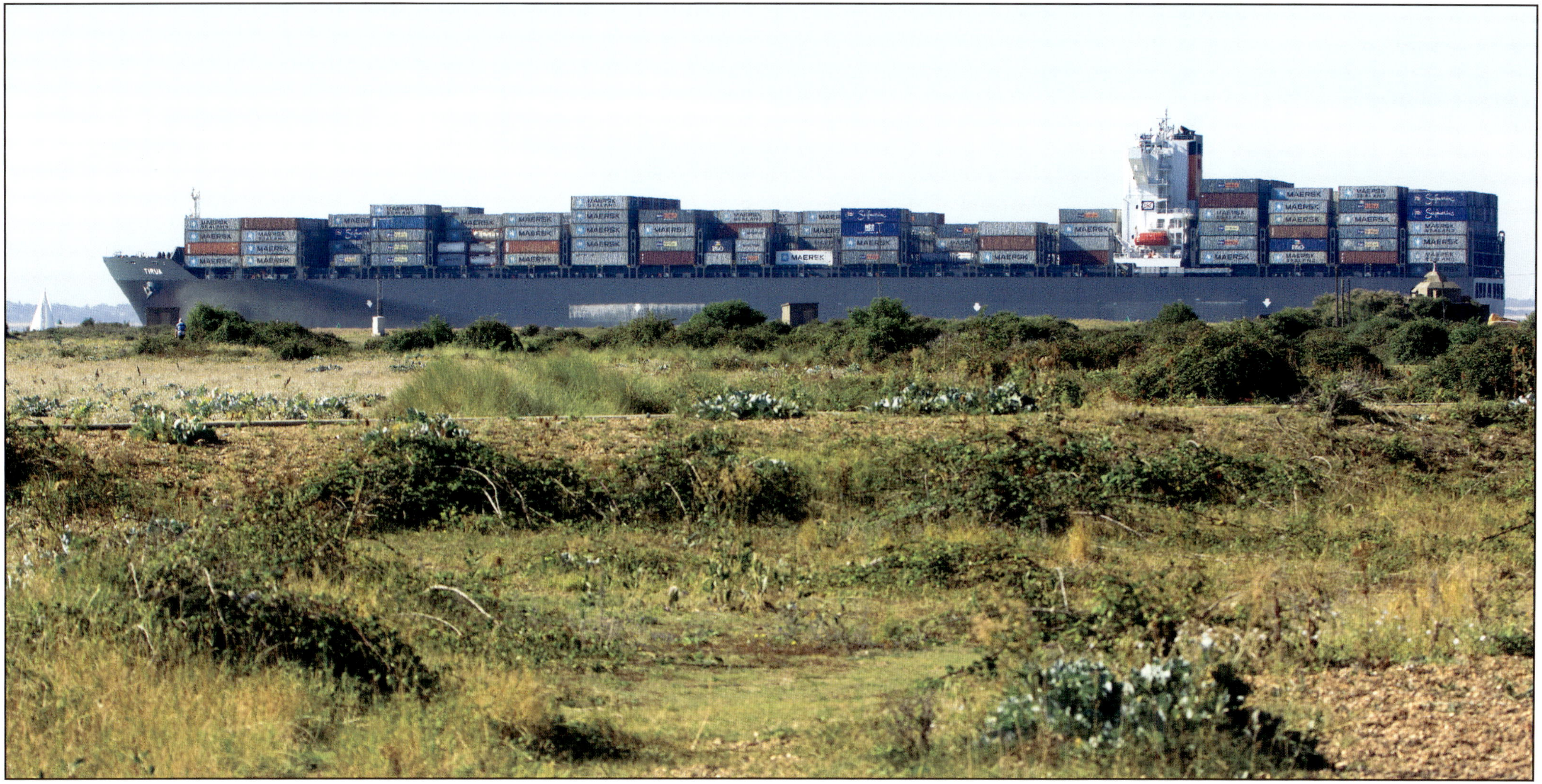

It's a surreal experience, seeing a monster ship laden high with containers apparently drifting slowly across the stony scrubland near Landguard Fort – another ship departing on yet another sea passage. This is a daily sight here as ships arrive at Felixstowe deep water port, do a quick turnaround to unload and load new containers, before heading out again to foreign destinations.

In the mid-1960s the port was at the forefront of developing containerised cargo handling in the UK. Now owned by Hutchinson Ports (UK) it is the country's largest and busiest container port and is operational around the clock. It has developed a mini-community in its own right – boasting a police force, ambulance and fire service, and rail terminal. In an effort to minimise road traffic and carbon emissions, more use is made of rail freight from Felixstowe, and with the introduction of short sailings on smaller feeder ships to other parts of the UK, heavy goods vehicles on the busy A14 route to the Midlands are significantly reduced. The vast infrastructure required to keep the port operating provides hundreds of jobs and is a major employer in the area. Suffolk's seafaring tradition lives on at Felixstowe.

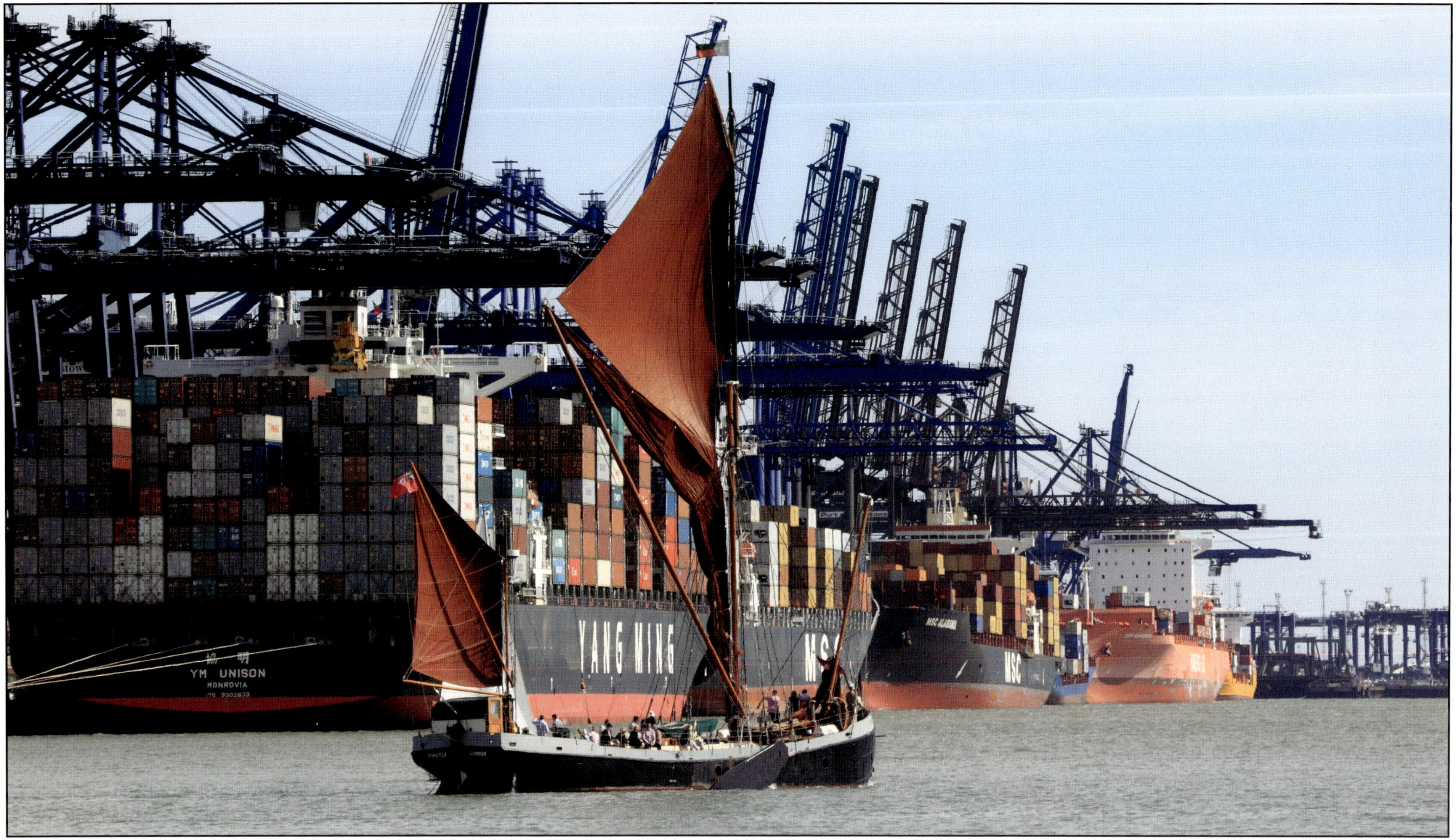

Thames sailing barge *Thistle* is dwarfed by the massive cranes and hulls of the container ships docked at Felixstowe Port. The largest of these world-girdling ships can carry over 11,000 containers on board – it would take nearly 800 sailing barges the size of *Thistle* to convey the same weight of cargo. *Thistle*, the oldest surviving iron Thames sailing barge, was built in Scotland in 1895, and was able to carry 200 tons of cargo when she plied her trade on the East Coast. The Rivers Orwell and Stour would have been familiar territory for her. She is now used for pleasure purposes, and frequently charters out of Ipswich docks.

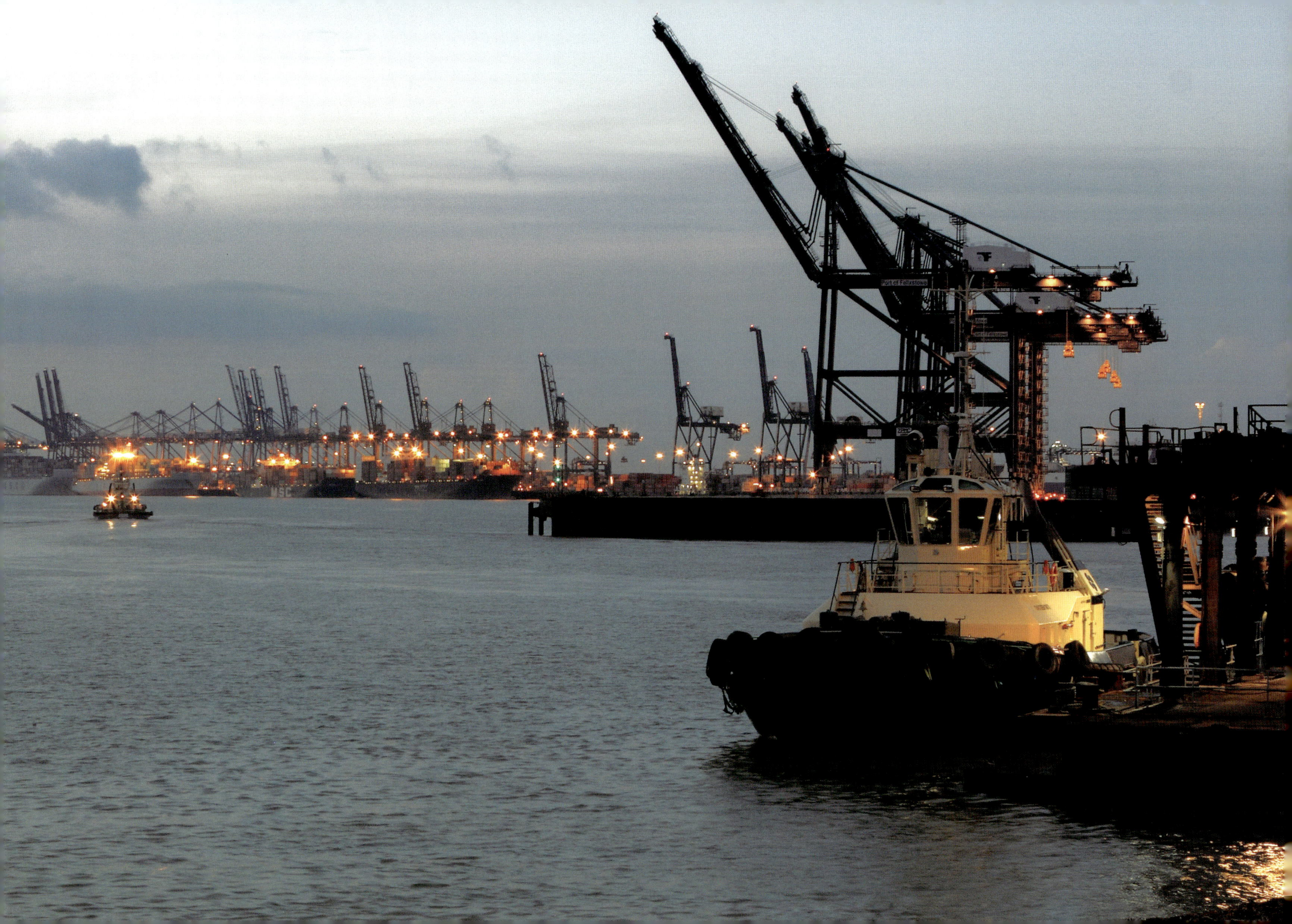
Port of Felixstowe

The River Orwell

The River Orwell is another Suffolk river that has a name change along its route from source to mouth. It sets out as the River Gipping with its source at Mendlesham. When it reaches Stoke Bridge in Ipswich it becomes the tidal River Orwell and broadens into an estuary at Ipswich docks, where it has been an essential commercial waterway since the seventh century. It then flows into the North sea at Felixstowe having merged with the River Stour en-route.

When Felixstowe became a major container port, traffic on the A14 (then the A45) was routed via Ipswich, causing heavy congestion. In 1982 the graceful sweeping bridge over the Orwell – The Orwell Bridge (opposite page) – was opened to bypass the town, and now carries over 60,000 vehicles a day. When it was built – by a Dutch contractor – it was the longest pre-stressed concrete span in the world.

The river is a popular boating area, and large marinas at Levington, Shotley and Woolverstone, as well as those in Ipswich, provide safe havens for boat owners to keep their craft.

Pin Mill (right) has long been associated with sailing barges and seafaring activities. Today it is a popular leisure centre with the famous Butt & Oyster public house, once believed to be a key haunt for smugglers, now offering good food and drink and playing its part in the tourist industry of the area.

Houseboats, many of them converted sailing barges, occupy the waterfront, adding a charm all of its own to this unique riverside hamlet.

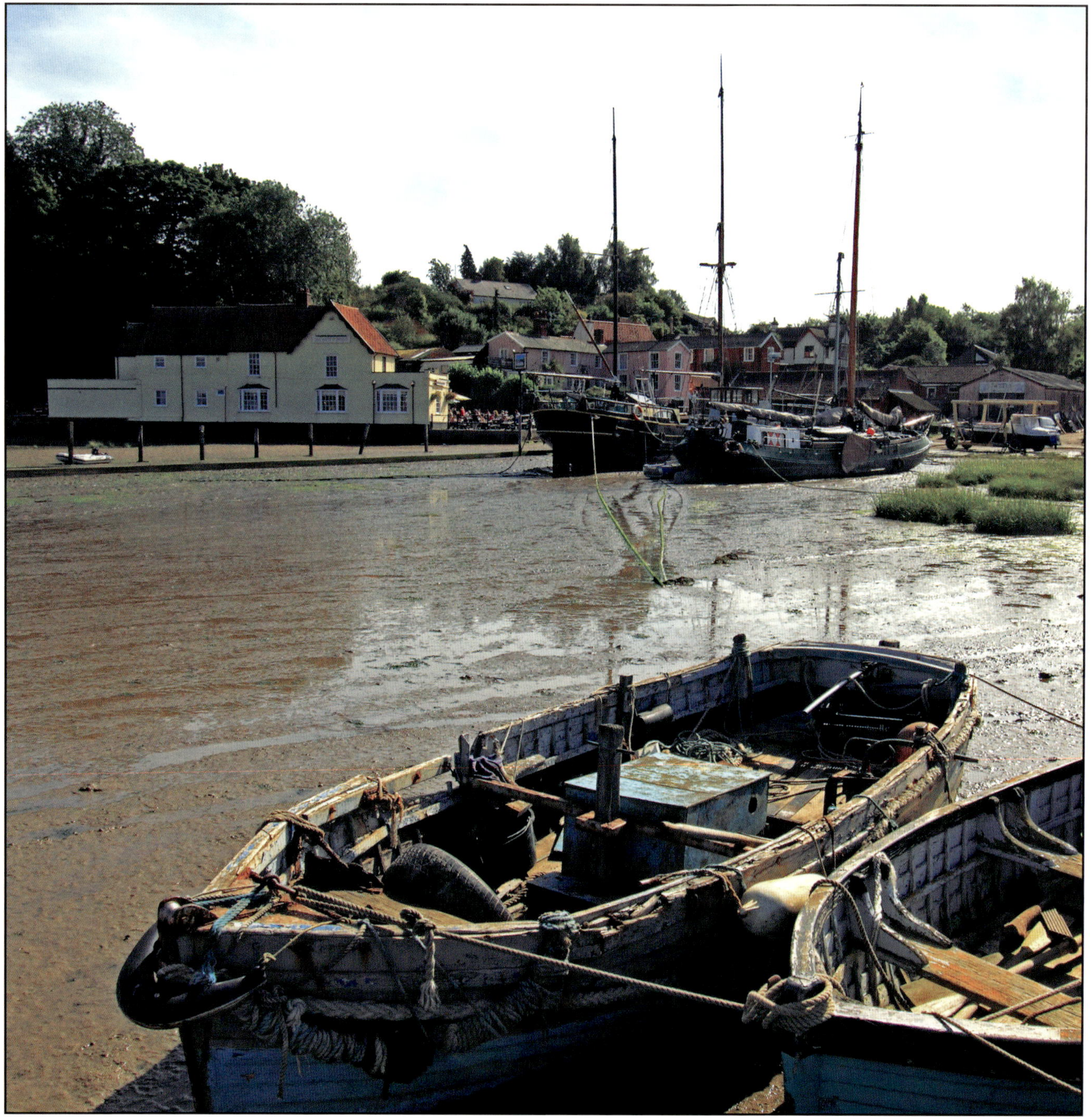

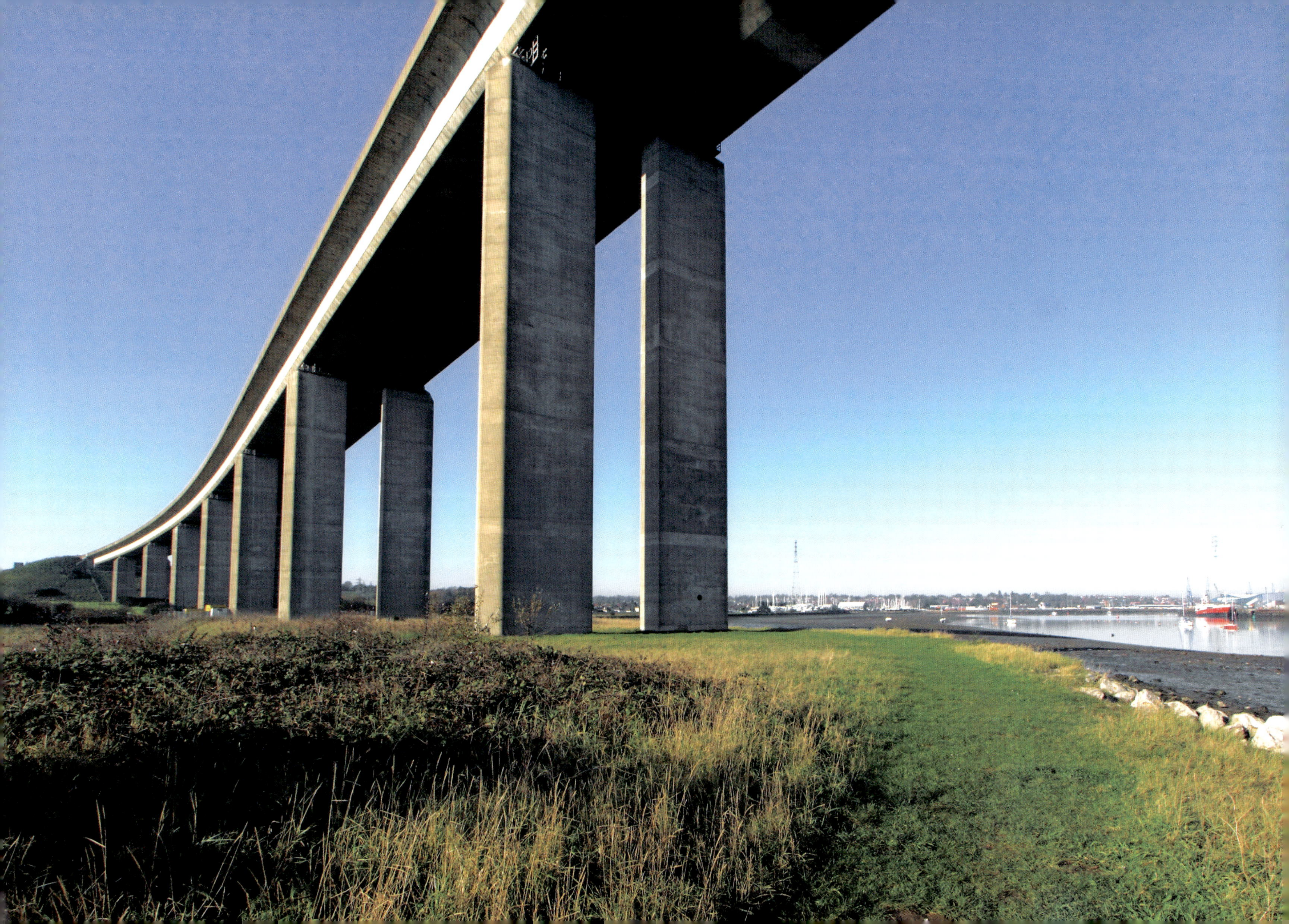

Ipswich – Suffolk's county town with a great past

Strictly speaking Ipswich doesn't qualify as being part of the Suffolk Heritage Coast, and has little connection with Benjamin Britten, who thought 'the town was rather down at heel', but I'm going to exercise some degree of artistic licence to include it in this book because of its historic significance to Suffolk and the coastal area – and also because I'm fond of Ipswich.

Ipswich is one of the oldest towns in England (then known as Gipeswic). Remains of the largest Roman Villa in Suffolk have been found here. King Raedwald, supreme ruler of the English, is associated with the town (Sutton Hoo is probably his burial site). Friesian potters from the Netherlands settled here in the seventh century and set up a large scale pottery, exporting their wares all over Europe from Ipswich docks. With growing prosperity the area of the Buttermarket was the upmarket part of town, with grand merchants' houses built to reflect its growing wealth from the wool trade. Ipswich docks became a *kontor* – a foreign trading post for the Hanseatic League of the Baltic ports. It was also one of the main embarkation points for puritans leaving for New England in the great migration in the 1630s. In 1797 Lord and Lady Nelson moved to the town and he was appointed High Steward of Ipswich.

Sadly the borough burghers of the mid-twentieth century allowed many beautiful timbered buildings to be demolished – I well remember as a teenager standing in despair watching ancient carved oak beams being thrown onto a demolition-site pyre in order to make way for car parks, and concrete monstrosities sprang up to replace the irreplaceable. It was a sad time architecturally for the town. Thankfully, before too much damage was done, the Ipswich Society was formed by people who cared about their heritage, and worked closely with the Borough Council, who created the Ipswich Building Preservation Trust to fund restoration, and bring about public awareness of Ipswich's historical inheritance. Since then great strides have been made to preserve and restore buildings, and Ipswich can be proud once again of its past, and look to build on that for the future.

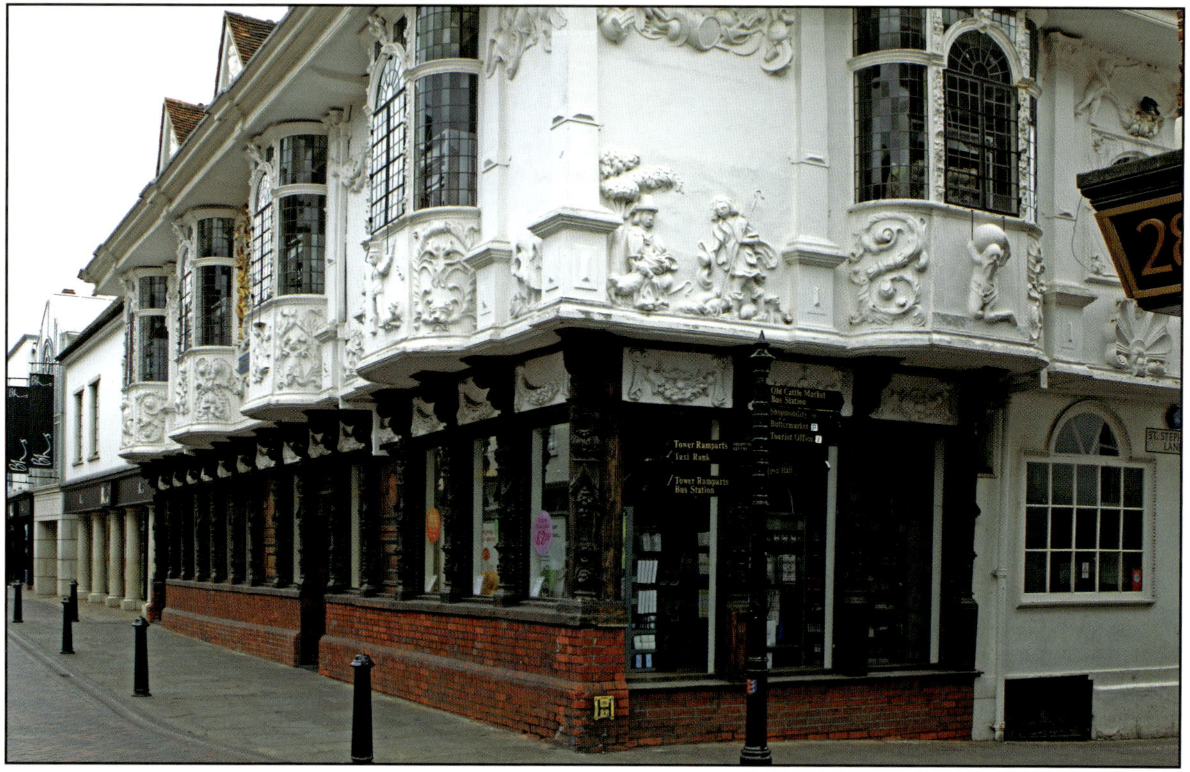

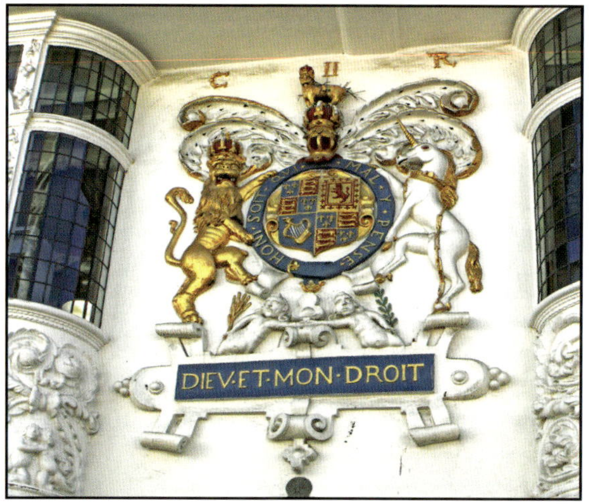

The most iconic building in Ipswich is, without doubt, *The Ancient House* in the Buttermarket. This fifteenth-century Grade 1 listed building was near to collapse in the late seventies, when it was bought by Ipswich Borough Council, who lavished money, love and care, to renovate it completely. The highly detailed pargeting plaster-work depicts a Tudor viewpoint of the world. King Charles II was said to have hidden from his enemies in a secret room here after the Battle of Worcester in 1651. His coat of arms appears on the front of the house (left).

Christchurch Mansion and Ipswich Town Football Club

You might well ask what the grand sixteenth-century Tudor brick mansion situated within Christchurch Park has to do with Ipswich Town Football Club. It's all to do with the Cobbold family, who live at Great Glemham and were friends of Britten, who had a liking for all sports. The mansion was due to be demolished in 1894, but was saved by Felix Cobbold, a wealthy local businessman and brewer, who bought it and then gave it to the town on condition they also bought the parkland surrounding it for the people of Ipswich.

The Cobbold family have been great benefactors of the town: Ipswich Town Football Club owes a great deal to them. Of its twenty-nine directors, one third of them have been Cobbolds. Of the eight chairmen, five of those have also been Cobbolds. It was under John Cobbold's chairmanship that two brilliant managers were appointed.

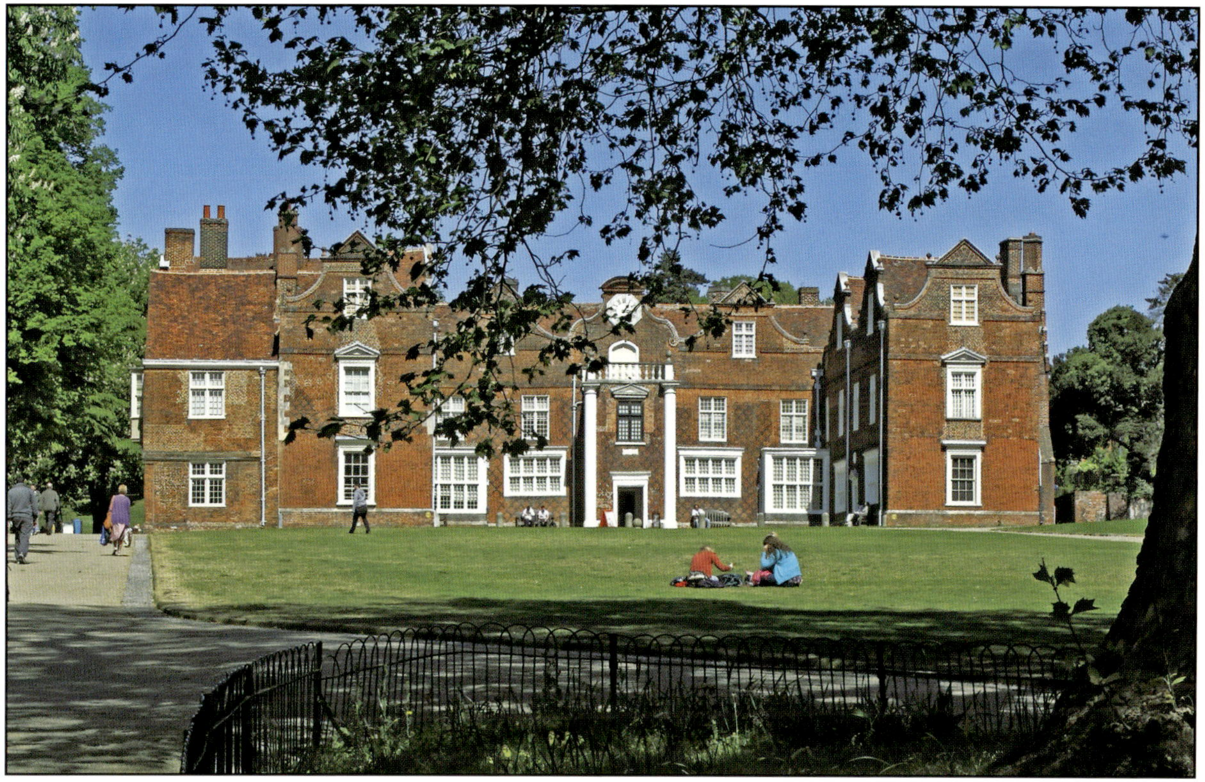

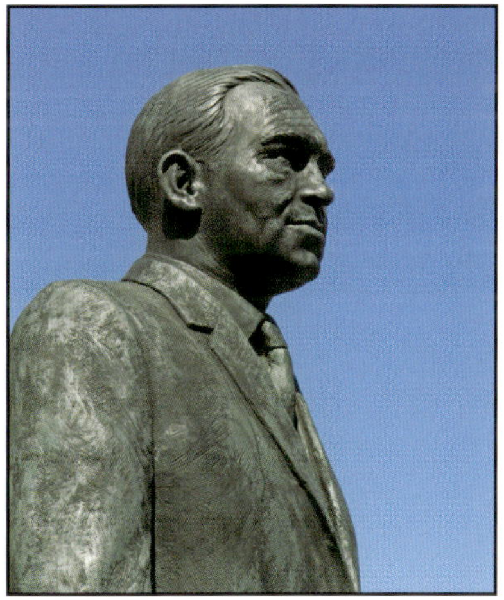

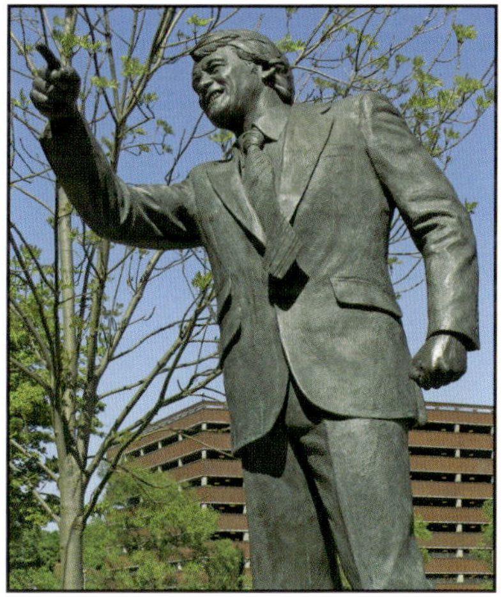

Two great Ipswich Town Football Club managers: Sir Alf Ramsey (left) and Sir Bobby Robson. Both these statues stand outside the Portman Road Football Ground.

Alf Ramsey, who within five years of his appointment took Ipswich Town from the then third division to the top of the football league (in their first year of promotion to that league), then went on to manage the England team, and became the only manager to lead them to World Cup victory. John Cobbold later appointed Bobby Robson, who took Ipswich to Wembley to win the FA Cup, and later to go on and win the UEFA Cup. He too was tempted away from the Ipswich manager's job to coach the England team.

Both those brilliant managers were awarded a knighthood. They succeeded in Ipswich by nurturing locally trained talent and moulding them into a homogeneous team, always with the full support of the Cobbold-led board, who allowed them, without interference, to get on with the job they did best.

St Nicholas Street and St Peter's Street

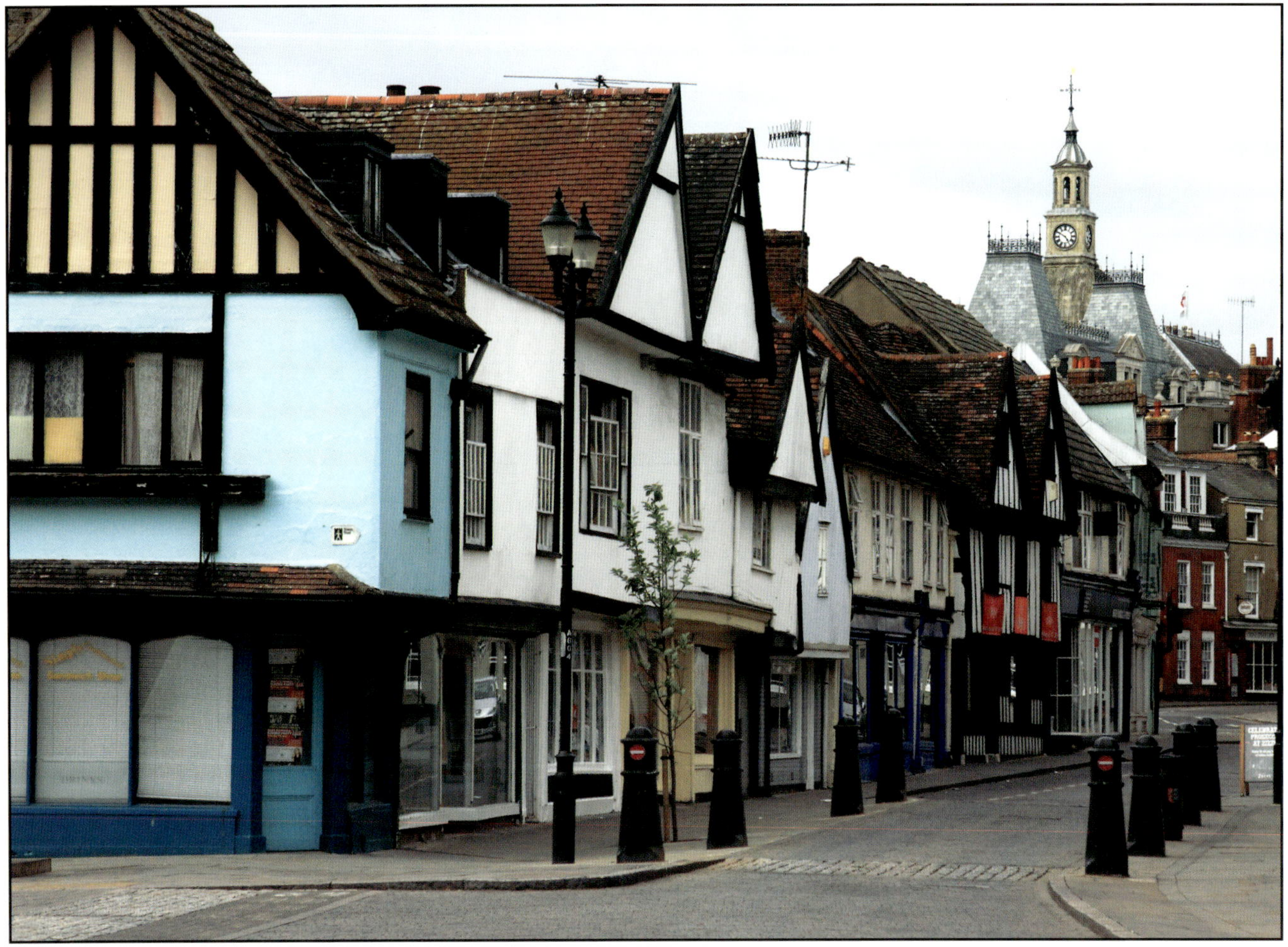

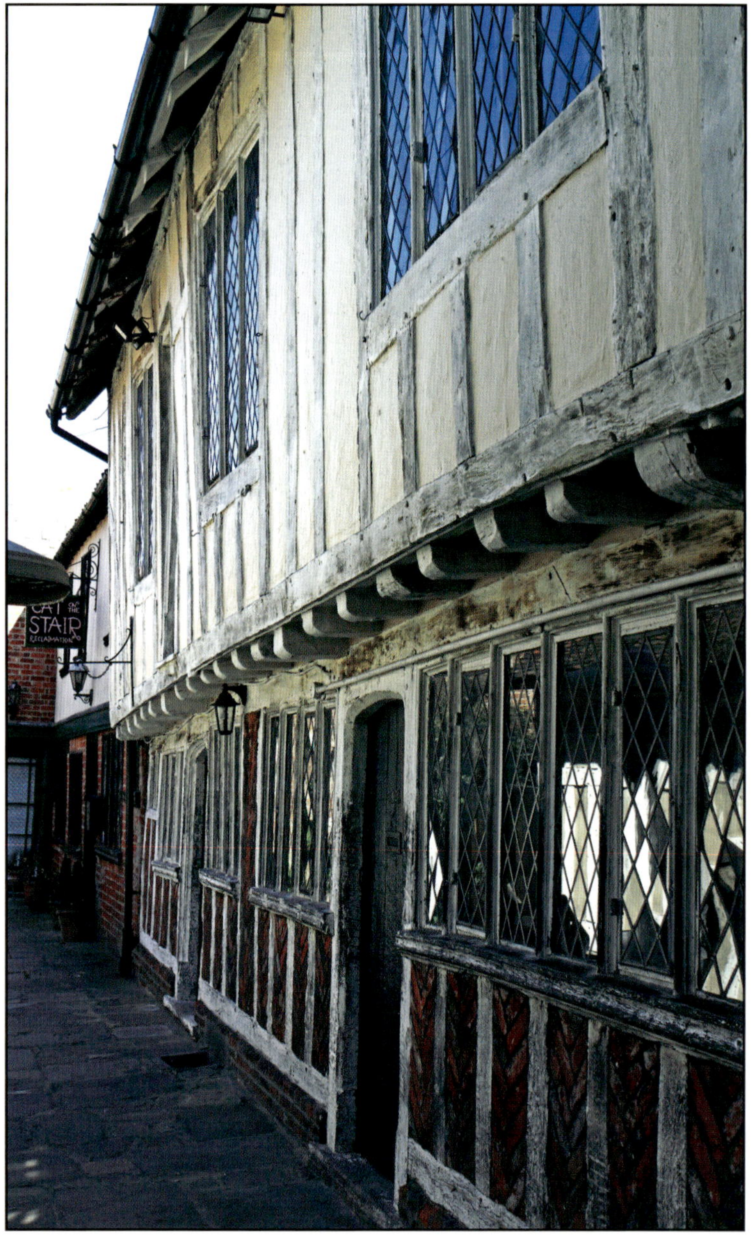

If, in this day and age, Benjamin Britten were to take a walk to Ipswich Waterfront from the Cornhill, leaving the Town Hall on his right (in the distance in top picture), past Giles Circus into St Nicholas Street and St Peter's Street, he would be passing some of Ipswich's most beautifully restored timber buildings dating back to Tudor times that, in his day, were in a sad state of dereliction. This is a street of restaurants, pubs and specialist shops. Look into the small alleyways, (right) and more timbered buildings are discovered tucked away almost out of sight. Here he would be seeing Ipswich's historical past at its best, much changed from when he walked down these sreets.

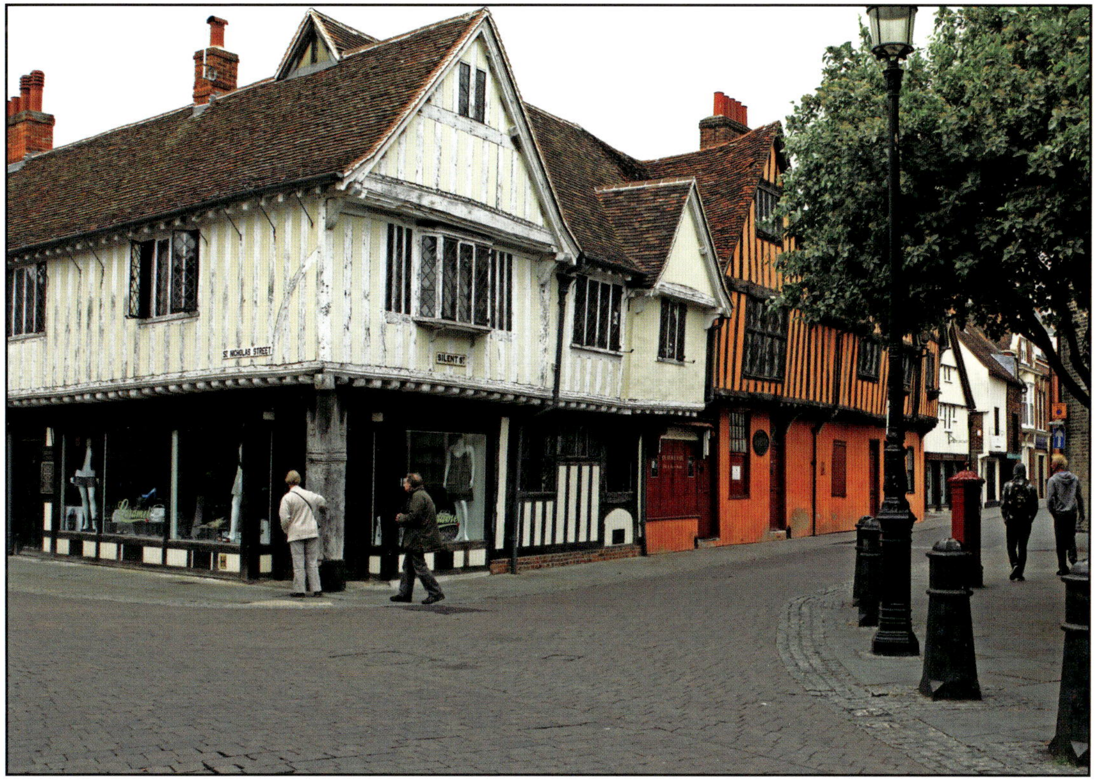

Cardinal Thomas Wolsey (1473-1530) was one of the richest and most powerful men in the country, and one of King Henry VIII's closest confidants – until his downfall after failing to secure papal consent to the king's divorce from Catherine of Aragon. He was born very near to where the above photograph was taken in St Nicholas Street. He is the town's most famous son, and Wolsey's Gate on College Street (right) is all that is left of his attempt to build a college in Ipswich that he hoped would rival any in Oxford.

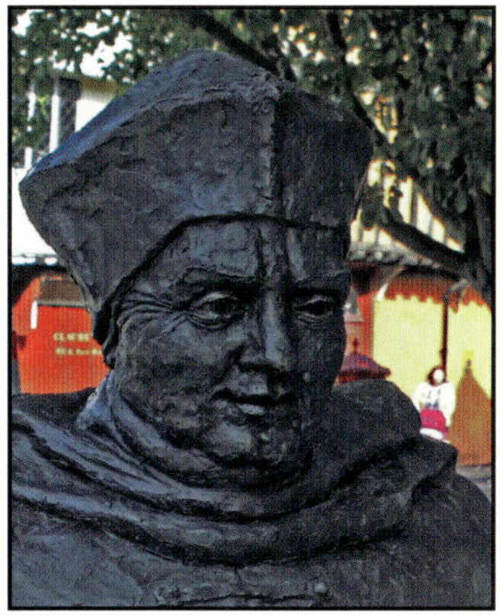

The redundant fifteenth-century St Peter's Church, originally destined to be Wolsey's College chapel (in the background), has been transformed into a centre for music and the arts. These are both a mere stone's throw away from Ipswich Waterfront, an area that has undergone exciting renewal development.

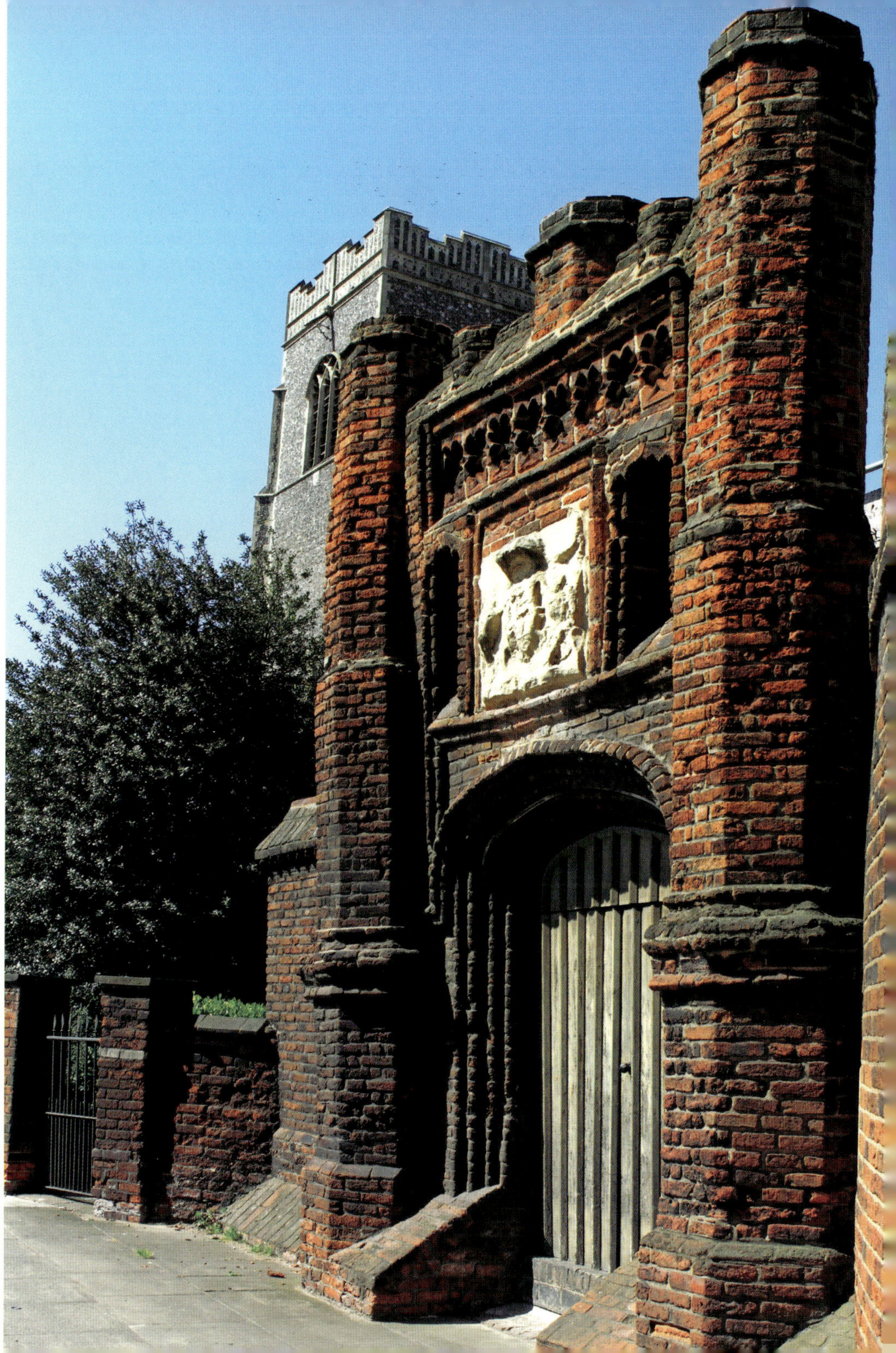

The Waterfront, Ipswich

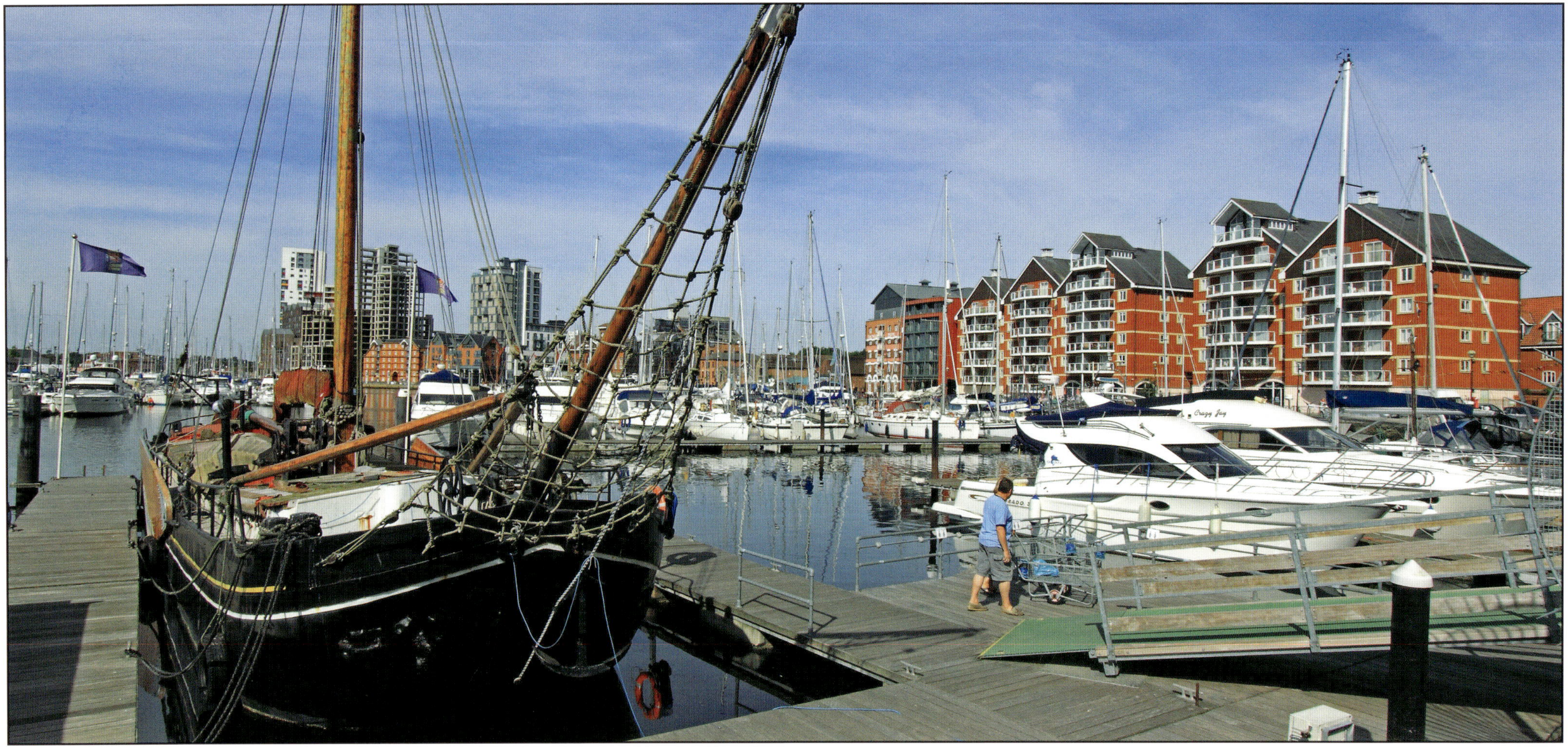

Ipswich docks have been the heartland of the town since Roman times. Towards the latter half of the twentieth century the old dock area around Stoke Bridge fell into decline, and redundant buildings deteriorated into a sad state of disrepair.

Since 1995 this area has gradually been reclaimed as The Waterfront, and taken on a new lease of life as a vibrant upmarket part of the town, centred around a marina, with shops, restaurants, cafés, hotels, apartments, and leisure facilities. The new University Campus Suffolk (UCS) building on the Waterfront (right), adds a feeling of youthful rejuvenation and a new beginning to this once run-down area. Cardinal Wolsey would have approved of the Waterfront siting of the college, I'm sure.

The UCS is the hub of six schools across five locations, at Bury St Edmunds, Great Yarmouth, Lowestoft, Otley and Suffolk New College Ipswich. All degrees are validated by the University of East Anglia and the University of Essex. UCS officially welcomed its first students in September 2007.

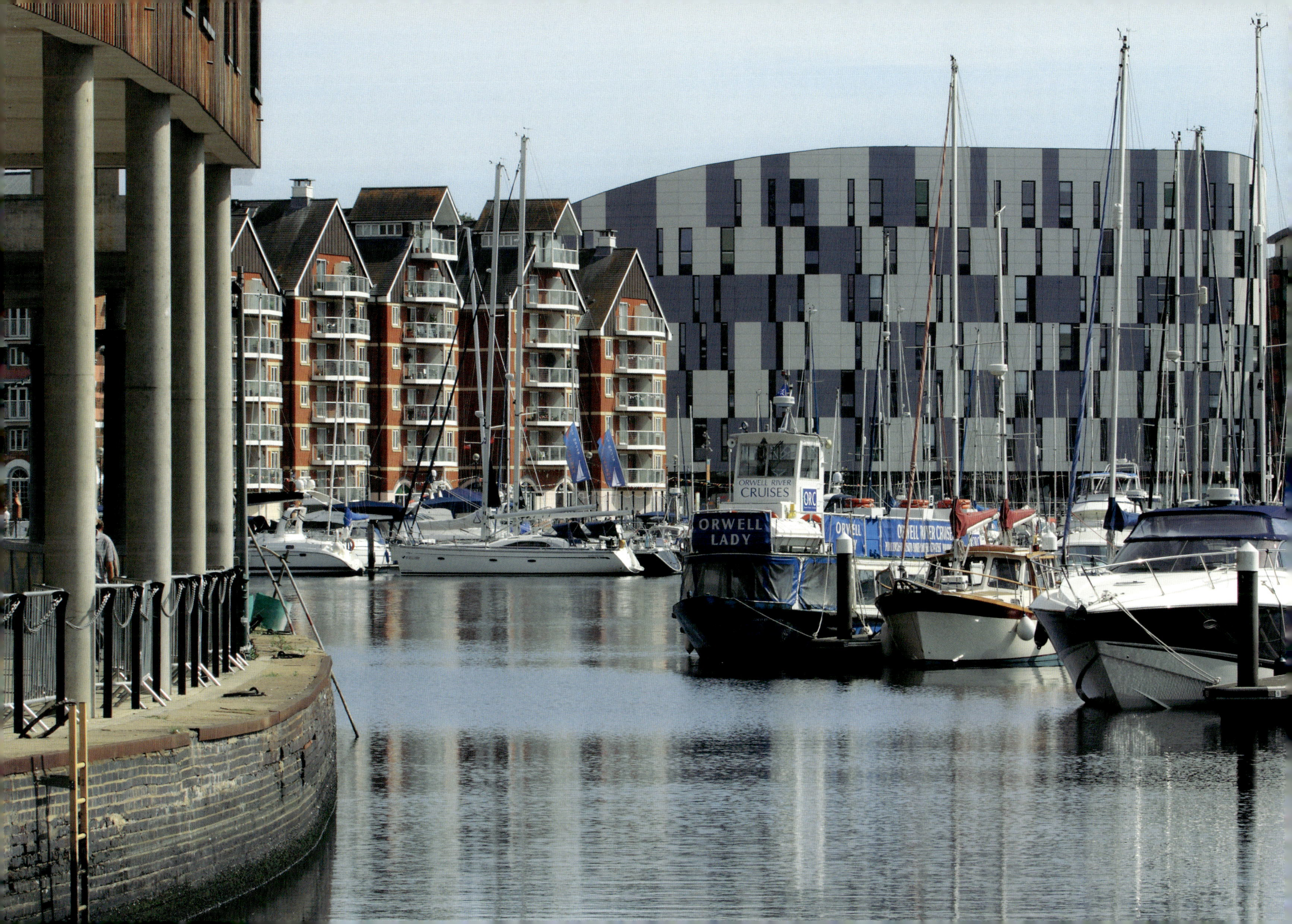
ORWELL RIVER
CRUISES
ORC
ORWELL
LADY

Familiar places

Having travelled along Britten's Suffolk Heritage Coast from Lowestoft to Ipswich, I briefly return to those places he knew best – places with big skies, crystal clear air, and with a history as rich as any place in England – and also to the Suffolk people, proven stalwarts in the face of adversity, who are respectful, proud, hard-working, and who are not in awe of anyone. These are Britten's people – the people who inspired him and whom he chose to live amongst, who made him feel most at ease, and who brought a smile to his face just by being in their company.

While doing pictures for this book I met a retired carpenter in Aldeburgh – I knew him from my school days as someone of few words who could sum up a situation in a sentence. I told him what I was doing and asked if he'd met Britten. 'Yes; I knew Ben,' he replied. 'He was a good bloke, always had time for a chat – I didn't like his music much though.' As any true Suffolk man will tell you, it's a real compliment to be called a 'good bloke' – Ben would have liked that. I've never heard a bad word said against him from any of the local born and bred people – and they are pretty good judges of character.

Opera is not to everyone's liking, and my carpenter friend was evidently not impressed by Britten's musical genius. However, Benjamin Britten is probably the most influential composer of the twentieth century, and his music is celebrated worldwide. Aldeburgh is synonymous with Britten, and Britten with Aldeburgh. It's probably because of that symbiotic relationship that local residents may not be as aware of the significance of this great man and his music as people from elsewhere are. I have been in situations abroad when the very mention of his name brings about looks of adulation. His genius will continue to enthral music lovers for generations to come.

The village of Orford from the marshes (right) with its castle and church will forever be linked with the Aldeburgh Festival and Benjamin Britten.

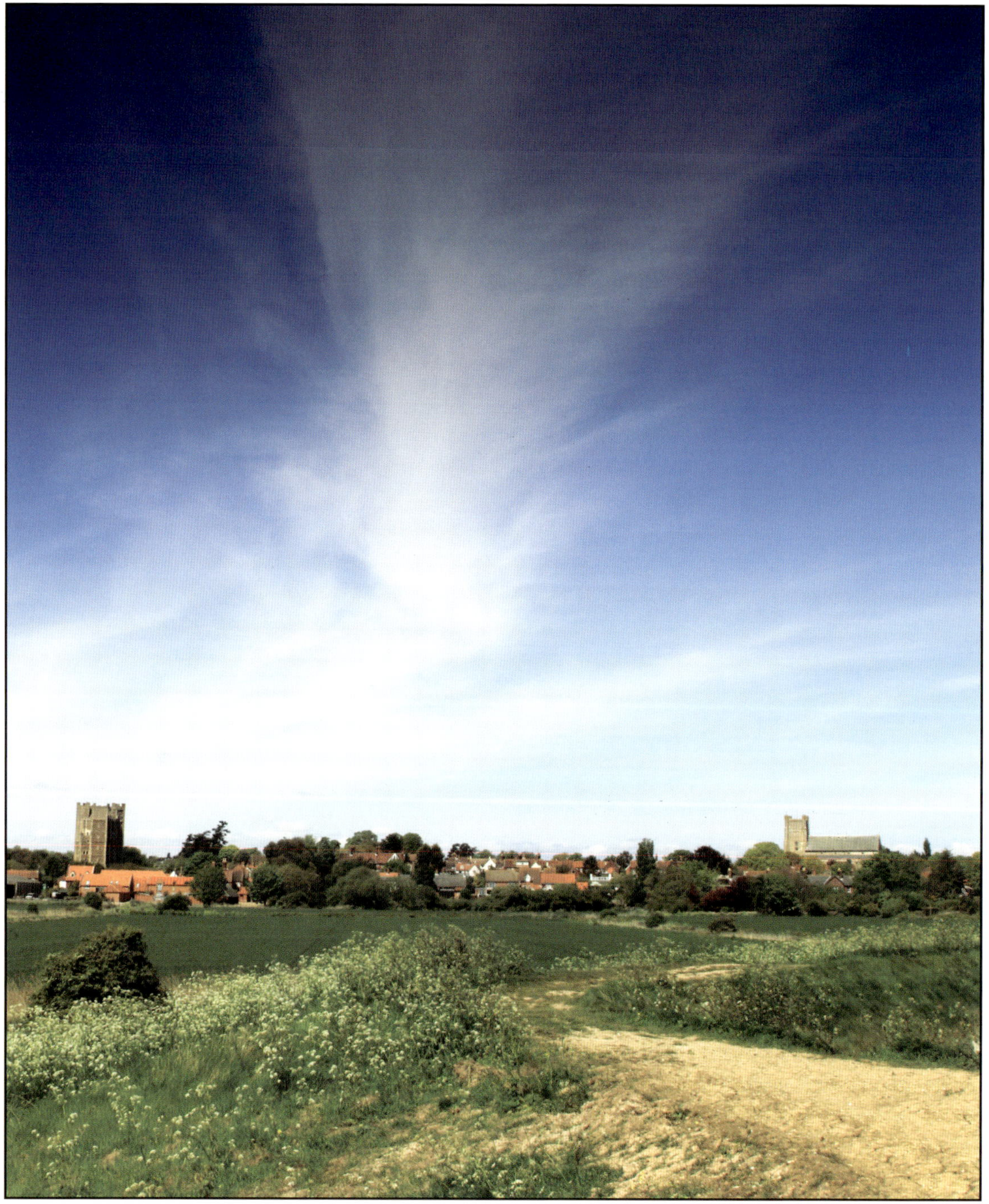

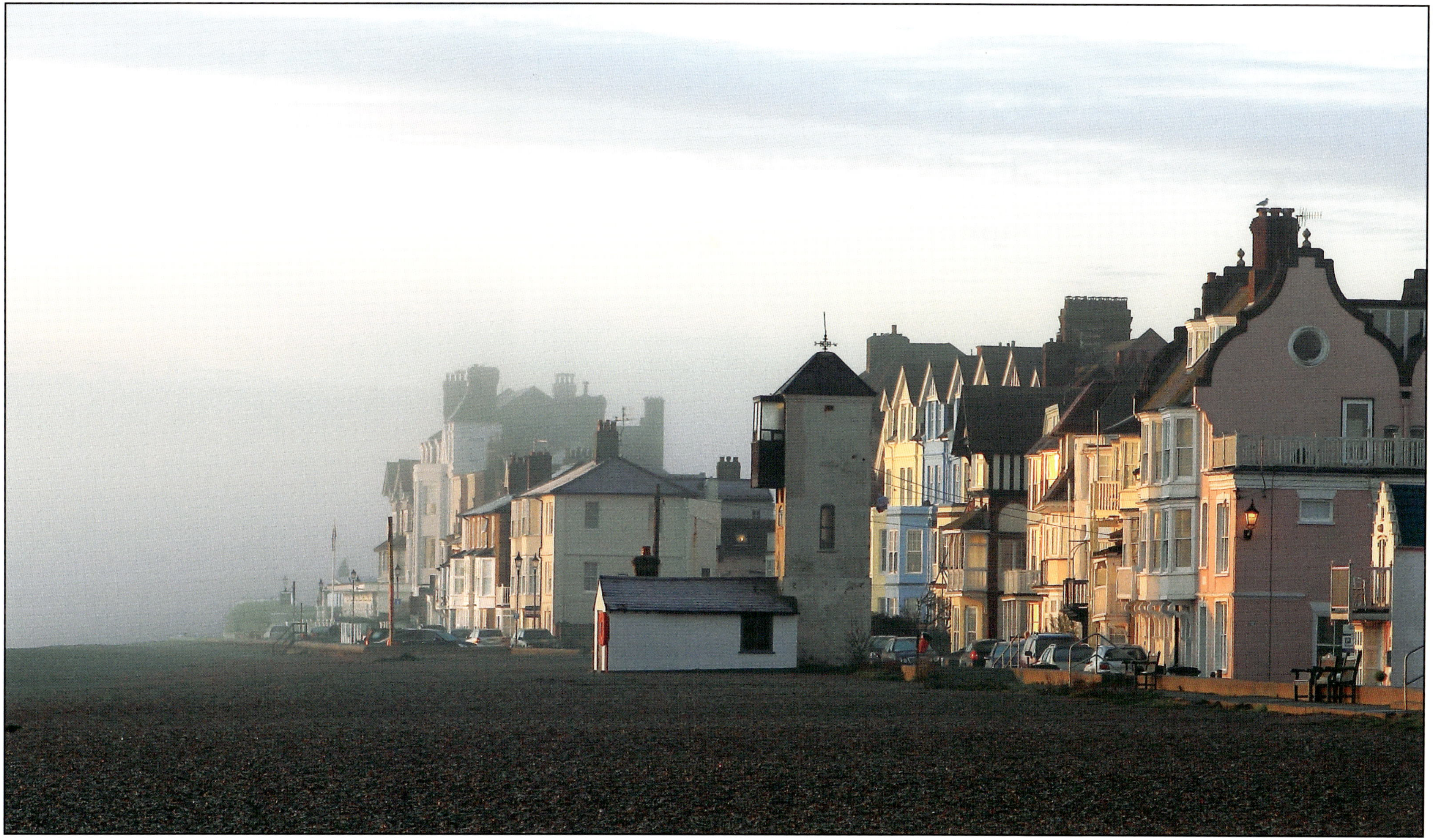

A misty morning on Aldeburgh beach as houses along Crag Path are bathed in the golden glow of the rising sun.
This atmospheric setting would have been familiar to Britten when he and Peter Pears lived on Crag Path.

Britten in his Suffolk workplace

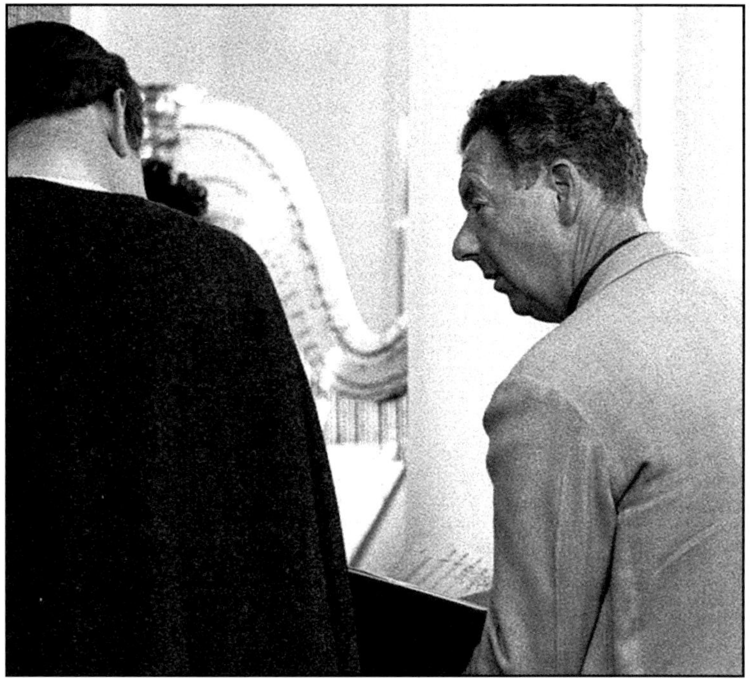

'In writing *Peter Grimes*, I wanted to express my awareness of the perpetual struggle of men and women whose livelihoods depend on the sea,' Ben wrote.

This most celebrated of Benjamin Britten's operas will remain a lasting tribute to the folk along Suffolk's coast, and to the Aldeburgh townspeople.

His music is now performed in the most prestigious concert halls throughout the world, but it was in venues local to Aldeburgh where he derived his greatest satisfaction when conducting his works. Suffolk churches, community halls and later, his beloved Snape Maltings Concert Hall, were his preferred working places and where he was happiest and at one with his music.

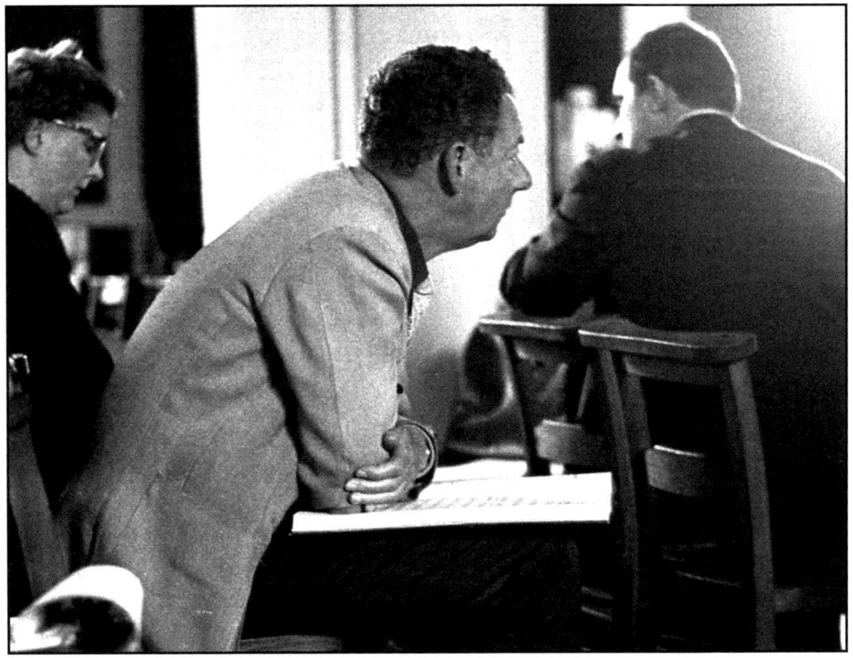

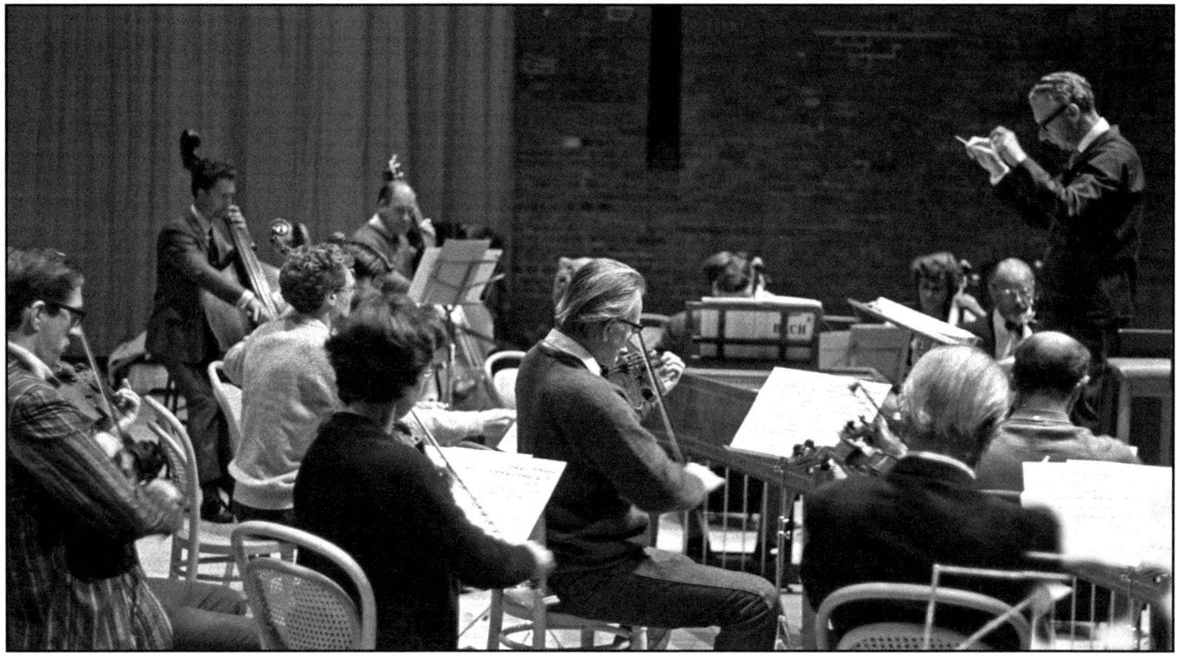

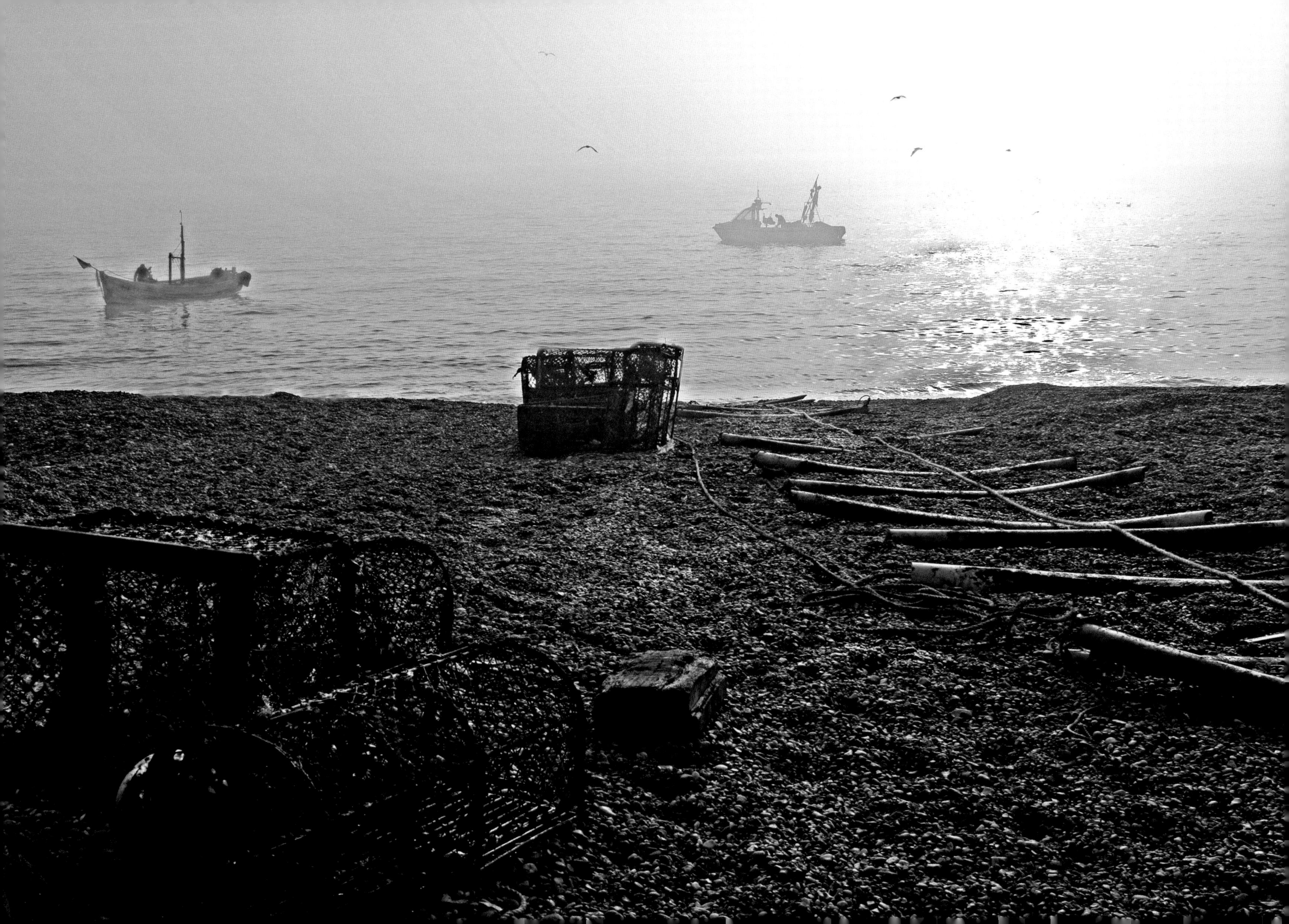

Journey's end

Edward Benjamin Britten, OM, CH, Baron Britten of Aldeburgh in the County of Suffolk, died on 4th December 1976 at Red House, with his lifelong partner Peter Pears and his devoted nurse Rita Thomson at his bedside. He is buried in the churchyard of Aldeburgh parish church with a simple headstone marking his grave. Sir Peter Pears died ten years later and is buried beside him.

My association with Britten lasted a decade during the sixties before I moved on to do other things. It was an exciting time to have been involved with him as he spearheaded the Aldeburgh Festival into an international festival of music and the arts, and to see the development of the splendid Snape Maltings Concert Hall.

I will confess to not having been a great fan of Britten's music in my younger days. This was in the swinging sixties, and I was in my early twenties enjoying the pop music and jazz of that time. When I admitted this to Ben, I think he rather enjoyed the idea that I was not a fawning sycophant, as so many people around him were. 'Maybe one day you will come to appreciate my music,' he told me. He was right of course, I did. I just wish he'd been around a little longer so I could have told him so.

Toward the latter part of his life he was courted by royalty, heads of state, and the greats of music and the arts, and had many honours bestowed upon him from all over the world. I always gained the impression he was most at ease with ordinary non-judgemental folk, especially the young. He was on Christian-name terms with people local to the Aldeburgh area: fishermen, tradesmen, builders – and a photographer – and they with him. With them he was gracious, polite, and a gentleman in every way.

My pictorial journey along Suffolk's Heritage Coast has inevitably left out towns or villages that some people would have thought should be included, and other places have been included that would appear to have no connection with Benjamin Britten. Ben was, however, inextricably connected with Suffolk, its people, and its wonderful Heritage Coast. He, and his music, were nourished by the very roots of his birth county.

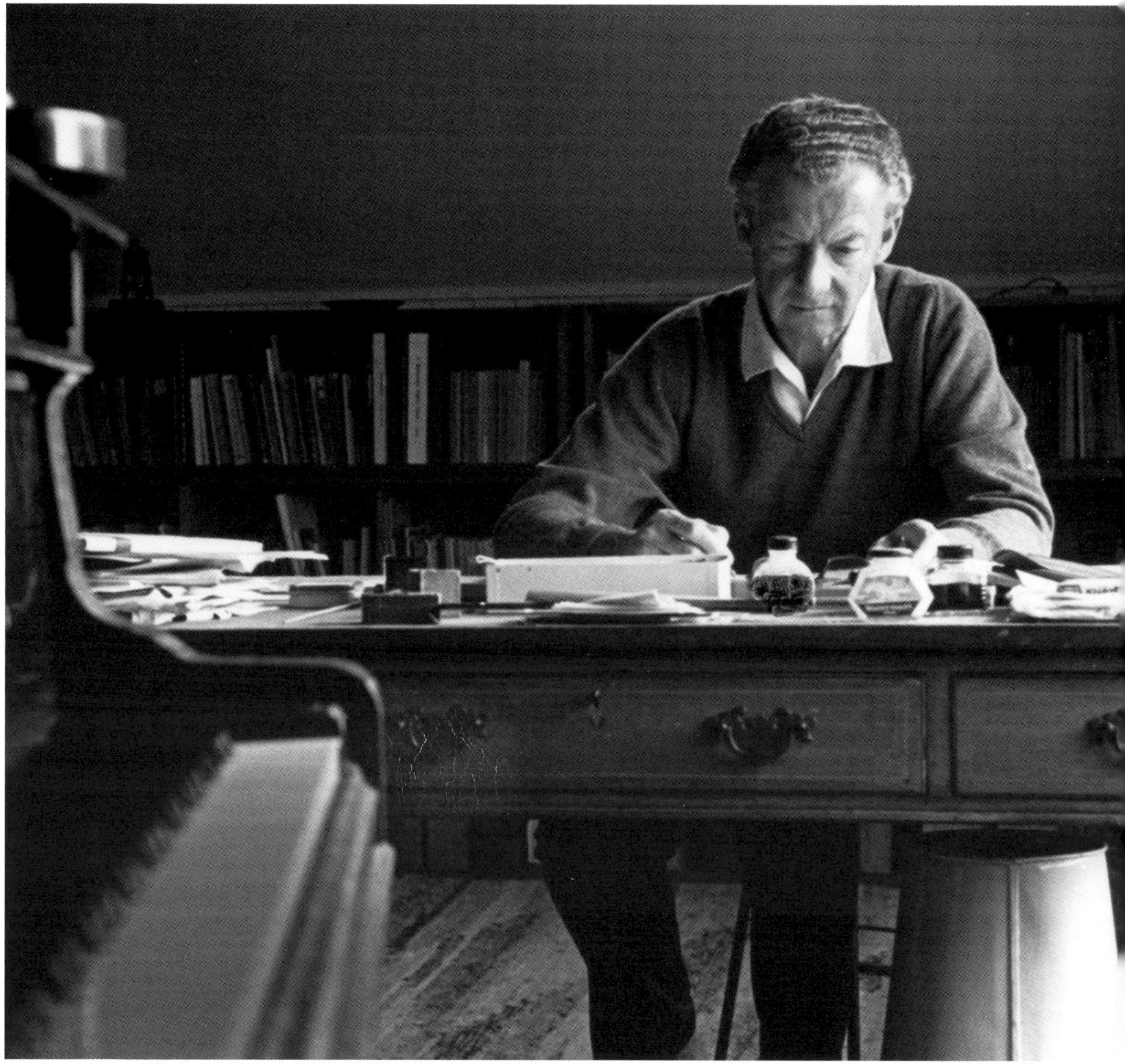

Benjamin Britten 1913 – 1976

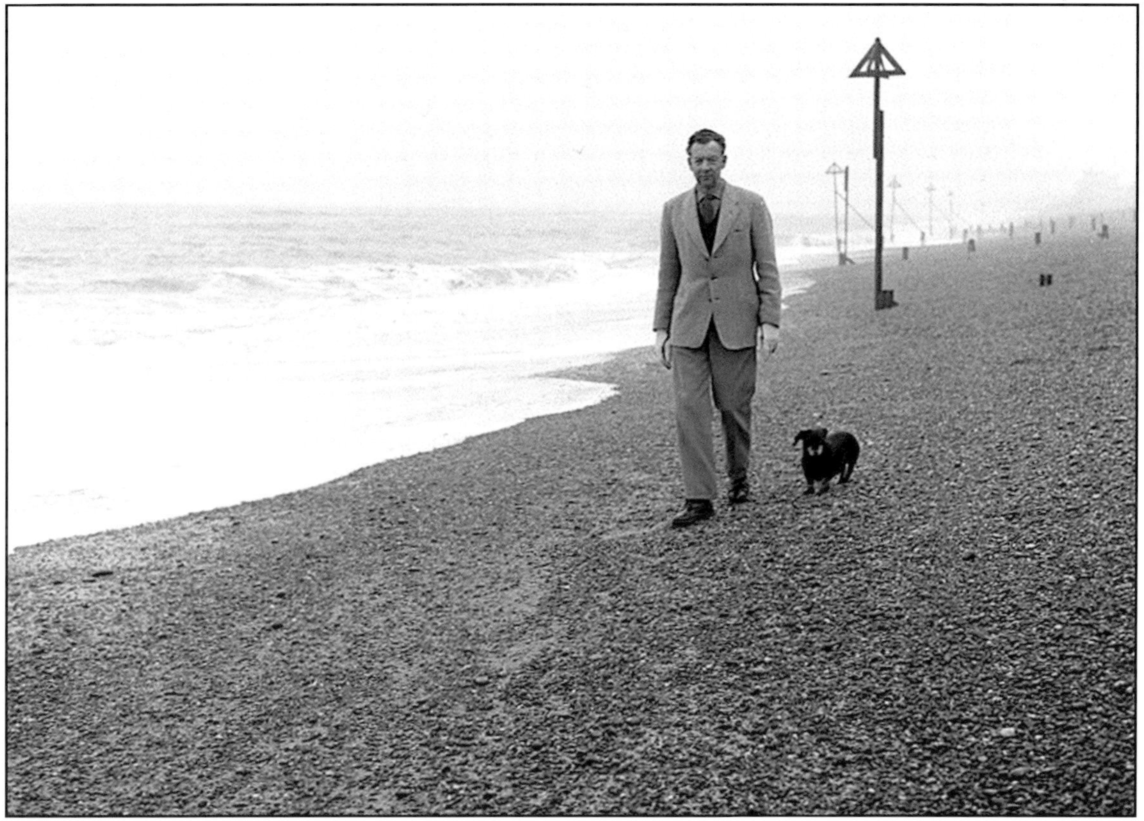

'I hear music when waves whoosh the shingle up the beach, and make the gulls call,' Ben remarked to me on one of our shore-side dog walks.

End note for photographers

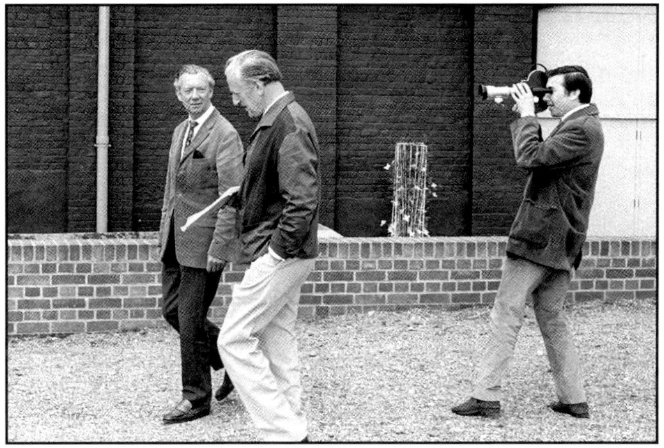

In this digital age where most mobile phones have an inbuilt camera capable of taking some extraordinarily good-quality photographs, I am often asked what was it like when I first became a professional photographer.

I was trained as a news cameraman in the late nineteen fifties, and was one of six staff photographers working for the East Anglian Daily Times in Ipswich. All newspaper cameramen wielded a heavy 5"x 4" double dark slide press camera in those days. Each slide held two sheets of cut film, so if you carried fifteen slides – about as many as one could comfortably carry in a very large camera case – that was a total of thirty photographs 'in the bag'. No matter how important the job, that was all the shots you had, you had to make every picture count. The flashgun was a massive light that took a single bulb the size of a tungsten domestic light bulb; four of those was about all one could stuff into a case. Frequently they would explode when fired, sending shards of glass over the hapless subjects – no health and safety in those days!

The photographs I took of Britten when I was a self-employed freelance photographer were taken on 35mm single-lens reflex and roll film twin-lens reflex cameras. For television filming I used a 16mm Paillard Bolex H16 film camera (above). All film needed to be taken back to a darkroom and processed in chemicals and then prints enlarged onto bromide paper, processed again, and dried.

Today my cameras are all digital Canon cameras, with three Canon lenses – a 10-22mm wide angle, a 24-70mm zoom, and a 100-400mm telephoto. These cameras are auto-focus, auto-exposure, and can even eliminate camera shake. They can take up to ten shots a second and have the capabilities, if needed, to store more photographs than I will ever use on one SD card.

Instead of a darkroom I now use Adobe Photoshop and, sitting comfortably in front of my computer, I can zap pictures all over the world in seconds. Do I long for the return of the 'good old' photographic days? No. I'm still a great fan of black and white photographs, though.

Index